Built of Books

Built of Books

How Reading Defined the Life of Oscar Wilde

Thomas Wright

A John Macrae Book
Henry Holt and Company
New York

For my parents, Paul and Anne Marie Wright

Henry Holt and Company, LLC
Publishers since 1866
175 Fifth Avenue
New York, New York 10010
www.henryholt.com

Originally published in Great Britain in 2008 by Chatto & Windus

Library of Congress Cataloging-in-Publication Data

Wright, Thomas (Thomas Edward), 1973–
    Built of Books / Thomas Wright.—1st U.S. ed.
        p.   cm.
    Includes bibliographical references and indexes.
    ISBN-13: 978-0-8050-8993-6
    ISBN-10: 0-8050-8993-4
    1. Wilde, Oscar, 1854–1900—Books and reading.   2. Authors, Irish—19th century—
Biography.   I. Title.
    PR5823.W75 2009
    828' .809—dc22
    [B]

                                                              2008037762

Henry Holt books are available for special promotions and premiums.
For details contact: Director, Special Markets.

First U.S. Edition 2009

Title page and part opening illustrations by John Vassos

Printed in the United States of America

1   3   5   7   9   10   8   6   4   2

Contents

PART I

Built Out of Books

Contents

CONTENTS

Appendices

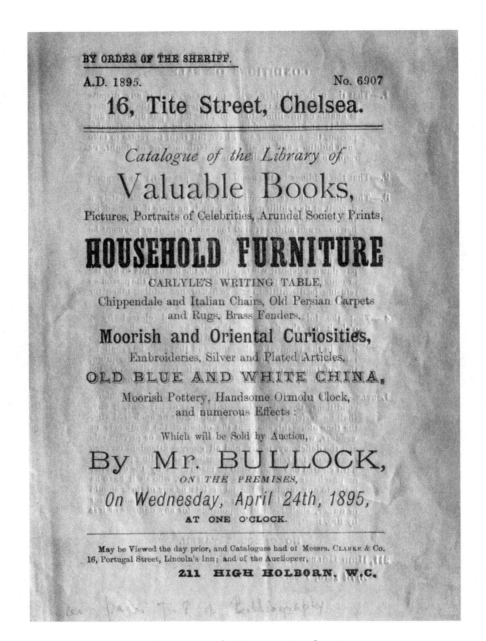

A.D. 1895.   No. 6907

16, Tite Street, Chelsea.

Catalogue of the Library of

Valuable Books,

Pictures, Portraits of Celebrities, Arundel Society Prints,

HOUSEHOLD FURNITURE

CARLYLE'S WRITING TABLE,

Chippendale and Italian Chairs, Old Persian Carpets
and Rugs, Brass Fenders,

Moorish and Oriental Curiosities,

Embroideries, Silver and Plated Articles,

OLD BLUE AND WHITE CHINA,

Moorish Pottery, Handsome Ormolu Clock,
and numerous Effects :

Which will be Sold by Auction,

By Mr. BULLOCK,

ON THE PREMISES,

On Wednesday, April 24th, 1895,

AT ONE O'CLOCK.

May be Viewed the day prior, and Catalogues had of Messrs. CLARKE & Co.
16, Portugal Street, Lincoln's Inn; and of the Auctioneer,

211 HIGH HOLBORN, W.C.

Front page of the 'Tite Street Catalogue'.

List of Illustrations

Every effort has been made by the author and publishers to trace the holders of copyrights in quotations and illustrations. Any inadvertent mistakes or omissions can be rectified in future editions.

Chronology of Wilde's Life

1854	16 October	Oscar Fingal O'Flahertie Wilde is born at 21 Westland Row, Dublin to Lady Jane Francesca Wilde ('Speranza') and Sir William Robert Wills Wilde. He is their second son, his brother William having been born in 1852.
1855		The Wilde family moves to Merrion Square.
1857		Wilde's sister Isola is born.
1864–71		Attends Portora Royal School, Enniskillen.
1867		Death of Isola Wilde.
1871–74		Studies Classics at Trinity College, Dublin.
1874	17 October	Matriculates at Magdalen College, Oxford, where he studies 'Greats' (Classics).
1876	19 April	Death of Wilde's father.
1878	19 July	Achieves a First in 'Finals' at Oxford.
1879		Moves to London.
	May	Wilde's mother and elder brother move to London.
1880		Writes his first play *Vera; Or, The Nihilists*.
1881	June	Publication of *Poems*.

1882		Lectures in the USA and Canada on art and Aestheticism.
1882–83		Writes *The Duchess of Padua*.
1883–84		Lectures throughout England on art and Aestheticism.
1884	29 May	Marries Constance Lloyd in London.
1885		Wilde's career as a journalist begins in earnest. He starts to review regularly for the *Pall Mall Gazette*, and continues to do so until 1890.
	1 January	Wilde and his wife move into 16 Tite Street, Chelsea.
	5 June	Wilde's first son, Cyril, is born.
1886		Wilde meets the seventeen-year-old Robert Ross, and embarks on his first significant homosexual affair.
	February	Compiles a list of his favourite, and least favourite, books for the *Pall Mall Gazette*.
	3 November	Wilde's second son, Vyvyan, is born.
	18 November	Wilde's review of Harry Quilter's *Sententiæ Artis* appears in the *Pall Mall Gazette*.
	24 November	Lectures on Thomas Chatterton.
1888	May	Publication of *The Happy Prince and Other Tales*.
1889	January	Publication of 'The Decay of Lying'.
	July	Publication of 'The Portrait of Mr W.H.'.
1890		Publication, in two parts, of 'The True Function and Value of Criticism', later reissued as 'The Critic as Artist'.

	20 June	Publication of the original magazine version of Wilde's novel 'The Picture of Dorian Gray'.
1891	February	Publication of 'The Soul of Man under Socialism'.
	April	Publication, in book form, of the enlarged version of *The Picture of Dorian Gray*.
	May	Publication of *Intentions*.
	July	Publication of *Lord Arthur Savile's Crime and Other Stories*.
	July	Wilde meets Lord Alfred Douglas.
	November	Publication of *A House of Pomegranates*.
	October–December	Wilde is the 'great event' of the social season in Paris. During his stay he writes *Salomé*, in French.
1892	20 February	West End production of *Lady Windermere's Fan*.
	May	Publication of the limited edition of Wilde's *Poems*.
1893	22 February	Publication of *Salomé*.
	19 April	West End production of *A Woman of No Importance*.
	October	Rents rooms at Nos 10 and 11 St James's Place.
	9 November	Publication of *Lady Windermere's Fan*.
1894	9 February	Publication of the English version of *Salome*.
	June	Publication of Wilde's poem *The Sphinx*.
	June	Douglas's father, the Marquess of Queensberry, confronts Wilde in his library at Tite Street.
	9 October	Publication of *A Woman of No Importance*.
1895	January	West End production of *An Ideal Husband*.
	February	West End production of *The Importance of Being Earnest*.
	February–March	Wilde discovers Queensberry's insulting card at his club and prosecutes him for libel.

	3 April	The Queensberry trial opens.
	5 April	Queensberry is acquitted and Wilde is arrested.
	6–26 April	Wilde awaits trial in Holloway prison.
	24 April	Public auction of Wilde's library and household effects.
	26 April	Wilde's first trial opens. The jury fail to reach a verdict. A new trial is set for 20 May.
	25 May	At his second trial Wilde is found guilty of committing acts of 'gross indecency' and sentenced to two years' hard labour. He is taken to Holloway prison.
	November	Transferred to Reading Gaol.
1896	3 February	Death of Wilde's mother.
1896–97		Wilde writes *De Profundis*.
1897	19 May	Wilde is released. He crosses the Channel to Dieppe and then settles at Berneval-sur-Mer.
	September	Leaves Berneval for Naples.
1898	February	Moves to Paris, which remains his base for the rest of his life. Publication of *The Ballad of Reading Gaol.*
	7 April	Death of Constance in Genoa.
1899	February	Publication of *The Importance of Being Earnest.*
	July	Publication of *An Ideal Husband.*
1900	30 November	Wilde dies in Paris.

'One of the greatest of the many worlds'

O N 24 APRIL 1895, while Wilde was in Holloway prison awaiting trial, the entire contents of his house in Tite Street, Chelsea were sold at the demand of his creditors. The Marquess of Queensberry, whom Wilde had unsuccessfully prosecuted for libel, had been awarded £600 legal costs, and it was his insistence on payment that led to the sale of Wilde's goods.

Wilde's effects were 'sold by Auction, by Mr. Bullock, on the premises at one o'clock'. The cover of the sale catalogue advertised the choicest items on offer – 'portraits of celebrities', '[Thomas] Carlyle's writing table', 'Old blue and white China' and a 'library of valuable books' (see page viii). Wilde had accumulated this collection of books since his adolescence, transporting the volumes between the various bachelor residences he occupied before he settled at 16 Tite Street in 1885 with his wife. There, he had set out the books on the shelves of his luxurious ground-floor library.

At the auction, Wilde's 'House Beautiful' was plundered by a frenzied crowd of curiosity hunters who had come in search of mementoes of the 'monster'.[1] After his arrest on 5 April, on charges of 'sodomy' and 'gross indecency', Wilde had become the most notorious figure in England. During the sale, the white front door of No. 16 was left open, giving the jostling crowds access to the house and licence to loot it. People pushed each other in a frantic attempt to help themselves to the finest items; some forced the locks on the rooms that had been shut up.[2] A scuffle broke out between a group of people and a number of Wilde's friends. The police were called in to quell the disturbance.[3]

Inside the library, just to the right of the house's entrance, the auctioneer's men took Wilde's books down from the shelves, then carted them out to the auctioneer. The sale was conducted right in front of the library window. Members of the public crowded the room, eyeing bargains and perhaps pocketing volumes that caught their eye. Piles of letters and manuscripts, that had been emptied out of Wilde's mahogany desk before it was carried outside, were strewn across the floor. Bidders pored over them, and riffled through Wilde's books, in a prurient search for references to his 'crimes'.[4] Wilde's large cast of the bust of Hermes, the Greek god of liars and thieves, looked on at the mayhem from the corner of the room.

In front of the house there was pandemonium. The auctioneer was surrounded by a sea of bidders, comprised, in the main, of antiques dealers and second-hand-book dealers who had come in search of bargains. They were not disappointed. They had the opportunity of acquiring private letters and manuscripts, even though the public sale of these was illegal;[5] they also had the chance of picking up Wilde's beautiful furniture and books at knock-down prices.

The books were hastily bundled together and sold as job lots. Lot 114 consisted of 'about' one hundred unidentified French novels. Extremely personal items were auctioned off, such as first editions of Wilde's works that he had inscribed to his wife and two sons.[6] Wilde especially lamented the loss of his sumptuous *éditions de luxe*, and the 'collection of presentation volumes' he had received from 'almost every poet of my time'. He also deeply regretted the dispersal of the 'beautifully bound editions of' his 'father's and mother's works', and the 'wonderful array' of 'book prizes' that had been awarded to him as a student.[7]

The volumes were sold for a song. The first lots fetched derisory sums, the last next to nothing. The hundred or so French novels that comprised lot 114 (which must have cost Wilde around five shillings each) went for the grand total of 35 shillings. Twenty-five beautifully bound volumes of the classics (i.e. Greek and Latin texts) were knocked down at the price of an ordinary Victorian novel.* The auctioneers' men grouped the books indiscriminately, with little consideration of their value. Unique presentation copies of Wilde's own works were sold along with volumes on angling.

A surviving copy of the sale catalogue, which lists some of Wilde's books, and which was annotated by a bidder, suggests that Wilde's library contained around two thousand volumes, along with numerous magazines, periodicals, scrapbooks, photograph albums and parcels of manuscripts. The entire collection was sold for about £130 – roughly the same as Wilde's weekly expenditure on food, drink, cabs and hotel rooms.[8]

Most of the books went the way of a large paper edition of Wilde's fairy tale collection *The Happy Prince and Other Tales* [1888], which bears the inscription of the book dealer 'H. Parsons of Brompton Road'.[9] Parsons acquired it as part of lot 53, which included eight other extremely rare editions of Wilde's works. He paid £8 5s., and doubtless sold them on for at least five times the price.

Wilde hoped that his friends would buy some of the books on his behalf, but it is highly unlikely that they were able to out bid the dealers.[10] A few did, however, manage to acquire certain volumes for him when the dealers put them on the open market. One friend bought several books which he came across by chance in a shop on Chelsea's Queen's Road, with the intention of restoring them to their

---

* Lot 96, which went for 34 shillings; the standard price of a Victorian three-volume novel was 31 shillings.

former owner.[11] Other acquaintances, horrified by the idea that Wilde's cherished volumes (some of which were adorned with extremely personal inscriptions) were being displayed in booksellers' windows, purchased and eventually returned them to Wilde.

The overwhelming majority of the books were bought from dealers by individuals with no connection to Wilde, and, in time, sold on again to be scattered throughout the world. Wilde's Tite Street library, which had taken over thirty years to build, was destroyed in a single afternoon.

When Wilde learned the fate of his books he was inconsolable. Five days after the sale he wrote despondently to his lover Lord Alfred Douglas from Holloway prison: 'I hope you have copies of all my books [i.e. the first editions of Wilde's published writings]. All mine have been sold.'[12] Two years later he would describe the loss of his library as 'the one of all my material losses the most distressing to me'.[13]

Wilde's anguish should not surprise us. Like many nineteenth-century gentlemen, he regarded books as his 'friends', and his collection as both a record of his life and as an emblem of his personality. Books were extremely personal objects to him, and he delighted in making them uniquely his own. He inscribed his name on their title-pages in his elegant hand; he also habitually marked and annotated them. Most of Wilde's marginalia express his readerly response to a text; some are of a more private character. His copy of Theodore Tilton's volume of poems, *Thou and I*, contains the following note in his hand: 'Tilton brought me to see the old room where Poe wrote "The Raven", on Friday, Nov. 10 [1882]. An old wooden house over the Hudson, low rooms, fine chimney piece, very dull Corot day, clergyman with reminiscences of Poe, about chickens'.[14] Wilde never kept a diary, and laughed at those earnest and egotistical souls who did; scribbling in books was probably the closest he ever came to doing so.

Yet Wilde's library was far more than a museum of personal mementoes: it was the source of so much that was vital in his life. From it he derived the remarkable intellectual culture which suffuses and animates his writings.

That culture was exceptionally broad and profound. A brilliant classicist, Wilde was highly proficient in Latin and Greek. He was also a reader of modern and medieval French and Italian, and knew enough German to read Goethe. Wilde was, too, in Coleridge's famous phrase, a true 'library cormorant' who fed off a varied diet of books. His library included volumes on folklore, ancient and modern history, Japanese art and the music hall, and works from countless intellectual disciplines such as science, philosophy, archaeology, philology, comparative mythology, art history and literature.

Books were the greatest single influence on Wilde's life and writings. He sometimes referred to the volumes that most affected and charmed him as his 'golden books'. These were the books that revolutionised his conception of the world, the books in which he recognised an aspect of himself for the first time. As events in his biography, these readerly encounters were as significant as his first meetings with friends and lovers.

Yet Wilde did not so much discover as create himself through his reading: he was a man who built himself out of books. He poured scorn on the notion that each of us has a fixed 'inner' self that represents our essential 'nature' – that self was, he believed, a fiction invented by the political, economic and cultural powers that be. It could, therefore, be rewritten by the artist in life, with a little help from his favourite books. Wilde used these volumes as 'prompt books' for the various roles he assumed during the different phases of his life. Soon after his liberation from prison he discarded his 'natural' name (itself a thoroughly literary concoction) for the alias Sebastian Melmoth; the surname was derived from the doomed itinerant hero of the Gothic novel, *Melmoth the Wanderer*. As Wilde spent some of the final period of his life roaming the continent, he may be said to have lived up to his pseudonym.

Life for Wilde could be made to imitate art; it might also be viewed through its filter. He always came to life via books, literally seeing reality through them. Of an acquaintance he would say, 'she might have walked straight out of a page of Thackeray'; an everyday incident was described as having 'a little of Browning' in it. It is even possible that Wilde could see *only* the things he had read about: all other external phenomena may have been a flux of inchoate data that his mind failed to register. Certainly, in an immediate and instinctive sense, things only became real to Wilde if they had first been subjected to the alchemy wrought by the artistic imagination – his own, or another artist's. His feelings were never fully experienced until they had been expressed poetically or in the form of quotations. Friends had to be baptised anew with names derived from literature if they were to assume a clear outline and significance. Alfred Douglas was dubbed, at various stages of their relationship, Hylas, Narcissus, Alcibiades and Harpagon.

Wilde's reading was the chief inspiration for his writings. He was essentially a pre-modern author who adapted and conflated the books he read, rather than a Romantic writer concerned with originality and self-expression. His works are saturated with allusions from his vast and miscellaneous reading: they form a little library of exquisite echoes. Books also played a crucial part in the presentation of Wilde's public persona. When he was interviewed, he would surround himself with volumes; in photographs he sometimes poses book in hand.

Keenly aware of the power of appearances, Wilde knew how to use books — the traditional symbols of authorship and learning in Western iconography — to convey his culture and his literary achievements.

Wilde devoured and luxuriated in books. When he was sick, and when the prison doors were closed upon him, books were the first things he asked for. He turned to them, too, as he crawled towards death in his final years, for comfort and consolation, eloquently describing them, at that time, as 'one of the greatest of the many worlds God has given to each man'.[15]

Wilde talked books and often talked like a book; he talked so well that he seemed to talk books away. He told stories based on books and countless anecdotes and jokes about them; in his writings, his characters are frequently compared to books. One is 'like an *édition de luxe* of a wicked French novel, meant specially for the English market', another as 'dowdy' as a 'badly bound hymn-book'.[16] If people could be books, books could also be personified. The first edition of *Salomé* (1893) was an irrepressible little minx who required a 'stern look', once in a while, from an eighteenth-century tome to restrain her from dancing on the library shelves.[17] Wilde also lost books, and lost himself in them: a fictional character based on him has a fall while riding, because he 'thinks of something he's been reading, and mistakes his horse for a bookcase'.[18]

Books appear at every stage on Wilde's life's way from his boyhood, in which he 'loved literature . . . to excess',[19] to his death, surrounded by books in a cheap Parisian hotel. For Wilde, books were a lifelong romance.

Built Out
of Books

[handwritten, top margin:] gold dust / black lead. / Golden opinions — ounce of lead

ΑΔ. ἀλλ' ἀνατρέψω 'γὼ αὖτ' ἀντιλέγων
    οὐδὲ γὰρ εἶναι πάνυ φημὶ δίκην.
ΔΙ. οὐκ εἶναι φῄς; ΑΔ. φέρε γὰρ ποῦ 'στιν;
ΔΙ. παρὰ τοῖσι θεοῖς.
ΑΔ. πῶς δῆτα δίκης οὔσης ὁ Ζεὺς   865
    οὐκ ἀπόλωλεν τὸν πατέρ' αὑτοῦ
    δήσας; ΔΙ. αἰβοῖ τουτὶ καὶ δὴ
    χωρεῖ τὸ κακίν· δότε μοι λεκάνην.
ΑΔ. τυφογέρων εἶ κἀνάρμοστος.
ΔΙ. καταπύγων εἶ κἀναίσχυντος.   870
ΑΔ. ῥόδα μ' εἴρηκας. ΔΙ. καὶ βωμολόχος.   910
ΑΔ. κρίνεσι στεφανοῖς. ΔΙ. καὶ πατραλοίας.
ΑΔ. χρυσῷ πάττων μ' οὐ γιγνώσκεις.
ΔΙ. οὐ δῆτα πρὸ τοῦ γ', ἀλλὰ μολύβδῳ.   875
ΑΔ. νῦν δέ γε κόσμος τοῦτ' ἐστὶν ἐμοί.
ΔΙ. θρασὺς εἶ πολλοῦ. ΑΔ. σὺ δέ γ' ἀρχαῖος.
ΔΙ. διὰ σ' οὐ φοιτᾶν
    οὐδεὶς ἐθέλει τῶν μειρακίων·
    γνωσθήσει τοι ποτ' Ἀθηναίοις   880
    οἷα διδάσκεις τοὺς ἀνοήτους.
ΑΔ. αὐχμεῖς αἰσχρῶς. ΔΙ. σὺ δέ γ' εὖ πράττεις.   920
    καίτοι πρότερόν γ' ἐπτώχευες,
    Τήλεφος εἶναι Μυσὸς φάσκων,
    ἐκ πηριδίου
    γνώμας τρώγων πανδελετείους.   885
ΑΔ. ὤμοι σοφίας ΔΙ. ὤμοι μανίας
ΑΔ. ἧς ἐμνήσθης
ΔΙ. τῆς σῆς, πόλεώς θ' ἥτις σε τρέφει
    λυμαινόμενον τοῖς μειρακίοις.   890
ΑΔ. οὐχὶ διδάξεις τοῦτον Κρόνος ὤν.
ΔΙ. εἴπερ γ' αὐτὸν σωθῆναι χρὴ   930
    καὶ μὴ λαλιὰν μόνον ἀσκῆσαι.
ΑΔ. δεῦρ' ἴθι, τοῦτον δ' ἔα μαίνεσθαι.

[handwritten margin notes:] this free thinking is being spread abroad · standard of easie · you will you take it · unco good, reckon · magnanimous / god boy / Davil elegis

ADNOTATIO CRITICA

870 τυμβογέρων Nauckius ad Aristoph. Byzant. p. 98 ǁ 878 vulgo
διὰ σὲ δὲ contra metrum: corr. Hermannus ǁ 880 vulgo γνωσθήσει
ποτ': καὶ metro scilicet flagitante praefigunt nonnulli, τοι inseruit Hermannus quod ante ποτ' facile excidere poterat

[handwritten, bottom margin:] old dotard — misty ideas. + / quite behind the age, not very (out of / unison with them)

Annotations in Wilde's copy of Aristophanes' Nubes (The Clouds).

1. 'Hear the song of Oscar!'

HEN WILDE MADE his entrance on to the world's stage on
16 October 1854, his mother came up with a name that
produced intensely romantic vibrations: Oscar Fingal
O'Flahertie Wilde.* Christening was a matter of the utmost importance
for Wilde – like one of his fictional heroes, he believed that 'names
are everything'.[1]

Lovely names, he thought, could make even the ugliest objects beautiful: cigars were vile things, but when called 'nut-brown cigarettes' they
became charming.[2] Wilde's friends too, were altered forever when he
baptised them anew with names drawn from books. What unimaginative
people referred to as the 'real' world could be transformed, apotheosised,
and endowed with meaning through words, which took its brazen
objects and magically turned them into gold.

It was imperative then, that the bloody, screaming baby boy was
licked quickly by language into shape and significance, and elevated
from the mundane and formless world of nature to the golden world
of words. Wilde's mother, a famous poetess, proved equal to the task
by conferring on her second son a name both marvellous and musical
(Wilde's elder brother, Willie, had been born in 1852).

Two of Wilde's names, 'Oscar' and 'Fingal', were drawn from

---

* Later Wilde also adopted 'Wills' as a middle name, because of a family connection with
the Roscommon Wills's.

James Macpherson's celebrated eighteenth-century *Ossian* poems, which were based on ancient Celtic mythology; O'Flahertie was the name of a famously fierce Irish clan.[3] Fingal is Macpherson's name for Fionn MacCumhaill, the legendary Irish poet and warrior king. Oscar is Fingal's grandson, and the son of the poet Ossian. According to one Celtic legend, a version of which Wilde would narrate years later, Ossian is enchanted by a fairy woman called Niamh, who carries him over the seas to Tír na nOg, the Celtic country of the eternally young, where the fairy child Oscar is born. After three hundred years, Ossian yearns to revisit the land of his fathers. Niamh warns him never to dismount from his horse in the land of mortal men – if he does, the three hundred years he has spent in Tír na nOg will suddenly catch up with him. But alas, when he returns, Ossian's foot does touch the earth; his three hundred years suddenly fall upon him, and he is bowed double, and his beard sweeps the ground.[4]

Macpherson's reconstruction of Celtic mythology, which draws on the rich oral folk traditions of Ireland and Scotland as well as on ancient manuscripts, has an epic flavour. It is full of archetypal stories concerning warriors, bards and women of ethereal beauty, who people a misty landscape haunted by ghosts and memories. The style too, with its solemn and plangent music and its extravagant formulaic epithets, has an epic grandeur. The young warrior Oscar is hailed as 'the chief of every youth', 'the King of many songs', 'Oscar of the future fights', and 'Oscar of the dark brown hair'. His father and grandfather continually exhort him to heroic deeds: 'O Oscar, pride of youth . . . Pursue the fame of thy fathers . . . Their deeds are the songs of bards.' Oscar takes up their challenge, and resolves to seek renown. Though he may fall, his death will be fully recompensed, so long as some future bard shall announce at the feast, 'Hear the song of Oscar!'

Lady Wilde, who liked to be referred to by her pen-name Speranza, chose the names precisely because they were 'grand, misty, and Ossianic';[5] she doubtless hoped they would inspire her son to deeds of greatness. She had glorious plans for her two boys, describing them as 'all I have to live for'.[6] She looked forward to the time when Wilde's brother Willie would be 'a Hero and perhaps President of the future Irish Republic'.[7] She harboured similar ambitions for her second son, later urging him to take the English parliament by storm as an MP; failing that, he must become the most celebrated writer in English since Byron.

Speranza encouraged her youngest boy to emulate his legendary namesake by dressing him in the garb of an Ossianic hero. In the earliest surviving photograph of Wilde, taken when he was about two, he wears what appears to be the costume of an ancient Celtic warrior.[8] (see plate 1). The infant looks out with his dark and heavy-lidded eyes; his expression is serious, his physique robust and his bearing stately. Even at that early date, he seems to have no difficulty in living up to his heroic name.

Speranza often read poetry to her children, and her fondness for Macpherson, as well as for other versions of the Oscar legend, makes it highly likely that Wilde imbibed the myths surrounding his name from his mother.[9] Perhaps he heard them as he lay in bed in the Wildes' grand house in Dublin's fashionable Merrion Square, or in the nursery there. He would not, of course, have understood all of the words, but they would have enchanted him like a magical incantation or a piece of marvellous music. Wilde was described, by a visitor to the house, as 'an affectionate, gentle, retiring, dreamy boy',[10] and such boys are often susceptible to poetry's sound and suggestiveness.

The fertile fancy of the dreamy boy was doubtless fired by the heroic images, as his mother declaimed Macpherson's sonorous phrases: 'O Oscar!' (she pronounced the name 'As-car') 'be thou like the age of Fingal. Never search thou for battle; nor shun it when it comes.' And with what delicious melancholy must she have read the passages that narrate his death. 'Ossian, carry me to the hills!' the blood-soaked warrior whispers at his last. 'Raise the stones of my renown . . . place my sword by my side.'

Speranza would have performed the poem with gusto. Flamboyant, exuberant and innately theatrical, she described herself as 'wild, rebellious' and 'ambitious'. 'I wish,' she told a friend, 'I could satiate [myself] with Empires, though a Saint Helena were the end.'[11] Instead, she satisfied herself by writing the fervent Irish Nationalist poetry that made her famous throughout Ireland, and by creating a grand personality. As part of her self-fashioning, she continually improved on 'facts' by lying about her age and ancestry; through such means, she kept her two *bêtes noires*, nature and the 'real' world, at a safe distance. Children often regard their parents as all-powerful sources of comfort and authority, but Speranza, who thought of herself as 'first cousin to Aetena and half-sister to Vesuvius'[12] must have seemed goddess-like to the young Wilde. He worshipped and adored her.

Wilde was, in a sense, born out of a book and, when he looked back on his baptism, he was well pleased. He delighted in Celtic mythology, which, he said, revealed 'the loveliness of the world . . . through a mist of tears'; his renditions of some of its famous episodes formed part of his repertoire of spoken stories. He also adored the 'passionate melancholy' of the *Ossian* poems. Macpherson's verse, he argued, had revolutionised 'dull' eighteenth-century literature and offered the Romantic poets of the succeeding century a 'well of undefiled pure poetry' to draw from.[13]

Most of Macpherson's first readers accepted his claim that the poems were collated from the writings of the ancient bard Ossian. Historians of ancient Ireland quoted them as authoritative sources;

Speranza in her mid-fifties, painted by J. St. C. Liddell.

archaeologists dated their finds according to the events they described. By Wilde's time, however, Macpherson's 'hoax' was quite exploded: it was widely known that the poet had conflated ancient oral and written sources with many passages of his own invention. The fact that *Ossian* was a 'forgery', or what might be called a 'bastard' book, did not concern Wilde in the slightest. He defended the poet, on the grounds that 'to censure an artist for forgery was to confuse an ethical with an aesthetical problem'.[14]

Wilde was delighted by the sound of his name as well as by its provenance. As a two-year-old, he entertained a group of drawing-room guests at Merrion Square by reciting it repeatedly: 'Oscar, Fingal, O'Flahertie, Wilde . . . Oscar, Fingal, O'Flahertie, Wilde'.[15]

While his school companions later laughed at these romantic appellations, Wilde relished them. He signed his early poetical publications, and autographed many of his own books, with all of his names; in later life, he lamented the fact that he was forced to drop some of them. 'A name which is destined to be in everybody's mouth must not be too long,' he explained. 'It comes so expensive in the advertisements . . . All but two of my names have been thrown overboard. Soon I shall discard another and be known simply as "The Wilde" or "The Oscar".'[16]

2. 'The Irish imagination'

THE 'GOLDEN BOOK' of Wilde's early childhood was not really a book at all. The boy grew up surrounded by the traditional Irish folk tales his parents told him, the bulk of which were not published until long after his infancy.

In the nineteenth century, Ireland possessed one of the richest oral cultures in the world. The ancient Bardic schools, in which Irish poets were taught the elaborate art of Gaelic oral poetry, had been forcibly closed by the British plantation settlers of the seventeenth century, as part of the suppression of the culture of the native Catholic population that had accompanied their appropriation of its land. Yet the indigenous culture, and the spirit of the Bards, endured in the performances of traditional peasant story-tellers known as *seanchaí* who specialised in popular folk tales, which they narrated in Gaelic or English.

Wilde's parents, and many members of their Merrion Square circle, were fascinated by Ireland's native oral tradition.[1] Their interest is noteworthy because they belonged to the Anglo-Irish elite, which had, in many instances, ancestral links with the British settlers and strong cultural ties with England. Educated, English speaking, and almost exclusively Protestant, the Anglo-Irish comprised the overwhelming majority of Ireland's urban middle and upper class, and formed its professional and governing establishment. They ruled the country under the English Union, which had annexed Ireland to the United Kingdom in 1801.

The Wildes' interest in Ireland's Catholic peasant culture was a corollary of their Nationalism. Notwithstanding their Anglo-Irish background, both of Wilde's parents were passionately committed to the Nationalist cause, which campaigned for the abolition of the English Union. Speranza, who had been brought up a Protestant and who had English blood, vehemently denounced the Union in the fiery words of her verse. She also took the exceptional step of having her children baptised twice – first as Protestants, then as Catholics. Her son's famous penchant for enjoying the best of both worlds, and for entertaining opposite, and often contradictory, positions, was thus fixed at a very early date.

Wilde's father, Sir William Wilde, was the finest eye and ear surgeon of his generation, a keen amateur archaeologist and a leading Irish antiquarian. He was also one of the country's first folklorists. He collected tales from the peasants who came to him for medical treatment, sometimes accepting a story as payment for his services. Many of these tales were recounted in English, but some were narrated in Gaelic, a language in which he was fluent. Sir William garnered hundreds of traditional yarns on his frequent tours of the West of Ireland, from the renowned *seanchaí* of the region and from the labourers who worked on the estate he owned at Moytura, on the shores of Lough Corrib. During family holidays there, young Oscar often listened to the peasants' tales in the company of his father. The stories entranced father and son, taking them back, according to one of their neighbours, 'to the dawn of time, which in Ireland began the day before yesterday'.[2]

Sir William committed many of the tales he heard to paper, and published a small selection of them in magazines and in the volume *Irish Popular Superstitions* (1852). Speranza wrote a favourable review of one of his magazine pieces, and it may have been her article that first brought the couple together. Sir William wanted to publish as many

Wilde's father, aged around fifty, dressed in the regalia
of the Chevalier of the Swedish North Star.

of the stories as he could because he believed that print would preserve Ireland's oral culture, whose existence was seriously threatened by the depopulation caused by the Great Famine of 1845– 49. At his untimely death in 1876, at the age of sixty-two, Sir William's monumental labour of love remained unfinished. Speranza completed his work, editing and revising the remainder of the transcribed tales, perhaps with the help of her son, for publication, in two books, in the 1880s and 1890s.[3] The adult Wilde owned and cherished both volumes. He penned an anonymous notice of one of them in which he described Speranza as an 'Irishwoman telling Irish stories, impelled by . . . tradition . . . and with a nursery knowledge at first hand of all characteristic moods of the Irish imagination'.[4]

The folk stories published by the Wildes comprise a teeming, grotesque and luridly coloured world. The chief protagonists are the little people, or the fairies, who are mischievous or malevolent, according to their mood or race. Sometimes they are content simply to upset a milk churn, but woe betide the farmer who takes away their dancing ground, because their retribution is swift and lethal. They take a devilish delight in stealing the most beautiful newborn babes and substituting them with demons. The only means of discovering if a child is a fairy changeling is the terrible trial by fire, in which the baby is thrown on to the flames. In one of the Wildes' stories a child is hurled into a fire, where it turns into a black cat, then flies up the chimney with a terrifying scream.

It is a typically gruesome and bizarre episode from tales which articulate the very real fear of the fairies then still prevalent among the Irish peasantry and shared perhaps even by high-class Dubliners such as the Wildes.[5] The tales record the fate of many children who have been carried off by the little people. They are usually whisked away to fairy palaces of pearl and gold, 'where they live in splendour and luxury, with music and song and dancing and laughter and all the joyous things, as befits the gods of the earth'. If the fairies are of the Sidhe race they transport their child captives to Tír na nOg, where they pass their lives in pleasure until Judgment Day, when they are annihilated.[6]

The folk tales Wilde imbibed as a child form an autonomous fairyland, making little concession to the 'primary' or everyday world. They eschew ordinary rationale for the weird logic of dreams. Like inventions of the unconscious they are fragmentary, and move swiftly from horror to comedy; they also contain episodes of extreme violence and thinly veiled eroticism. Powerful human desires and impulses are personified in a cast of exemplary and mythical beings including witches, leprechauns, banshees, saints and talking animals. This is, in other words, a literature concerned with the inner landscape of man's fears and desires. Its realism does not lie in its accurate representation of the external world but in its articulation and excitement of intense feelings and sensations. Wilde's mother later expressed this idea when she congratulated her son on one of his own fairy stories: 'no matter', she said, 'how strange and fantastic the incidents, yet the pathos, the human pathos is always real'.[7]

Wilde later objected to works of conventional realism in part because they made little appeal, or reference, to man's inner world. They offered instead an objective picture of nature, uncoloured by the unconscious or the imagination, which only addressed the reader's reason. He praised, instead, those artists (and writers) who see the world 'not merely [with] actual and physical vision, but with that nobler vision of the soul which is as far wider in spiritual scope as it is far more splendid in artistic purpose'.[8]

Wilde believed that the external world became more significant and familiar when viewed in a 'mythopoetic' rather than an objective fashion.[9] Nature, he claimed, is brought to life, and becomes identifiable to us, through the stories we tell about it: thus the Greeks, in their myths, 'peopled the grove and hillside with beautiful and fantastic forms', in order 'to make Nature one with humanity'.[10]

The folk tales that cradled Wilde performed precisely this function. Some of the legends in his parents' anthologies inspired the place-names of modern Ireland; they include stories in which the deeds of the little people leave indelible marks on the Irish landscape, such as the hollows that are still known in Ireland as 'fairy glens'. Most of the tales are attached to a particular place: it is as though they have grown up, irresistibly, from their native soil. Wilde loved the legends associated with the area around Lough Corrib, near Cong, in County Mayo, where his family had their country home. As a boy he was told that Finvara, the King of the Fairies, held his court at the Lough; he heard too, that weird female figures, carrying flames in their hands and thought to be the *genii loci*, haunted the summits of the rocks.[11] Sir William decided to have the Wildes' holiday home built at Moytura because of a tale connected with the place. The house marks the site of the legendary Battle of Magh-Tura fought between the Fir Bolg and the Tuatha-De-Danann tribes. At that bloody clash, at which the sworn enemies contended for lordship over all Ireland, the giant magician Balor was slain when a stone was hurled into his evil eye.

Sir William saw the conflict literally written in the landscape. An inspired amateur archaeologist, he was able to identify the land's characteristics with the help of an ancient manuscript account of the conflict. On one occasion, wandering over the hills near their home with a copy of the manuscript in his hand, he suddenly stopped and ordered his labourers to dig. Buried beneath the earth they found a square chamber made of flagstones, with a small ornamented urn inside containing human bones, which Sir William believed to be those of a heroic Fir Bolg youth.

Wilde often assisted his father on his archaeological digs, so it is possible the boy witnessed this remarkable act of divination.[12] He certainly knew of the discovery, as he would later describe Moytura as 'a beautiful place which stood upon the scene of the greatest battle in the Irish legends . . . where the ground was full of memories, and crammed with ancient monuments'.[13]

An account of the find is given in Sir William's engaging book *Lough Corrib: Its Shores and Islands* (1867), Wilde's copy of which has survived. 'To Oscar,' reads Sir William's inscription, 'on his birthday. With the author's love. 16 Oct, 1867.'[14] It is a rare and beautiful memento of their relationship, and of the time they spent walking and talking their way across the hills and fields of the West of Ireland.

On their rambles, Sir William mapped the land with so many legends, songs and poems that, in the imagination of his boy, the scene and the songs became one. When he fished in Lough Corrib, young Oscar, who was a keen angler, would try to lure the great melancholy carp that lay on its bed by singing them a Gaelic song he had learned from his father, *Athá mé in mu codladh, agus ná dúishe mé* (I am asleep, do not wake me.)[15] Poetry and nature were married in Wilde's mind and, from a tender age, he believed that words might exercise a supernatural power over the material world.

Wilde adored the scenery of the 'delightful, heathery, mountainous, lake-filled region'[16] of the West no doubt in part because it was so deeply interfused with poetry and myths. Given his bookish vision of the world, it is likely that he saw it directly as a legendary and poetic landscape: 'This wild mountainous country,' he said, finding in it an echo of his own name, 'is in every way magnificent and makes me years younger than actual history records.'[17] The idea that the West of Ireland magically preserves one's youth suggests that it may have been coupled in Wilde's mind with Tír na nOg, which is apt because the area was believed to be haunted by fairies of the Sidhe race, whose home was the country of the young.

In the stories published by the Wildes, the Celts are portrayed as childlike, sentimental and superstitious; they are 'a nation of poets' to whom the presence of God and the invisible powers are ever near. They love 'splendour, grace of movement, music and pleasure' and adore beauty above all things. They are protean, airy, generous and sensitive, and contemptuous of logic and common sense.[18]

Wilde accepted, and indeed exemplified, this idea of the Celtic identity. In the first journalistic profile written about him he describes himself as 'the offspring of a fervid and emotional race' to whom 'the intangible delights of the beautiful are the realities of life'.[19] Throughout his writings he celebrates the creativity, quick artistic sense and poetic genius of the Celtic race which, he claims, always 'leads in Art'.[20]

There was a political edge to Wilde's encomia to the Celtic nature. Like his parents, he was, in his own words, a 'recalcitrant patriot' who openly criticised England's control over his country and supported Charles Stewart Parnell's Home Rule campaign for Irish autonomy; he even joked, on one occasion, that his answer to the 'Irish Question' was that the Irish should govern England. His praise of the Celt was often coupled with caustic criticism of Anglo-Saxons. He followed his mother in characterising that race as philistine, rapacious, insensitive to beauty, and suffering from a fatal want of imagination.

The folk tales that nurtured the young Wilde often illustrate political issues. They make explicit reference to events such as the 'troublous times of '98' when the English quashed a Nationalist rebellion, as well as to the Great Famine of the 1840s. Stories concerning that tragedy, which many believed to have been the English government's responsibility, seem to have made a strong impression on the boy: 'How tragic,' he said years later, 'stories of the Irish Famine are! My father . . . used to tell me marvellous tales about it.'[21]

Like the profusion of poems dedicated to Ossianic lore in the nineteenth century, folk tales (in their published form) were part of the Gaelic cultural revival which celebrated, and also attempted to forge, a strong national Irish identity. This identity would, it was hoped, be capacious enough to appeal to both the Catholic peasantry and to Anglo-Irish Protestants such as the Wildes. The tales and the Ossianic poems certainly succeeded in shaping Wilde's own cultural identity: 'French by sympathy, I am Irish by race,' he proudly declared in adulthood; 'and the English,' he added, 'have condemned me to speak the language of Shakespeare'.[22]

The folk tales and Ossianic legends formed the landscape of Wilde's adult imagination. He spoke fondly 'of the beauty and glamour of the old Celtic legends',[23] and retold Irish folk tales at dinner parties in Paris and London.[24] During these performances Wilde imitated, in an alien urban context, the *seanchaí* he had encountered as a boy in the West of Ireland.

When he picked up his pen too, Wilde drew on the reservoir of images, scenes and phrases he had absorbed in his infancy. His own fairy tales, with their talking animals, ghosts, mermaids and spells, transport us back to the world of Celtic Faëry.[25] His novel *The Picture of Dorian Gray* (1891) also draws on the legends of Tír na nOg, and is saturated with motifs and echoes from Celtic mythology.[26] That story fulfils two prophecies his parents made in their anthologies. Speranza hoped that some of the tales would one day inspire a work of genius in a writer of the stature of Goethe; Sir William looked forward to a time 'When we have a novelist . . . possessing the power of fusing ancient legend with the drama of modern life'. 'Then, and only then,' he said, 'will Irish history be known and appreciated.'[27]

What was true of Wilde's art was also true of his life. Fairyland serves as the perfect metaphor for the marvellous worlds of burnished gold he sought to inhabit in his daily existence as well as to create in his books. 'My father,' as Wilde's son Vyvyan put it, 'lived in a world of his own; an artificial world . . . in which the only things that really mattered were art and beauty.'[28] It is indeed tempting to think of Wilde as one of the eternally young, lured away one evening from his bed at Merrion Square by the grace and beauty of a Sidhe fairy and magically conveyed to Tír na nOg, the land from which his heroic Ossianic namesake hailed.

3. 'Words that are winged with light'

WHEN WE TRY TO envisage Wilde's early experiences of literature we should not primarily think of him curled up in bed with his head in a book – an image familiar to us from the childhoods of Dickens or Proust. Instead, we must picture that almost unimaginable thing: an Oscar Wilde who sits in silence and listens to others. He is listening to his parents' voices, the one powerful and rotund, the other excitable, shrill and volatile, as they narrate traditional tales or recite verse. In his childhood, Wilde did not encounter literature exclusively, or perhaps even chiefly, in printed form – it was poured into the portals of his ears.

The set of brilliant Anglo-Irish intellectuals who regularly congregated at the Wildes' house at No. 1 Merrion Square evidently believed that the Celtic soul best expressed itself in the sociable and physical medium of 'living speech'. Rhymers such as the Catholic convert Aubrey de Vere would often recite their verses at the Wildes' receptions; members of the coterie also put on some of Shakespeare's plays. The intellectual discussions Wilde heard at his parents' dinner table were, too, a crucial part of his oral literary upbringing. He is described as having 'at eight years old, heard every subject demolished at his father's dinner table, where were to be found not only the brilliant geniuses of Ireland, but also the celebrities of Europe and America'. It was here 'that the best of his early education was obtained'.[1]

This description of the dinner table arguments at Merrion Square calls to mind the Greek symposium evoked by Plato. It is quite possible that the debates were modelled on classical lines, because Speranza referred to them as 'Athenian converse with the best minds'.[2] Over the course of the discussion, anecdotes and stories were told, to illustrate a point or simply to entertain, Sir William being renowned as one of the finest storytellers in Dublin. Aphorisms would often illuminate the discourse – Speranza held that epigrams were far more effective than rational arguments. Books were constantly referred to and précised; quotations were cited, or perhaps made up. The debates were a wonderful example of the happy marriage of the oral and the written literary traditions, a union of which Wilde would be the brilliant child.*

The young Wilde was brought up by his mother to regard poetry as the apotheosis of oral literature. In a preface to one of her own volumes of verse, Speranza encourages the reader to recite the poems aloud.[4] Her delight in declaiming poetry is well documented. On one occasion, during one of the Wildes' intermittent periods of financial embarrassment, the bailiffs called at Merrion Square. Loftily ignoring them, Speranza lay down on the sofa with a copy of the plays of the Greek tragedian Aeschylus, from which she proceeded to recite passages with 'exalted enthusiasm'.[5]

In a letter Speranza describes the way Wilde's brother's 'pretty

* In later life, Wilde would become a master of the oral arts. He was widely acknowledged as one of the greatest storytellers of his, or perhaps any, age.[3] In his critical writings, he argued that the true test of literature was the spoken word, and urged writers to 'return to the voice'. And this is precisely what he did himself. Not only did he excel, as an author, in 'oral' forms such as the dialogue and the drama, but virtually all of his works began life as stories he told to friends. His writings contain a conspicuous oral residue, too, with their stock characters, formulas and elaborate repetitions. This is why we are often compelled to read them aloud.

graceful head' would rest on her shoulder while she read ' "The Lady Clare" to him from Tennyson or . . . [Longfellow's] "Hiawatha", two favourites of his'.[6] This may surely also stand as an emblem of young Oscar's experience. Willie Wilde was only three years old when Speranza wrote her letter, a remarkably early age at which to acquire a personal, and indeed discerning, taste in literature. Oscar must have been introduced to verse at an equally tender age; indeed, there may be some truth in his later claim to have been acquainted with the work of Walt Whitman 'almost from the cradle'.[7]

The experience of hearing his mother recite verse taught Wilde that poetry is primarily an oral art. In adulthood he recited from memory poets such as Shakespeare and Charles Baudelaire in the company of his friends; he also gave public performances of his own verse. Wilde learned that a poem's sound should be savoured above all of its other qualities — an idea perhaps inculcated by a steady infant diet of Longfellow and Tennyson. In later life, he lingered lovingly over musical words such as 'amber' and 'narcissus', even licking his lips with bliss as he pronounced them. He thrilled to melodious poetic phrases, declaring Tennyson's line 'Now lies the Earth all Danaë to the stars' to be poetry at its most perfect. He also derived intense pleasure from beautiful examples of alliteration, evincing a particular fondness for the seventeenth-century poet Andrew Marvell's line 'Like golden lamps in a green night'.

Wilde absorbed from his mother the idea that poetry is essentially a form of word music: instead of attempting to convey a message or trying to represent the 'real' world, verse should offer listeners intense sensual pleasure through its melody. When he later recited his own verse Wilde 'chanted' it in his 'melodious Irish voice'.[8] 'Chant' was a word Speranza used to describe her own recitations, so perhaps Wilde deliberately imitated his mother in his public performances.[9] He would employ the same musical term in his famous definition of the poet as a singer who builds 'his song out of music, repeating each line over and over again to himself till he has caught the secret of its melody, chaunting in the darkness the words that are winged with light'.[10]

For Wilde, poetry was a potent form of magic, and the poet a sort of magus. 'Words!' he wrote, 'Mere words! How terrible they were! . . . what a subtle magic there was in them! They seemed to be able to give a plastic form to formless things . . . Was there anything so real as words?'[11] Poetical words, he believed, give form to inchoate feelings; indeed with 'their mystical power over the soul', they often create 'the feeling from which [they] should have sprung'.[12]

Wilde's idea of poetry as a species of magical word music may have been derived from the Irish Bards. His parents regaled him with stories of that ancient order, many of which are included in their anthologies of folklore. According to these yarns, Bards recited poetry from memory, or gave extempore recitals comprised of stock motifs, to the accompaniment of a golden harp. Their gift derived from the magical Bardic potion or from the fairies, whose delicate and captivating music was said to enter their souls as they lay sleeping. This is eminently appropriate, for the Bards often 'swayed the hearts of their hearers as they chose, to love or war, joy or sadness, as if by magic influence, or lulled them into the sweet calm of sleep'.[13] Bards also commanded the power of prophecy and the power of the curse.

The Bards generally resided at the courts of kings, where their supernatural powers and the enchantment of their song secured them a status second only to that of their regal lords. They were allowed, as a special privilege, to wear clothes of four colours, 'a state of things', Wilde commented, 'which I would wish to see revived for the benefit of modern poets'.[14] This aside suggests, in its witty way, that the Bards were not merely historical curiosities for him, but the archetypal ancestors of modern rhymers. When Wilde remarks, in 'The Decay of Lying', that the imaginative 'liar' will one day 'lead' society, we may read this as a veiled prophecy that the Bards will regain their prominent place in the world, in the modern guise of the 'liar' or storyteller.[15] Wilde himself would later charm and 'lead' London society by the performances of his stories he gave at dinner parties. Both here and in his essentially oral method of composition he may have been consciously assuming the mantle of the Bards. That is certainly how it appeared to his friends, one of whom said that Wilde had 'inherited the soul of some far away bard who invented his chants as he sang them'.[16]

4. 'Soul-forward, headlong'

WHICH POEMS DID Speranza recite to her son? Perhaps she began with those she knew best: her own. The young Wilde was intimately familiar with his mother's verse: in his first surviving letter, written when he was fourteen, he asks Speranza to send him a magazine containing one of her poems. Four years earlier she had dedicated an edition of her verses to 'my sons Willie and Oscar Wilde'. 'I made them indeed', she declares in the dedication, 'Speak plain the word COUNTRY. I taught them, no doubt / That a country's a thing one should die for at need.'[1]

Speranza's poems are patriotic, grandiloquent and sometimes inflammatory. She also commanded a quieter power, penning conventional Romantic verses, but Wilde preferred her in fiery political mode. His favourite poems were her ballad on the trial and execution of the Sheares Brothers in 1798 for having 'sought to free their land from thrall of stranger [i.e. the British]', and her passionate verses on what her son called 'our unfortunately unsuccessful [Nationalist] *rebellion of '48'.*[2] He read both poems, 'with much effect and feeling', during a lecture he gave in America in 1882.

In that lecture, Wilde also quoted from, or mentioned, many of the other Irish poets he had grown up with as a boy. These included Samuel Ferguson, the author of lovely lyrics on mythological themes, Thomas Moore, whose melodies 'were made to be sung by beautiful Irish maids to beautiful Irish music,'[3] and the most famous patriotic poets of the middle of the century, Clarence Mangan and Thomas Davis. It was Davis – the leader of the Young Ireland movement, which campaigned for the repeal of the English Union – who had first inspired Speranza to take up her pen. His poetry, and that of his Nationalist contemporaries had, Wilde said, 'kept alive the flames of patriotism in the hearts of the Irish people'.[4]*

Speranza's taste in English and American poetry was modern and Romantic; Whitman, Matthew Arnold, Longfellow and Wordsworth were the poetic gods of her idolatry. Wilde was heir to her taste and, in his youth, he favoured Romantic over Classical verse. Even in his later years he would remark that there were two ways of disliking poetry: one was to dislike it, the other was to like Alexander Pope. His preference for Romantic verse is hardly surprising, given his delight in the music, emotiveness and magical potency of poetry, along with his fascination with the ancient figure of the Bard.

Speranza passed on to her son many of her predilections. He delighted in the work of her great heroine, Elizabeth Barrett Browning, hailing her as the greatest poetess since Sappho and ranking her *Aurora Leigh* alongside *Hamlet* and Tennyson's *In Memoriam*. Barrett Browning's masterpiece is an impassioned and delightfully rambling autobiographical poem, concerning a woman's struggle to find the intellectual, physical and social space in which to write. 'So much do I love it,' Wilde later told William Ward, an Oxford friend to whom he gave the volume as a gift, 'that I hated the idea of sending it to you

---

* Many of the poets Wilde referred to in his lecture can be placed in the ancient Irish Bardic tradition. The verses of Moore and Mangan are wonderfully melodic; other authors consciously drew on Irish folklore and mythology for inspiration. Aubrey de Vere, whom Wilde also mentioned in the lecture, consciously attempted to revive the ancient Bardic tradition in poems such as 'Inisfail', which Wilde was certainly familiar with.[5]

without marking a few passages I felt you would well appreciate – and I found myself marking the whole book.'[6]

Wilde's book gift has survived.[7] In its margins he provided Ward with a running commentary. Next to a passage on Puritanism he wrote: 'read all this delightfully satirical';[8] alongside a frightening description of an old woman he scribbled the word 'terrible'. In the letter that accompanied the present Wilde praised the poem's sincerity, calling it 'one of those books that, written straight from the heart – and from such a large heart too – never weary one'.[9] His notes testify to the appropriately earnest mood in which he read it. He marks touching passages on love, emotionally charged sections on women's fight for independence, and passionate lines on the sacred role of the poet in modern society.[10] Barrett Browning describes the ardour with which she reads her favourite poets: 'We gloriously forget ourselves and plunge / Soul-forward, headlong'. This captures the spirit in which Wilde perused her poem, so it is fitting that he marked the lines.

Wilde inherited his mother's profound admiration for Tennyson. He was beguiled by the melodious music of the Poet Laureate, and regarded him as the apotheosis of a specifically English tradition whose earlier exemplars included Chaucer and Spenser. This tradition was, he said, characterised by a 'sympathy with passion', a fondness for 'sensuous imagery as opposed to ideas', and by its joyous celebration of 'the variety of life'.[11] It is possible that Speranza read to her son from the 1858 edition of Tennyson's *Poems* that later found a place on the shelves of Wilde's Tite Street library.[12] This little quarto volume, which contains poems such as 'The Lotos Eaters', 'Locksley Hall' (Speranza's favourite) and 'The Lady of Shalott', had a special provenance: it was inscribed to her by the Scottish author Carlyle. As she, in turn, passed it on to her son, it may serve as a symbol of the poetic legacy she bestowed upon him.[13]

Just as Speranza famously banned the word 'respectable' from the parties she hosted at Merrion Square, she displayed scant concern for a poet's moral 'respectability'. She allowed, and indeed probably encouraged, her son to read Algernon Swinburne and Dante Gabriel Rossetti, two poets regarded as scandalous in Victorian England, because of the frankly pagan character of their 'fleshy' verse. Swinburne's *Poems and Ballads* contains breathless poems sung with 'lips full of lust and of laughter' in which the poet cries out to be filled with pleasure 'Till pain come in turn'. Wilde was ravished by the book's 'very perfect and very poisonous' verses,[14] the first in English literature, he claimed, to 'sing divinely the song of the flesh'.[15] He would, he declared years later, rather have written *Poems and Ballads* than any other book.

Wilde loved the 'artistic completeness of the workmanship' of Rossetti's verses which, he said, affect one 'like a deferred resolution in Beethoven'. He admired the poet's genius for drawing 'the quintessential music out of words'.[16] Once again, it was the 'sweet and precious melodies' of the poems that appealed to Wilde, just as it was surely the delicious music of the following lines that made them especially dear to him:

> The cuckoo-throb, the heartbeat of the Spring;
>> The rosebud's blush that leaves it as it grows
>> Into the full-eyed fair unblushing rose;
> The summer clouds that visit every wing[17]

Wilde was greatly impressed, by the 'strength and splendour' of Rossetti's 'dominant personality'. 'Personality' was one of the qualities he looked for in verse, along with 'perfection' of craftsmanship. These attributes were exquisitely blended in the writings of the favourite poet of his youth, John Keats, the 'god-like boy', whom he placed alongside Shakespeare and the Greeks in his poetic pantheon.[18] In fact, when Wilde later came to compile a list of books he advised the readers of the *Pall Mall Gazette* to 're-read', Keats was the only poet he included.* To Wilde, Keats was a master among minstrels, a sacred 'Priest of Beauty'. When he later visited the poet's grave (which he called 'the holiest place in Rome') he was so overwhelmed that he prostrated himself upon it.

Wilde would come to see Keats as the presiding spirit of his own early poetry, in which he often echoes the Bard of Hampstead. When he was particularly satisfied with one of his own poetic efforts, Wilde would say that even his 'dear friend' Keats had approved of it. This reverence would endure into adulthood when he purchased some of Keats's letters at an auction. He also owned the manuscript of Keats's 'Sonnet in Blue', which he proudly displayed in the drawing-room at Tite Street. 'I am half enamoured of the paper that touched his hand,' Wilde wrote, 'and the ink that did his bidding, [I have] grown fond of the sweet comeliness of his charactery'.[19]

Another poet the young Wilde loved, 'as one should love all things, not wisely but too well'[20], was Shakespeare. We do not know the precise moment the boy entered the fiery-coloured world of the Bard's plays, nor can we identify the specific volume that provided a portal into it. Speranza may have read to him from the 1833 edition of Shakespeare's works contained in Sir William's library, or perhaps she used the three-volume illustrated Cassell edition that later formed part of Wilde's adult library.[21]

The nineteenth-century child often started with the Lambs' famous *Tales from Shakespeare*, or other prose versions of the plays, before moving on to the expurgated editions that had been produced by

---

* Wilde's list of 'Books to re-read', along with his suggestions for 'Books to read' and 'Books not to read' offers a succinct statement of his readerly taste. It is reproduced in Appendix I of this book (see pp. 317–8).

editors such as the American Thomas Bowdler, which excised or altered Shakespeare's salacious passages. Children were then ready to encounter the plays in their pristine form. As Rossetti passed through all of these phases before the age of seven, it is probable that Wilde was introduced to Shakespeare before his seventh year. While it is possible that Wilde began with the Lambs' *Tales*, it is highly unlikely that his parents inflicted a Bowdlerised Shakespeare on him.

Whatever door young Wilde used to enter the Shakespearean universe, the experience must have been an intense one. He found himself in the middle of that field of electrifying energy, in which every idea, emotion, style and character, is balanced by its opposite, and in which the possibilities of thought and life seem infinite. It is a world made out of all-powerful, magical and rhythmical words that would have acted on Wilde like intoxicating music. The encounter marked him for life, burning Shakespeare's words indelibly into his memory. He knew many of the plays so well that, in later years, he could identify even the slightest misquotation when he saw them performed on the stage.

In adulthood Wilde recalled his passionate boyhood affair with literature: he had loved it, he remarked, 'to excess.'[22] A childhood and adolescent ardour for poetry was common among writers in the nineteenth century. The poet Francis Thompson, an acquaintance of Wilde's, remembered being 'overwhelmed by feelings of which he knew not the meaning' at the age of seven on first encountering Shakespeare and Coleridge. Another of Wilde's friends, Edmund Gosse, 'listened, as if to a nightingale', during his boyhood, to the Latin of Virgil. Although it was incomprehensible to his child's ears, it revealed to him 'the incalculable beauty that could exist in the sound of verses', and the wonder of poetry 'took hold of his heart forever'.[23]

The experience of falling in love with poetry was one of the most important of Wilde's life, and not only in terms of literature. It convinced him that the poet was 'the supreme artist . . . lord over life and all arts',[24] and it stirred within him the ambition to be a Bard. The exact moment Wilde dedicated himself, with vows, to poetry, is unknown to us, but it is pleasant to imagine it having occurred during one of Speranza's recitations. At any rate, Wilde later said that it was his mother who inspired him to write verse.[25] Speranza would be involved at every stage of its production too, annotating his early efforts, some of which were penned in notebooks that belonged to her. When his poems first appeared in magazines she compiled a scrapbook of them, and frequently offered her enthusiastic criticisms. Of 'Magdalen Walks' she wrote: 'the last lines have a bold, true thought, bravely uttered . . . I recognise <u>you</u> at once . . . there is Oscar!'[26] When Wilde won the prestigious Newdigate poetry prize for *Ravenna* (1878) at Oxford she was even more effusive. 'Oh Gloria, Gloria! . . . we have *genius!*' she wrote to her darling boy, 'you have got *honour* and *recognition* – and this at only 22 [he was actually 23] is a grand thing.'[27]

5. 'A good book and a good fire'

O NE DAY, WHEN the Wildes were having dinner at Merrion Square, Sir William asked the three-year-old Oscar to fetch him a book from his library.[1] Wilde jumped down from the table and scampered off downstairs to the book-lined room on the ground floor. We can imagine him standing there in the middle of the library, casting his eyes rapidly over the spines in search of the relevant title.

To have been entrusted with this task the young Oscar must have known his father's collection well. Having the run of that 'library containing the best literature' was, he later remarked, vitally important for his early education.[2] The collection was comprised of the finest literature of various European cultures in their original languages; it also boasted volumes on subjects as diverse as theology, midwifery, metalwork, astronomy and ornithology. The age, size and provenance of the books were as heterogeneous as their contents. There were folio and octavo volumes which hailed from American, English and continental presses.[3] This vast emporium of multi-coloured editions of all shapes and sizes must have dazzled Wilde's infant eyes.

Speranza also possessed an extensive collection of modern and ancient literature. At Merrion Square she does not appear to have had a room set aside for her books, and they were probably scattered all over the house. The drawing-rooms at No. 1 were, she said, 'a lumber of books'. She planned to organise the volumes, 'but', she told a friend, 'time and courage failed me – so they are covering the floor'.[4] Throughout her life Speranza preferred to leave her books in a state of mild disorder, piling them up from floor to ceiling, or leaving them lying around on the furniture. As the young Wilde played around the house he would have bumped into books at every turn. Perhaps he even incorporated them into his games, as his own children did years later, when they made stilts by strapping books to the soles of their feet. Despite the markedly oral nature of Wilde's early literary education, his was also an eminently bookish childhood – he grew up surrounded by mountains of books.

As Speranza described herself happiest with 'a good book and a good fire'[5] we can picture mother and son in front of a roaring fire in the nursery at Merrion Square. Young Oscar was probably curled up in her lap, though he would have had to vie for that privilege with his brother Willie and his young sister Isola, who had been born in 1857. As Wilde's childhood is likely to have been crowded with all the usual incidents of infant disease, such as whooping cough and measles, his mother is also likely to have read to him when he lay ill in bed. In later life Wilde certainly turned to literature for comfort when he was sick.

Wilde would have received his first reading lessons from his mother and his nurse, as well as from the various French, German and English governesses employed to look after and educate the children at Merrion Square. During the 1850s two principal methods of teaching children to read were in vogue. One of these continued the ancient 'hornbook' tradition of instruction by emphasising spelling and the learning of letters. The other, known as the 'whole-word method', began with the association of entire words with sounds and pictures, thus encouraging the child to go 'straight from the printed form of a word to its enunciation'.[6]

Nineteenth-century primers based on the second method focus on the sound of words. Infants are encouraged to learn catchy nursery rhymes such as 'Wee Willie Winkie', and rhythmic phrases such as 'I am not six; but I can bat. A man, an ox, a cat, a fox'. Given his parents' sensitivity to the oral and aural aspects of literature, as well as the erratic nature of Wilde's adult spelling,[7] it is likely that he was taught with the whole-word method. It is hard to think of a better education for a poet who would savour sound above sense.

From these 'First Reading Books' the nineteenth-century child typically progressed to illustrated collections of nursery rhymes and to fairy tales, such as 'Little Red Riding Hood' and 'Jack the Giant Killer', along with stories by Hans Andersen and the Brothers Grimm. Children derive great satisfaction from the clearly defined narrative sequences of these tales, with their archetypal beginnings and emphatic conclusions. The tales offer them templates for ordering their own experience – they learn to construct narratives out of everyday occurrences; to *think* in stories. This was a mental habit that Wilde undoubtedly acquired as a boy. Years later he told one friend that he instinctively thought in the form of stories, rather than with abstract ideas.[8]

At some point in his childhood, the young Wilde became an accomplished enough reader to retreat, alone, into a private world of books. There are examples of writers, such as Robert Louis Stevenson, who were so enamoured of hearing stories that they deliberately put off learning to read for themselves until as late as six or seven years old. It is not impossible that Wilde was similar. He told a friend that he was never a precocious child, and there is a noticeable dearth of the sort of anecdotes relating to his childhood reading that are so common in the lives of other writers. Given the adult Wilde's celebrated gift for speed-reading, however, along with the fact that he had two clever and loving parents, the chances are that, like Swift and Dickens, he would have been able to read by himself around the age of three or four.

From that time onwards Wilde probably began to build up in his bedroom, on the top floor of the house, his first collection of books. In a lecture, Wilde described how the eighteenth-century English poet Thomas Chatterton had loved, as a boy, 'to covet the privacy of his little study', reading there 'from the moment he waked . . . until he went to bed'.[9] This may be an echo of his own experience. If it was, then it must have been an extremely novel one for a boy brought up to associate books with company, and the printed word with the spoken voice. Wilde was no doubt allowed to read in his bedroom before lights out – and this may well be the origin of his lifelong habit of reading in bed. In fact, it would not be at all surprising to learn that mandatory night-time reading was one of the few regulations enforced in the Wildes' bohemian household.*

And what did young Wilde take to bed with him to read? One of the 'golden books' of his childhood was J.W. Meinhold's 1847 Gothic historical novel *Sidonia the Sorceress*. Wilde's mother, who was an accomplished translator of European fiction, produced a celebrated English version of this German book. Wilde would remember it fondly as 'my favourite romantic reading when a boy'[11] and he returned to it at various times in his adult life.[12] He must have been a gifted child reader to have perused the novel because it would present insurmountable difficulties to the average infant. Indeed, both its style and content suggest that it was aimed at adults as well as children.

Sidonia is set in the seventeenth-century land of Pomerania. The heroine is the beautiful and eloquent Sidonia von Bork, an outsider, by her lowly birth, to the world of the court, which she is determined

---

* Wilde made bedtime reading mandatory for his lover Alfred Douglas when he was preparing for his Oxford exams. He drew up a mock timetable for Douglas's revision studies that included 'compulsory reading in bed' between midnight and 1.30. If 'found disobeying this rule', Douglas would, according to the timetable, be 'immediately woken up'.[10]

to conquer. Her plans to marry a duke are foiled when he learns that she has other lovers of far less exalted status than himself. Ostracised by the court, Sidonia turns to witchcraft. With the aid of Satan she puts a curse of sterility on the Pomeranian royal line, but when her spell is discovered she is burnt at the stake.

Before her demise Sidonia enjoys a series of picaresque adventures. These involve grisly murders, accidental decapitations and premature burials. There is a powerful erotic element in some of the episodes, which is often mixed with violence. The Sorceress has a voracious sexual appetite: she seduces priests and turns her nunnery into a 'Sodom and Gomorrah'. The sex and violence are mingled with a great deal of comedy. Sidonia is always ready with some quick-witted retort that would not have been out of place in the Wildes' drawing-room.

In the novel, humour follows hard upon the heels of horror. Reading it, Wilde must have been unsure whether to laugh or scream. Dickens referred to the principle of narrative heterogeneity as the 'streaky bacon' style. It was a style the young Wilde learned to love from *Sidonia* and from the Irish folk tales his parents told him. He would master it himself in works such as *Dorian Gray* and in plays where he consciously sought to 'produce tragic effects by introducing comedy'. A laugh, he believed, 'does not destroy terror, but, by relieving it, aids it'.[13]

Sidonia haunted Wilde's adult imagination, and traces of its influence can be found in *Dorian Gray*.[14] Another childhood favourite that he later turned to for inspiration was *Melmoth the Wanderer*, written by Charles Maturin, Wilde's great-uncle on his mother's side, in 1820.

Melmoth, a seventeenth-century Anglo-Irish gentleman, strikes a Faustian bargain with the Devil, exchanging his soul for a hundred and fifty year extension to his life. He soon tires of earthly pleasures, however, and tries to exploit a loophole in his diabolic deal, which allows him to elude his fate if he can find someone willing to exchange places with him. His search for a victim, often among the most wretched specimens of humanity, provides the novel with its chilling and tortuous plot; his failure to do so gives it its tragic end.

At many points *Melmoth* prefigures *Dorian Gray*. In one of the opening scenes a portrait of the eponymous hero is destroyed by his ancestor, just as, at the end of Wilde's novel, Dorian vandalises his own painted image. Melmoth's descendant hacks the picture to pieces then throws the fragments onto a fire. As he gazes at the flames a terrible voice suddenly comes out of nowhere: 'You have burned me,' it bellows, 'but those are flames I can survive − I am alive, − I am beside you.'

Wilde praised *Melmoth* as a pioneering work of European Gothic fiction. He admitted, however, that it was stylistically 'imperfect' and laughed at its absurdity.[15] Yet this is by no means a negative or an inappropriate response to a book that hails from the 'streaky bacon' school of writing: the novel exhibits no artistic decorum whatsoever, and Wilde's fondness for it can be regarded as a glorious example of what one of his acquaintances would call his 'infallible bad taste'.[16]

Wilde's childhood reading, dominated by folk tales, poetry and Gothic fiction, was probably atypical for the period, at least by the standards of middle-class Victorian England. He appears to have been spared the religious fare that formed the staple diet of many English children. There is no record of his having read enormously popular 'improving' books such as Mrs Sherwood's *The Fairchild Family*. Nor, so far as we know, was he force-fed the pious and mawkish children's literature of the day, which reached its apogee in Charles Kingsley's *The Water Babies*. Wilde maintained that it was a mistake to 'think that children are sentimental about literature; they are not: they have humour instead.'[17] It was a lesson he may have absorbed from his own youthful experience.

While the Wildes allowed their son the free run of their libraries, many Victorian parents rigorously censored their offspring's reading, providing for them carefully chosen 'selections' from the works of writers such as Alexandre Dumas or George Eliot. Even expurgated novels were forbidden to the children of strict English Protestant families. 'Never in all my early childhood,' remembered Edmund Gosse, 'did anyone address to me the affecting preamble, "Once upon a time" . . . I never heard of fairies.'[18]

One manual of advice concerning children's reading articulates the conventional Victorian attitude to boys' literature. 'The child soon becomes a boy, and is sent out into the rough world, where all the nonsense about giants and fairies is knocked out of him . . . To suit this hopeful young gentleman, the storyteller writes a *boy's novel*: take a boy for hero. Let him run away to sea. Wreck him on the coast of Africa, and land him among hordes of grinning Negroes. This is the boy's novel; and the boy . . . pronounces it "awfully jolly".'[19]

It is almost impossible to imagine such books being foisted on Wilde. His reading experience was, it seems, much closer to that of a number of English and Irish nineteenth-century writers, none of whom were reared in middle-class households. As a boy, the poet Shelley devoured Gothic fiction along with tales of magic and witchcraft; Maturin adored Shakespeare and Thomas Percy's famous collection of traditional medieval ballads, *Reliques of Ancient English Poetry*. The most striking comparison is with Rossetti, who, like Wilde, grew up in a bohemian and distinctly un-English environment — Rossetti's parents were Italian, and the language of their native country was spoken at home. As a boy, the poet-painter immersed himself in Irish folklore, Gothic fiction and Romantic poetry. Wilde was intrigued to learn of their common literary education when he read a collection of Rossetti's letters. He was especially charmed 'to see how my grand-uncle's *Melmoth* and my mother's *Sidonia*' had also 'been two of the books that fascinated his youth'.[20]

6. 'More than real life'

IN 1864, WHEN Wilde was nine years old, he was sent to Portora Royal boarding-school in Enniskillen, which is around a hundred miles north-west of Dublin. Wilde would later claim to have attended the institution for 'about a year', yet he was actually there for seven, returning home to Merrion Square only during the vacations. The year 1864 marks a definite, and perhaps a painful, rupture in his life, which had, by all accounts, hitherto been fairly idyllic.

Portora Royal, which was known as 'The Eton of Ireland', had a distinctly English ethos. It was one of the 'Royal Schools of Ulster', founded at the time of the British plantation of the seventeenth century, and it catered exclusively for the children of elite Anglo-Irish Protestants like the Wildes – most pupils being the sons of colonial officers, landed gentry or high-ranking professionals. Its aim was to mould competent and resilient young men capable of governing the country under the English Union, to instil in them a respect for authority through strict discipline, and to confer on them an awareness of their social and intellectual superiority.

The English Protestant ethos of Portora was reflected in the syllabus. History largely meant English history – a typical exam question being 'Name the British possessions in Further (Eastern) India.' Ecclesiastical history began after the Reformation, geography made scant reference to Ireland, and Gaelic found no place in the classroom. To judge by the evidence of a prize Wilde won at the school, it is also likely that the literature taught there was predominantly of the English variety. He was awarded a two-volume *History of English Literature* by G.L. Craik, who argues that 'Irish language and literature [cannot] with propriety be included in a history of the English language' because they exercised no influence upon it.[1]

Pupils were expected to know the Protestant King James Bible almost by heart, and Wilde mastered it better than most. He won a prize for Scripture studies at Portora, receiving, as his award, Joseph Butler's theological book *The Analogy of Religion*. He must have disliked the volume intensely — twenty years later he would recall it when he drew up a list of books which he advised people 'not to read'.[2] Wilde probably resented having to learn the Holy Book parrot fashion — he later said that forcing the Bible on young children destroyed for them its charm and enchantment. His schoolboy labours would bear rich and abundant fruit, however, in his mature writings, which are saturated with stories, themes and phrases from the King James Bible. Wilde's intimate acquaintance with that book was one of Portora's most significant and enduring legacies to him.

Wilde also excelled in French. His copy of Voltaire's *Histoire de Charles XII*, bears the autograph and date 'Oscar Wilde September 2nd 1865', which makes it the very first book known to have been in his possession. On page 171 the ten-year-old boy has written the words 'Oscar 8 November 1865', no doubt to mark his remarkable progress with the demanding French text.[3]

Wilde was far less adept at science, and he regarded both the subject and its master as faintly ridiculous. His spectacular incompetence at mathematics was the one glaring blemish on his school record. This probably tarnished his otherwise excellent academic reputation, because Portora's headmaster regarded mathematics and Classics as the two most important subjects on the curriculum.[4]

Wilde redeemed himself with his performance in Classics. He was one of the finest classical students in the school, and would go on to become one of the most pre-eminent classicists of his generation in England and Ireland. It is likely that Wilde had a head start on his companions. His mother was widely read in the classics, the 'Roman orators and the Greek tragedians' being among her favourite authors.[5] She was particularly fond of the works of Greek dramatist Aeschylus and the philosophical dialogues of Plato, which, according to her, constituted the ideal manual for those wishing to shine in intellectual conversation. As these predilections were shared by her son, the chances are that she introduced these writers to him during his childhood. Wilde was probably familiar with some of the classical volumes contained in Sir William's library, which included several titles from the 'Oxford Classics' series, along with a Greek Testament and Liddell and Scott's folio-size Greek lexicon. The collection also boasted a copy of Lemprière's *Dictionary* of Greek myths, which must have fascinated a boy steeped in Celtic mythology and folklore.

From an early age Wilde displayed a preference for Greek language and literature over Latin. This may have been due to the light and melodic nature of Greek, compared to the heavier, more precise, Latin language. Wilde spoke of the rich 'music of vowelled Greek'[6] and described the idiom of the most famous of all ancient Greek poets as a species of word-music, characterising Homer as 'a true singer', who builds 'his song out of music'.[7] Wilde also loved the luminous quality of the language, later likening his perusal of a Greek Testament, after years of reading the King James Bible, to 'going into a garden of lilies out of some narrow and dark house'.[8] Its vividness inspired in him visions of rich sensual beauty at Portora. 'I seemed to see,' he recalled, 'the white figures throwing purple shadows on the sun-baked palæstra; bands of nude youths and maidens . . . moving across a background of deep blue as on the frieze of the Parthenon . . . [I] read Greek eagerly for love of it all, and the more I read the more I was enthralled.'[9]

Unlike Latin, Greek was, too, unencumbered with the baggage of cultural imperialism and the suppression of nationalist vernaculars. Under the Roman Empire culture and language had been monolithic and imposed from the capital, but in ancient Greece the cultures of a number of independent city-states had flourished. Wilde's 1887 review of a volume called *Greek Life and Thought* suggests that this political consideration may have informed his predilection for Greek. In it, he strongly objects to the book's virulent attacks on the ideal of the independent Greek city-state.

The real subject of the review is English rule in Ireland. *Greek Life and Thought* contains explicit and disdainful references to the Home Rule movement, which Speranza's son supported wholeheartedly. Wilde champions the 'political value of autonomy and the intellectual [and artistic] importance of a healthy national life', condemning the coercive politics of 'Bloody' Arthur Balfour, England's Chief Secretary to Ireland at the time.[10]

Aesthetic bliss and nationalist politics are unlikely, however, to have been uppermost in the minds of those who made Classics one of the cornerstones of Portora's curriculum. It was hoped that, through the study of Greek and Latin, 'all the intellectual faculties' of the student would be 'strengthened'. This aim manifested itself in a system of grammatical rote learning designed to sharpen the mind and discipline the memory. The pupil was taught, 'through grind and repetition',[11] the bewildering mysteries of sentence structure, verbs and linguistic gender. It is hardly surprising that Latin or Greek grammar books inspired loathing in the students. Indeed there is something highly appropriate in the fact that, when disobedient schoolboys were caned, they traditionally bit on classical grammar books to help them endure the pain.[12]

Unlike many of his companions, Wilde probably enjoyed his grammar lessons. Surviving copies of his classics books – which contain copious and meticulous annotations concerning syntax and grammar – and his dazzling success in classical examinations, which focused on linguistic issues, suggest that he was, in his own words, a lover of the 'small points'[13] of language and literature. A contemporary remembered Wilde as 'one of the very few students who could grasp the nuances of the various phases of the Greek Middle Voice and of the vagaries of Greek conditional clauses'.[14]

Having mastered the linguistic minutiae, Wilde was among the handful of boys capable of appreciating the aesthetic qualities of the classical texts. He was particularly accomplished in translation and original composition. 'The flowing beauty of his oral translations in class, whether of Thucydides, Plato, or Virgil, was,' one of his peers recalled, 'a thing not easily to be forgotten.' He 'startled everyone', too, 'in the classical medal examination, by walking easily away from us all in the *viva voce* on [Aeschylus's] *Agamemnon*',[15] in which the pupils were asked to translate various lines from the Greek tragedy.

Wilde's real forte was Greek composition. The composition of first-rate original poems in classical Greek is extremely difficult; it is a skill that few classical scholars today command. The student was asked to perfect a wide variety of Greek poetic forms, and to imitate diverse literary styles. It was, in other words, principally a technical exercise with an emphasis on linguistic and stylistic competence, rather than on self-expression. Wilde's gift for imitation, as well as his mastery of a vast repertoire of poetic forms, is evidenced by the verse he published in adulthood. In that poetry passionate themes and feelings, which may derive from his childhood immersion in Romantic verse, are often expressed with a restraint and technical precision acquired, in part, from his study of the classics.

Wilde's peers remarked on his long flowing locks, and his

inordinate love of beautiful clothes. His intense passion for elegant volumes also excited comment in the classrooms. 'We noticed,' one schoolboy recalled, 'that he always liked to have editions of the classics that were of stately size with large print.'[16] It was perhaps the first time that Wilde used books as props for the exhibition of his public persona.

There is conflicting evidence, however, regarding Wilde's juvenile bibliophilia. Far from being exquisite editions issued for the delectation of a bibliomane, the classical volumes that have survived from his student years are all standard school and college editions published in cheap and unattractive small print formats.[17]

On the other hand, Wilde did spend a vast amount of money on books at Portora, where there was no real need to do so, as the boys had the use of a lending library. His book bill for 1871 came to £11 5s. 9d. – a huge sum considering the annual board and tuition fees were only £45[18] and the price of most books no more than a few shillings. It is possible that he purchased, with this money, some of the beautiful 'half bound vellum'[19] editions of the classics that later stood on the shelves at Tite Street but which have not survived. On the balance of the evidence, it seems likely that the man who famously liked to have it both ways probably owned two sets of the classics at school – one for study, the other for aesthetic pleasure and public display.

Wilde was set apart from his fellows by the keen delight he took in some of his studies. 'Understanding and knowledge,' he recalled, 'came to me through pleasure, as [they] always come . . .'[20] A contemporary remarked on his 'real love for intellectual things, especially if there was a breath of poetry in them'. It was always Wilde, too, he remembered, who interrupted a lesson to ask the master a philosophical question that would instigate 'a disquisition on Realism and Nominalism and Conceptualism in which we were all asked questions and which proved most illuminating'.[21]

The other boys were equally impressed by Wilde's vigorous and colourful imagination. He delighted them with fantastic stories and descriptions of 'what I should have done had I been Alexander, or how I'd have played King in Athens, had I been Alcibiades'. In his performances he displayed an extraordinary facility for entering entirely into the world of books. 'As early as I can remember,' he said, 'I used to identify myself with every distinguished character I read about . . . The life of books had begun to interest me more than real life'.[22]

As 'real life' meant regimented boarding-school life, Wilde's comment is hardly surprising. The heaviness and solidity of a world where the importance of hierarchy, authority and discipline were either beaten into the boys or inculcated through various forms of propaganda must have appeared oppressive to one born, and brought up, for exceptions rather than rules. Portora was, in many ways, the converse of Merrion Square. It made little appeal to his poetic and oral sensibility, or to the Celtic, Nationalistic and 'Catholic' aspects of his identity. This may explain why Wilde rarely spoke of his time at the school, claiming instead to have been educated at home.

In 1867 Wilde had to face something far more terrible than tedium: on 23 February his little sister Isola, the 'radiant angel' and 'idol' of the family, died of an 'effusion of the brain'.[23] Wilde was given leave to visit her during her final illness. The doctor who attended the ten-year-old girl described young 'Ossie' as overwhelmed by an 'inconsolable grief' which would find expression in 'long and frequent visits to his sister's grave'.[24]

It is little wonder then that the young Wilde sought sanctuary in books. He remembered gorging himself on 'English novels and poetry' at Portora and 'dreaming away too much time' to master some of his schoolboy tasks. Unlike other pupils, who 'studied the schoolbooks assiduously', he elected to 'read everything that pleased me' – and it was very fortunate for Wilde that classical books happened to charm him.[25] His instinct was already guided by the artistic pleasure principle; even at that early stage, he had no doubt that his instinct was true.

It would be misleading, however, to caricature Wilde as a typically Romantic schoolboy who retreated from the monotony, toughness and tragedy of life into an imaginary world of literature. His adolescent immersion in books is certainly not the equivalent of an occasion when, during a childhood holiday, he ran away from his family to hide in a cave. On the contrary, there was something ostentatiously public about Wilde's bookishness at Portora — he made sure that his fellows knew of his intellectual precocity, and of his passion for literature. Books were sources of social power and distinction for Wilde, conferring on him a sense of uniqueness and superiority. This was confirmed publicly at examinations and prize-givings where he basked in the applause of the entire school.

7. 'At home with Lucien'

S O YOUNG WILDE often put his schoolbooks to one side, and turned instead to poetry and English fiction.[1] He would have read on his rambles around Portora's extensive and beautiful grounds, which encompassed copses of oak trees and a large lake, and in his dormitory before lights out. Although there was nothing exceptional about his schoolboy penchant for English novels, his taste was eccentric enough to inspire comment. His peers were surprised to hear him speak disparagingly of Dickens, the most popular novelist of the day. While Wilde admired the author's humour and his gift for caricature he loathed Dickens's moralising.[2]

Wilde's fellow pupils remarked on his veneration of the novels of Benjamin Disraeli, so it must have been a fairly unusual literary passion at Portora. The accepted wisdom on the works of the flamboyant Tory politician, who was Prime Minister for a few months in 1868, while Wilde was still at school, was that they were 'caviare to the general' reading public because of their 'pretentiousness, affectation, false English' and charlatanism.[3] True to form, Wilde's mother begged to differ, ranking Disraeli way above George Eliot and recommending him, along with Plato, as the ideal guide for those who wished to talk brilliantly in society.

Speranza literally passed her passion on to her youngest son by lending him several Disraeli novels.[4] Wilde was ravished by the books, declaring them infinitely superior to anything produced by Dickens.

As this is one of the Wildean literary judgements with which posterity has not concurred, it might be regarded as another example of his 'infallible bad taste'. But if it is 'bad' taste then it is surely something to be celebrated, because it derives from Wilde's idiosyncratic personality and his lack of conventional artistic 'decorum'.

There is something wonderfully trashy about Disraeli's novels. They are full of melodramatic scenes featuring beautiful young men and older, highly idealised, society women – as though Jane Austen has been rewritten in the style of Mills and Boon. Young Wilde must have giggled and wept his way through them. Victorian readers delighted in Disraeli's sentimentality, and read him for his brilliant evocations of English high society.[5] He presents a burnished world of fine wine, delicate food, clever conversation and people with long titles. Disraeli's novels are love letters to a society from which, as a non-university-educated Jew, he was excluded, at least until he had conquered Westminster. Yet if Disraeli is a terrible snob, he is also a haughty spectator, often diluting his sycophantic praise with heavy irony. It was a pose that must have intrigued Wilde.

Wilde imitates Disraeli throughout his writings, perfecting the novelist's aphoristic manner and frequently mimicking such delicious Disraelian nonsense as 'I rather like bad wine. One gets so bored with good wine.' Wilde became proficient, too, in echoing the very movement and music of Disraeli's prose. Speranza recognised the similarities between their writings. After congratulating Wilde on the 'epigrammatic style' of one of his short stories, and on his brilliant depiction of society women, she remarked, 'you could be another D'Israeli of fiction if you choose'.[6] She evidently hoped Wilde would model himself on Disraeli in other ways, urging him to embark on a career in parliament and encouraging him to create a sensation in high society.

Wilde used Disraeli's novels as manuals for success in society – his social triumphs made him feel, he said, like 'Tancred and Lothair',[7] two 'fashionable and brilliant young dandies' from Disraeli's fiction.[8] It is possible that he consulted the Prime Minister's novels to a similar end at Portora where, like Vivian Grey and Coningsby, two other Disraelian heroes, Wilde strove to impress his schoolboy peers with his intelligence, his fantastic stories, his dandified clothes and his and 'distant' manner.[9]

The most unconventional aspect of Wilde's adolescent taste was perhaps his love of French fiction. Wilde would always rate it far higher than its English equivalent, and even claimed the French had 'brought the art of fiction to a point beyond which human genius cannot go'.[10] French literature was synonymous, at least in middle-class Victorian England, with decadence and depravity; besides, much of it was probably beyond the linguistic resources of the average schoolboy. The young Wilde, however, professed himself 'particularly fond of French writings' which seemed to him to be, 'pervaded by an enthusiasm having some kinship with that peculiar to the Irish'.[11]

In stark contrast to middle-class English households, continental culture was regarded as neither immoral nor exotic at No. 1 Merrion Square. Intellectual celebrities from mainland Europe frequently dined with the Wildes; they also employed French and German governesses who taught the children their respective languages. Wilde probably became competent, rather than proficient, in German, and, as a boy, he 'cared little for German literature, excepting only Heine and Goethe'.[12]

Sir William's library contained numerous volumes in French and German; Wilde's mother owned countless continental works too, which were imported for her by Dublin book dealers. She translated a number of works from German, French and Italian, including

Dumas's novel *The Glacier Land* and several poems by Dante and Goethe. She was also proficient in several Scandinavian languages, and well versed in the literature of the region.

With his lofty disdain for the vulgar facts of geography, young Wilde probably thought that his Dublin home was fairly close to the continent. That impression must have been heightened by a childhood holiday in France. It was on this excursion that Wilde 'began to realise in some measure what he was', finding 'himself for the first time in a wholly congenial environment', where 'exquisite beauty' was everywhere. Along with Greek literature, the literature of France became the 'passion of his [early] artistic life'.[13] Wilde would remain an ardent Francophile for the rest of his days. He conferred on the race the status of honorary Celts, and praised their intellectual sophistication and their keen sensitivity to art and to the beautiful surface of life.

Wilde's love of French culture was intensified and perhaps even prompted by his reading. Three novels, which were written at the beginning of the nineteenth century by two acknowledged masters of imaginative realism, impressed him particularly – Balzac's *Lost Illusions* and *A Harlot High and Low* (whose hero is Lucien de Rubempré), and Stendhal's *Scarlet and Black*, which featured Julien Sorel. Wilde would nominate the pair as the 'two favourite characters' of his boyhood.[14]

Julien Sorel is a 'slim and shapely' boy, bent on achieving success in society. Through a passionate love of books this son of a provincial miller impresses the local gentry, who further his career. His reading teaches him how to divest himself of every trace of his lower-class provinciality and to comport himself correctly in the high-class Parisian circles to which he is introduced. He also imbibes from books the revolutionary Enlightenment philosophy that sets him firmly against the aristocratic world.

Julien successfully fashions himself as a young dandified nobleman.

The opportunity of marrying into a patrician family then presents itself. On the eve of his triumph, however, he commits the unpardonable social solecism of seducing the daughter of his noble Parisian employer. His tragic flaw is not lust, but satanic pride combined with a visceral class hatred. At the end of the book Julien is placed on trial for attempting to murder his previous aristocratic mistress. As a peasant, whose 'only crime' is to have 'risen in revolt against the lowliness of his station', he expects no mercy from the bourgeois jury, and is not disappointed when he is sentenced to death.

Lost Illusions, and its sequel *A Harlot High and Low,* form part of Balzac's multi-volumed *Comédie Humaine,* a kaleidoscopic portrait of early nineteenth-century French society. The hero of the novels, Lucien de Rubempré, is the son of a plebeian father and an aristocratic mother who has fallen on hard times. He makes it his life's mission to restore the family fortune. A course of impassioned adolescent reading liberates his mind and inspires in him the desire to become a renowned poet; he travels to Paris with only a manuscript collection of his verse in his pocket.

It is the old, old story of an impoverished young writer coming to a capital city in search of fame and riches; a tale of sink or swim, which ends with the hero going down. Lucien, who lacks the requisite social graces, and a thick enough skin, eventually admits defeat and returns to the provinces, where, after a time, he resolves to commit suicide. It is at this moment that he encounters his Mephistopheles. Vautrin, a.k.a. Jacques Collin, is a Napoleon of crime, who seduces Lucien with a vision of worldly success. At this point *Lost Illusions* ends. *A Harlot High and Low* takes up the story of Lucien's rise to prominence in Paris through nefarious means, and charts the spectacular downfall that follows his, and Vautrin's, exposure. The pair are eventually imprisoned and, in his cell, Lucien takes his own life.

Balzac's novels offered the young Wilde further guides to how to get ahead in literary and aristocratic society, and valuable tips on how to mould a marvellous personality from books. Wilde took Lucien as an exemplar, even going so far as to model his French on the poet's conversation. Years later Wilde would claim that 'The nineteenth century, as we know it, is largely an invention of Balzac. Our Lucien de Rubemprés . . . made their first appearance on the stage of the *Comédie Humaine*. We are merely carrying out, with footnotes and unnecessary additions, the whim or fancy or creative vision of a great novelist.'[15] He may well have been speaking from personal experience.

The schoolboys who surrounded Wilde must have paled in comparison with the dashing Lucien. 'After reading the *Comédie Humaine*,' as he put it later, 'one begins to believe that the only real people are the people who never existed . . . A steady course of Balzac reduces our living friends to shadows, and acquaintances to the shadows of shades. Who would care to go out to an evening party to meet Tomkins, the friend of one's boyhood, when one can sit at home with Lucien de Rubempré?'[16] So real, indeed, did Lucien appear to the young Wilde that he wept 'tears of blood' when he read of the poet's tragic demise in prison. 'I was never,' he recalled in adulthood, 'so affected by any book . . . [It was] one of the greatest tragedies of my life . . . It haunts me in my moments of pleasure. I remember it when I laugh.'[17]

8. 'Minute and critical'

IN HIS FINAL year at Portora, Wilde declared his genius to his peers. He won the Carpenter Prize for achieving the highest mark in an examination on the Greek Testament, for which he was awarded, at the school's annual prize-giving ceremony, a seven-volume edition of Edward Gibbon's *History of the Decline and Fall of the Roman Empire*.[1] A few months later he sat the entrance examination to Trinity College, Dublin, and came second only to a boy who would go on to become the college's Professor of Latin. Portora acknowledged his prowess by awarding him one of its three school scholarships to Trinity.

Wilde matriculated at Trinity as a Classical Honours student on 10 October 1871, six days before his seventeenth birthday. In his first year he resided at home in Merrion Square, a short walk from Trinity; the remaining two years of his time there were spent in college rooms. As an undergraduate, Wilde reprised the authors who had appeared on his entrance examination, and studied many others, to acquire, during his three years at college, a deep and catholic knowledge of classical literature.* Trinity's *University Calendar*, which

---

* In the entrance examination, Wilde was tested on four authors of his choice — two Greek and two Latin. The list of Greek writers included the epic poet Homer, the tragedians Euripides and Sophocles, and those masters of the philosophic dialogue, Plato, Lucian and Xenophon. On the Latin list there were the poets Virgil and Horace, the historians Sallust and Livy and the dramatist Terence.[2] The paper testifies to the breadth of classical culture

was handed to Wilde on his arrival, outlined the details of the course and the various examinations that lay ahead. His 'minute and critical knowledge' of ancient texts would, it informed him, be rigorously tested; he would be assessed, too, on his 'power of expressing the full meaning and force of an ancient author by writing such a translation of a given passage as may deserve commendation, not merely for its correctness, but for its excellence as a piece of English Composition'.[4]

The classical volumes Wilde used as a student are copiously marked and annotated. The annotation of ancient texts has a long history. Before the birth of printing, scholars 'glossed' manuscripts with footnotes and marginal notes in which they offered variant readings of a text and suggested emendations; they also included translations of words and phrases and cited parallel passages from other classical authors. The first printed editions of the classics, issued during the Renaissance, followed these early annotators by accompanying texts with Latin notes that contained similar information. In the margins of these volumes students then wrote their own annotations, which, likewise, generally concerned literary parallels, variant readings of the text and the translation of obscure words.

Wilde's annotations and markings conform very closely to these scholarly conventions. Their focus is generally on textual elucidation and on the fine points of language and grammar. The earliest of his extant volumes is a copy of Livy's *Roman History* which bears the date 'November 1868', when Wilde was still at Portora. It is full of marginal notes dealing with linguistic matters.[5†]

Portora offered its pupils. At Trinity Wilde revised many of these authors and augmented his knowledge by studying, among other writers, the Greek philosopher Aristotle, the Greek historians Herodotus, Thucydides and Isocrates and the Roman orator Cicero.[3]

† Similar annotations can be found in Wilde's undergraduate copies of Cicero's *Philippic Orations*,[6] a collection of the Roman politician's speeches, and his Aristophanes' *Nubes* (*The*

Wilde's copy of *The Bacchae of Euripides* edited by one of his Trinity tutors, R.Y. Tyrrell, has also survived.[8] On the title-page of the famous play, which concerns Dionysus and the riotous orgiastic rites of his followers, Wilde wrote 'Oscar Wilde T.C.D. Trinity [i.e. summer term], 1872'. Clearly intent on acquiring a 'minute and critical knowledge' of the text, Wilde underlines countless words and phrases which he then presumably looked up in his lexicon; he frequently glosses lines in the drama with notes such as 'Cf Xenophanes', 'Cf [line]342'.[9]

Wilde covered every available blank space of his Euripides and, in the process, damaged the spine and knocked its corners. All of his surviving classical texts are in very poor condition, with their tops and tails bumped and their hinges loose. Wilde had his rough scholarly pleasure with them, cramming the margins and end leaves full of notes and doodles, and sometimes even tearing out entire pages. He obviously used them exclusively for the purposes of study, which is doubtless why he purchased them in relatively cheap editions. The label of Galway & Co. bookshop, Eustace Street, is pasted in the endpapers of *The Bacchae*. Next to it Wilde has jotted down some sums in which he appears to calculate the relatively small amount of money he has spent, or is about to spend, on other books by Euripides as well as on volumes by the Latin poets Ovid and Horace.

Perhaps Wilde also bought his copy of *The Iliad of Homer* from Galway & Co.[10] This economically priced student edition of Homer's epic on the Trojan war is autographed 'Oscar F. Wilde Trin. Coll.D. August 1873'. The date suggests that he purchased books in accordance with the college syllabus, because '*Iliad*, XIII–XIV' was

---

Clouds), an amusing satirical play about the Greek philosopher Socrates. In the latter volume, Wilde circles obscure words and phrases, scribbling English translations in the ample margins. As was customary with Wilde, some of the annotations are in Latin and Greek as well as in English.[7] (See p. 10.)

taught in Trinity term of 1873.[11]* At Trinity, Wilde doubtless immersed himself fully in Homer's world of rosy-fingered dawns and wine-dark seas, and in the intense drama of the war between the gods, and among the heroes on the blood-soaked Trojan battlefield. A fellow student described him 'as a queer lad' who was 'ever moping and dreaming', and it was probably on ancient battles and the intricate web of doom that Wilde dreamed. To him, Homeric heroes such as Achilles and Odysseus were no mere 'Shadows in song'. 'No,' he commented, 'they are real' — far more real than the people who inhabit the everyday world.

Wilde's thoughts were carried away by Homer's winged words; but sometimes they wandered from his reading involuntarily. His classical volumes and the various notebooks he kept at university are covered with doodles and amusing sketches of dragons, people in profile and paper kites (See p. 65). The kites may be seen as symbols of the lightness and sensitivity of a mind which soared on the currents of its reading, yet they also testify to the fact that even the most dedicated of classicists was sometimes known to nod.

Generally, however, Wilde read hard, and with an intense and sustained concentration that would pay dividends in his exams. He arrived first out of his entire year in his 1872 Freshman Classical examinations. The following year he secured one of the college's ten foundation scholarships and also sat an examination for Trinity's prestigious annual Berkeley Gold Medal Prize. That year the exam was on *The Fragments of the Greek Comic Poets*, a multi-volume book edited by the German scholar Meineke.

* Most of Wilde's notes relate to the meaning of words and their age, gender and derivation, and to specific points of grammar; others offer English or Latin translations. Wilde again makes numerous cross-references, and compares certain passages to the works of other classical authors (at Book XXIII, lines 255–60, we find the note 'CF Bacchae [line] 1007'). This bears witness to Wilde's prodigious memory, because he had studied Euripides' play a year before he sat down with his Homer. (See p. 64.)

Annotations in Wilde's copy of The Iliad of Homer.

The notes Wilde made in preparation for the examination (along with the evidence of the paper itself)[12] display the meticulous nature of his reading at Trinity, as well as his impressive intellectual calibre. Contestants were asked to revise incorrectly transcribed lines of Greek comic verse and then translate them into particular styles of English. In his notes Wilde translated a fragment on the Homeric hero Odysseus into the colloquial English of the Elizabethan period.

Students then had to render, into the ancient Greek characteristic of the comic verse fragments, an English passage beginning 'A good sherries-sack hath a twofold operation in it'. This complex task must have been relatively easy for Wilde, because his notes include brilliant Greek verse translations of the poems of Wordsworth, Shakespeare and Arnold. His efforts were certainly accomplished enough for the

Pages from Wilde's Trinity College Notebooks.

examiners who awarded him the coveted Gold Medal. It would prove
to be the most useful of all Wilde's academic prizes. Whenever he was
short of funds in later life, it was the first thing he pawned.

Ironically, Wilde's spectacular triumphs may have prompted his
premature departure from Trinity. Buoyed up by his success he
attempted to secure one of the two Classical scholarships Magdalen
College, Oxford advertised in 1874. At the examination in June of that
year, which took place in Oxford, Wilde appeared insouciant,
ostentatiously asking the invigilator, on numerous occasions, for extra
paper. His arrogance was justified: he achieved the highest mark of all
the candidates by some distance, and secured a substantial scholarship
of £95 per year. Thus Wilde would finish at Oxford the degree course
he had begun in Dublin, matriculating at Magdalen on 17 October

1874, the day after his twentieth birthday. His intellectual prowess made an instant impression on the English public school boys who were now his peers. Wilde 'came up having read much more than the rest of us', one of them recalled; the extent of his classical culture 'excited awe'.[13]

9. 'How to love Greek things'

ONE OF WILDE'S tutors in Greek at Trinity was the Reverend and Doctor John Pentland Mahaffy, a towering intellectual figure and a brilliant and paradoxical conversationalist. Wilde later called him 'my first and my best teacher . . . the scholar who showed me how to love Greek things'.[1]

Mahaffy's stylish and engaging *Social Life in Greece*, published in 1874, may serve as a symbol of his influence on Wilde. In the acknowledgements, the doctor thanks 'Mr Oscar Wilde of Magdalen College' for having 'made improvements and corrections all through the book'.[2]

The Greeks, Mahaffy declares in his introduction, are 'men of like culture with ourselves . . . thoroughly modern, more modern even than the epochs quite proximate to our own'. Their works are living things, in Goethe's phrase, intended for those who are alive, and not 'mere treasure-houses of roots and forms to be sought out by comparative grammarians'.[3] Mahaffy advises students to eschew the disinterested 'scientific' curiosity of the linguist, and urges them instead to engage passionately with the past. They are to use ancient texts to explore the concerns and problems of their own period, bringing contemporary questions, and their own interests, to bear on their reading; they should also allow the alien aspects of Greek literature and culture to challenge their modern assumptions. From this dialogue, both the ancient text and the student would, he hoped, emerge enriched and altered.

One facet of Greek culture that was alien to nineteenth-century civilisation was its approbation of 'homosexual' love.[4] In Greek society this sometimes took the form of a relationship between an older and a younger man, an institution referred to as *paiderastia*. Mahaffy argues that the romantic sentiment which animated that union inspired the heroism of countless Greek warriors, as well as several key aspects of the philosophy of Socrates. *Paiderastia*, he notes, was fully recognised by Greek law and enjoyed an exalted position in the hierarchy of social, cultural and spiritual relations.

'There is,' Mahaffy remarks, 'no field of enquiry, where we are so dogmatic in our social prejudices, and so determined by the special circumstances of our age and country.'[5] As we cannot see beyond the limits of our own historical horizon, it is absurd of us to speak of universal 'rights' and 'wrongs', and to condemn Greek homosexuality as 'unnatural'. As to the epithet '"unnatural"', Mahaffy continues with customary panache, 'the Greeks would answer probably, that all civilisation was unnatural . . . and that many of the best features in all gentle life were best because they were unnatural'. In fact, 'So different were Greek notions on this point from ours, that they would have thought our sentimental (i.e. heterosexual) relationships . . . *unnatural*'.[6] It was a daring statement at a time when men who engaged in sodomy could be imprisoned for life in England.

Social Life in Greece offers the fullest and frankest discussion of homosexuality in all nineteenth-century classical scholarship. Some commentators have been unable to resist the temptation of attributing it to the disciple, Wilde, rather than to his master. Yet there is neither the evidence nor the need to do so. The tenor of the discussion seems 'Wildean' because Mahaffy's audacious and epigrammatic style profoundly influenced his pupil.

The strategy of engaging the Greeks in a frank dialogue, and exploring the controversial results of that exchange, was also adopted by the renowned Victorian man of letters John Addington Symonds, whose commentaries on the classics deeply fascinated Wilde at this time. The first volume of Symonds's *Studies of the Greek Poets*, issued in 1873, was 'perpetually' in Wilde's 'hands' at Trinity.[7] The second volume came out in 1876, while he was at Oxford. On the title-page, he wrote, 'Oscar F. O'F. W. Wilde. S.M. Magdalen College, Oxford, May '76.'[8] The date indicates that Wilde purchased the book hot off the printing press.

Studies is an elegantly written survey of most of the surviving corpus of Greek literature. Like Mahaffy, Symonds urges his contemporaries to engage the ancients in a stimulating intellectual conversation. The overwhelming question for Symonds is how modern classicists might set about this, separated as they are from the Greeks by such an interval of time, and by countless cultural differences. He encourages students to visit the landscapes of Greece and southern Italy which are, he says, still imbued with the ancient Greek spirit; he also advises them to focus on the many points at which modern and ancient cultures touch. *Studies* identifies numerous parallels between the two cultures – Mozart is compared to Aristophanes, and Aeschylus to Whitman and Shakespeare. Wilde borrowed this last comparison during an oral exam at Oxford: questioned by the examiner on Aeschylus, he 'talked of Shakespeare [and] Walt Whitman'.[9] Symonds's book clearly made a powerful impression on Wilde. In his copy he marked its central arguments; he also transcribed numerous lines from it into his undergraduate notebooks, sometimes verbatim but more often summarising Symonds's ideas and adapting his language.[10]*

Wilde's wholehearted approval of Mahaffy's and Symonds's approach

---

* Wilde's annotations give the impression of a student engaged in an animated dialogue with the author. 'Perhaps so;' he says, for example, of the notion that the poet Hesiod had a low opinion of females, 'but the Greeks attributed to Hesiod a panegyric on women.'[11]

to ancient culture is evinced throughout his *oeuvre*, where he frequently applies Greek ideas to modern issues. Thus the prophecy, contained in his political essay 'The Soul of Man under Socialism', that machines will one day carry out all unpleasant manual tasks is directly inspired by Aristotle's *Politics*.[12] Wilde's approval is also evidenced by his undergraduate reading of another Aristotlean work, the *Nicomachean Ethics*.

This wide-ranging survey of ethical issues was one of Wilde's set texts at Oxford. He was also obliged to read Sir Alexander Grant's annotations and introduction to the work. In contrast to Mahaffy and Symonds, Grant belonged to the Historicist school of criticism, then, as now, prominent in academic circles. Historicists seek to understand literary works exclusively within their historical context and often deny their relevance to the modern world. Grant argues that Aristotle's *Ethics* has no purpose beyond offering readers 'a portrait of a graceful Grecian Gentleman' of the fourth century BC.[13]

The annotations in Wilde's copy of J.E.T. Rodgers's edition of the *Ethics*, which is inscribed 'Oscar Wilde, Magdalen College, October 1877', illustrate his passionate opposition to this view.[14] Interleaved with the Greek text are around 200 pages on which Wilde has written copious notes in English and Greek. In them he creates a bridge between the past and the present by comparing Aristotle to modern writers such as David Hume and Tennyson;[15] he also makes the perceptive observation that 'one of the reasons why we think the *Ethics* shallow' is precisely because it has so 'saturated modern thought'.[16]

Wilde uses Aristotle to wrestle with broad, moral and philosophical issues still relevant in his own day. 'The great questions,' he muses, are, 'what is good for man?' and 'how it is possible to know the right and do the wrong?'[17] He clearly believed that the Greek philosopher still offered readers possible answers to these eternal questions. Both in his marginalia and in the notebook entries he made on the *Ethics* he addresses Aristotle as a contemporary; at times, it is as though the philosopher is standing beside his desk as he scribbles away – 'Doing and making. Is this a sound difference?' Wilde asks the ancient sage at one point.[18]

In the light of these comments it comes as no surprise to find the remark 'Grant is quite foolish' among Wilde's marginalia.[19] Nor did Wilde's hostility to the scholar mellow with the passing of the years. A decade later he would include Grant's edition of the *Ethics* in the list of books he strongly advised people 'not to read'.[20]

Although Mahaffy was no historicist, he was keenly interested in archaeology and social history; he also travelled extensively in Greece in order to acquire an intimate knowledge of the land and its peoples. Here again, the Trinity don was exceptional, at a time when the focus of classical scholarship was the philological study of ancient texts. In Wilde's eyes, the fact that Mahaffy had visited Greece, 'and saturated himself there with Greek thought and feeling', elevated him above the other dons.[21]

Mahaffy's imaginative use of archaeology and topography to illuminate ancient literature is exemplified in his *Rambles and Studies in Greece*. He enthusiastically identifies the rock at which 'Plutarch sat', and is thrilled at the prospect of filling out 'the idle descriptions and outlines of many books with the fresh reality itself'.[22] He describes the sites of a number of archaeological excavations he visited, and uses the finds made there to explicate classical texts.

Once again, Wilde assisted his mentor, this time by proof-reading *Rambles and Studies* before its original publication in 1876. In the spring vacation of the following year, when Mahaffy returned to Greece to gather material for an enlarged edition of the book, Wilde accompanied him.

Mahaffy and his young protégé visited Corfu, Olympia, Argos, Mycenae, Arcadia and Athens. Wilde's account of their odyssey unfortunately survives only in the form of a draft fragment. In it, he extols the beauty of Greece's low mountainous coast, the gorgeous dress of its people and their rich and sensuous skin colouring.[23]

The excursion caused Wilde, then in his third year at Magdalen, to miss the beginning of Trinity term. He hoped the college authorities would turn a blind eye to his tardiness, and wrote to them in advance to explain the reasons for it, estimating that he would arrive ten days into the new semester. 'Seeing Greece,' he nonchalantly explained to the Dean of Arts, 'is really a great education for anyone and will I think benefit me greatly, and Mr Mahaffy is such a clever man that it is quite as good as going to lectures to be in his society.'[24]

This was not simply an excuse. Wilde genuinely believed that the 'chance of seeing' the ruins and excavations at Mycenae and Athens would be advantageous to his studies. Magdalen disagreed. When Wilde returned from Greece over three weeks into term, the authorities decided to rusticate him (i.e. send him down for the remainder of the term), implicitly punishing his, and Mahaffy's, approach to the classics, as well as his late arrival.[25] Wilde was infuriated by the severity of the sentence and the philistine attitude it displayed, claiming, years later, that he 'was sent down from Oxford for being the first undergraduate to visit Olympia'.[26] Yet he never regretted his decision. The trip animated Greek art and literature for him, infusing it with 'a living reality'.[27]

Like his master, Wilde believed that archaeology could be used to elucidate classical texts. After his graduation from Oxford he became a member of the pro-archaeology Hellenic Society, and in 1879 he made an impressive, though ultimately unsuccessful, application for an archaeological studentship at Athens.* Wilde cannot, therefore, be

---

* Archaeology must also have appealed to Wilde as a link between his classical studies and the Celtic culture of his childhood, during which he had assisted his father's excavations of ancient Celtic sites. In *Rambles* Mahaffy makes the association between the cultures explicit by comparing finds in Greece and Ireland.

characterised as an out and out anti-historicist – it would be more accurate to describe him as a scholar who recognised the value of the historicist approach but considered it limited in scope and application. The ideal, as ever with Wilde, was to balance two apparently contradictory approaches; classicists should, he thought, produce historically sensitive interpretations that also spoke directly to the present.[28]

During their 1877 jaunt, Wilde and Mahaffy visited Heinrich Schliemann's excavations at Mycenae. The celebrated German archaeologist had, earlier in the decade, located the site of Troy, not by scientific methods but through his profound knowledge of ancient literature and by an instinct even more inspired than that of Sir William Wilde. At Mycenae he performed a similarly miraculous act of divination by unearthing countless skeletons and a hoard of regal treasure.

During one dig, which took place about a year before Wilde's visit, Schliemann found a golden mask with a skull beneath it. Always one for the grand theatrical gesture, the archaeologist exclaimed, in awestruck tones, 'I have gazed upon the face of Agamemnon', and announced that he had discovered the tomb of the ancient King of Argos. Modern scholarship is extremely sceptical about this, and also about many of Schliemann's other claims: Agamemnon is now universally regarded as a purely legendary figure. Wilde and Mahaffy would certainly have harboured similar doubts about the assertion, but these did not necessarily diminish the archaeologist's achievement in their eyes. Soon after the visit Mahaffy would hail the German as a divinely inspired genius.

The story of Agamemnon was dramatised by Aeschylus. The narrative of his bloody tragedy, which bears the King's name and forms the first part of the celebrated *Orestean* trilogy, is inexorable and harrowing. Agamemnon was the commander of the Greek army that sacked Troy to avenge the seduction of Helen, the famous Grecian beauty, by the Trojan prince Paris. Before the siege, Agamemnon sacrificed to the gods his daughter, Iphigenia, to ensure the success of the mission.

The play opens nine years after the victorious conclusion of the war when Agamemnon returns home to his wife Clytemnestra at their palace in Argos. Clytemnestra welcomes him into the palace, then kills him with an axe, with the help of her lover Aegisthus, with whom she rules after Agamemnon's death. The origins of the tragedy are buried in the past: Clytemnestra seeks retribution for Iphigenia's murder, Aegisthus avenges his father, a victim of Agamemnon's father's cruelty. The consequences of the homicide reverberate into the future: years later, Agamemnon and Clytemnestra's son Orestes slays both Aegisthus and his mother. As punishment for his matricide, he is pursued and tormented by the terrible snake-haired goddesses known as the Furies.

Wilde regarded the *Agamemnon* as Aeschylus' masterpiece. Indeed, he probably concurred with Mahaffy, who extolled it as 'the greatest of [all] Greek tragedies' for its 'deep philosophy . . . grandeur and gloom'.[29] Given his mother's 'furious admiration' for J.S. Blackie's translation of Aeschylus' plays,[30] as well as her fondness for declaiming from them, Wilde probably first encountered it as a boy through one of her dramatic recitations. He certainly knew it, practically by heart, during his time at Portora, where he 'walked away' from the entire school in an oral examination on the drama.[31]

Aeschylus' play would prove to be one of Wilde's lifelong literary romances — he often returned to it in later life. Or perhaps it would be more accurate to say that it returned to him: as we shall see, rather like the Furies who hunt down Orestes, *Agamemnon* would pursue Wilde right up to his final years.

10. 'How to grow'

FROM THE MEMOIRS of his Oxford contemporaries, Wilde emerges as the fully formed character we know and love. He swaggers through their pages, supremely self-assured in manner, intellectually intrepid and precocious, with his striking dandified dress and towering physique, scattering epigrams and poems in his wake. Temperamentally romantic and mercurial, he is irreverent towards all forms of authority; he is also possessed of an irrepressible energy. That energy manifested itself in flamboyant speeches and an addiction to nonsense and fun. 'How brilliant and radiant he could be,' one of his peers remembered. 'How playful and charming! . . . how he revelled in inconsistency!'[1]

Wilde struck his English peers as utterly other. 'There was,' one said, 'something foreign to us, and inconsequential, in his modes of thought, just as there was a suspicion of a brogue in his pronunciation, and an unfamiliar turn in his phrasing.'[2] So far as his brogue was concerned, Wilde seems to have conformed, gradually replacing it with an English drawl, no doubt because of the unwelcome attention it attracted: 'My Irish accent,' he later remarked, 'was one of the many things I forgot at Oxford.'[3] Yet in other respects Wilde relished his outsider status. He charmed his new companions with Irish wit and munificent hospitality, shocked them with Nationalist political views that evinced a 'strong feeling against England',[4] and dazzled them with virtuoso displays of linguistic and mental dexterity that they regarded as characteristically Celtic.[5]

Wilde's effervescent manner was, too, an expression of his joy at being at Oxford. He called the city 'the most beautiful thing in England'; 'nowhere else,' he maintained, 'are life and art so exquisitely blended, so perfectly made one.'[6] The surface of life was so lovely there that even 'the food, the wine, the cigarettes' were invested with the charm and suggestiveness of 'artistic symbols';[7] it required no imaginative effort at all on his part to transform it into 'the capital of Romance'. The physical city encompassed by Broad Street and Christ Church meadows and the invisible city adumbrated by Oxford's poets over the centuries were, in his mind, one and the same place. Wilde was in his element.

Oxford, Wilde believed, sharpened a student's sensitivity to literary beauty. It certainly seems to have had that effect on him as he returned to the exquisite lyrics and odes of the Romantic poets he had worshipped in his youth. The city, he said, made 'the earth lovely to all who dream with Keats', and opened 'high heaven to all who soar with Shelley'.[8] It is no coincidence that much of Wilde's own poetry dates from his Oxford days of 'lyrical ardour and . . . studious sonnet writing'.[9] He lived and breathed poetry at Magdalen, often 'spouting yards of verse', at student parties, 'either his own, or that of other poets whom he favoured, and spouting it uncommonly well'.[10]

Poetry gushed out of Wilde during rambles with his friends, around Magdalen's bird-haunted Addison's Walk, or further afield to Iffley or Sandford Lock, when he would recite verse from memory or read it out from a book.[11] He also enjoyed reading in the more comfortable setting of his rooms, which were in Chaplain's Quad in his first year, in Cloisters in his second and third, and in the sumptuous three-room set on the Kitchen Staircase in his last.

Wilde loved to curl up with a book in bed. In one letter he

mischievously described himself as 'lying in bed . . . with Swinburne (a copy of)';[12] in another, he mentioned *The Imitation of Christ*, the pious manual for Christian living penned by the fifteenth-century German monk Thomas à Kempis. Wilde read the book before going to sleep on the principle that 'half-an-hour's warping of the inner man daily is greatly conducive to holiness'.[13] In the list of contents in his copy, it is rather amusing to find a little cross next to the chapters 'Of inordinate affections' and 'Of resisting temptations'; curiously, the chapter 'Of talking too much' is unmarked.[14]

'[Wilde] liked to pose as a dilettante trifling with his books,' a friend remembered, 'but I knew of his hours of assiduous and laborious reading, often into the small hours of the morning . . . in his small and stuffy bedroom, where books lay in apparently hopeless confusion . . . in every corner . . . though he knew where to lay his hand on each.'[15] This evokes the confusion and disorder typical of most undergraduate bedrooms, and is reminiscent of the bookish chaos that reigned in the drawing-rooms at Merrion Square.

The cigarettes Wilde chain-smoked were doubtless responsible for the stuffiness, although the room in question – probably Wilde's bedroom on the Kitchen Staircase – had a window opposite the bed, which gave a view of Magdalen bridge and the River Cherwell. We can imagine Wilde perched on the little seat in front of it, looking up from his copy of Swinburne or Keats whenever he was disturbed by the noise of the traffic flowing over, or under, the bridge, or by the sound of footsteps on the creaking winding wooden staircase outside his door. He would have been distracted too by the aromas of cooking that wafted up from the kitchens right below his window.

Although he loved reading in his rooms, Wilde sometimes left them to read elsewhere. He visited Magdalen's luminous library, with its mahogany shelves, its pungent perfume of venerable volumes and its superb views of the cloisters and New Buildings's lawns. It was

An undergraduate's room at Magdalen in the late nineteenth century.

inaccessible to most undergraduates, but Wilde was permitted to use it on account of the scholarship he had won after his brilliant performance in the entrance examinations.

Years later he recalled a visit he made to the library during his first term for the purpose of checking a reference. A book he was reading cited some lines from Dante's *Inferno*, which concerned the terrible punishment meted out to those who are 'wilfully melancholy'. Wilde was incredulous when he read it – surely the Florentine poet, who was usually so full of pity, could not have been so severe on such a venial sin – so he decided to verify the quotation. Leaving his rooms he sauntered around Magdalen's cloisters with his distinctive elephantine gait, his footsteps echoing as he went, until he reached the library on the north-west side. Having climbed the steep stone stairs, he entered the long room, located a copy of the *Divina commedia* and took it down from the shelves. He turned to the relevant passage to find that the citation had indeed been correct. Yet the whole idea still seemed 'quite fantastic' to him.[16]

It is unlikely that Wilde lingered long in Magdalen's valley of the shadow of books. He acquired his own copies of many of the volumes he read as an undergraduate from Oxford's numerous bookshops. On one spending spree he bought a large batch of Cardinal Newman's works.[17] Wilde adored the 'simple' yet 'subtle' writings of England's most famous convert to Roman Catholicism, and was himself almost beguiled by the allure of Rome during his student years.[18]

Although he had been baptised a second time as a Catholic, during his youth Wilde had dutifully professed the Protestant faith of his Anglo-Irish forebears. At Oxford, however, he irritated his Anglican peers intensely by talking endless 'nonsense regarding Rome' and by adorning his rooms with 'photographs of the Pope'.[19] This may have been a corollary of Wilde's need to assert his Celtic identity in an alien, and sometimes hostile, English environment. He stopped short of conversion, however, when the staunchly Protestant members of his father's family threatened to cut him off with a shilling: 'to go over to Rome,' he reflected ruefully, 'would be to . . . give up my two great gods "Money and Ambition".'[20]

At Oxford Wilde took the Honours School course of Latin and Greek languages and literature. Officially called *Literae Humaniores* it was commonly known as 'Greats'. To this day, Oxonians refer to Greats as an endurance test because of the course's exacting demands.*

---

* A glance at the Finals examination paper Wilde sat in the Trinity term of 1878 confirms this notion. To score well in the translation section the undergraduate had to know, virtually by heart, a number of works by Aristotle, Plato, Cicero, Xenophon, and the Greek and Roman historians Thucydides and Sallust. In answering the Ancient History essay

One of Wilde's Oxford book bills bears witness to the arduous requirements of Greats. The invoice, from Thomas Shrimpton's bookshop situated on 'the High', was made out to 'WILD [*sic*] ESQ. Mag. Coll'.[21] Wilde's acquisitions not only included set texts such as a modern edition of Thucydides, but also several secondary commentaries such as George Grote's *Plato and the other Companions of Socrates*. The Greats student was obliged to work his way through mountains of such scholarly criticism and to acquire an in-depth knowledge of academic debates.

In addition, the Shrimpton's bill lists a 'Hints to [Examination] Answers' guide, which Wilde purchased before his Finals exam in 1878.[†] Handbooks such as this offered undergraduates strategies for answering essay questions and advised them on how to successfully 'cram' in the run up to their examinations. Wilde dedicated the weeks preceding an exam to intense study – he speaks of setting aside 'six weeks' for a course of focused 'reading' prior to Finals.[22]

Wilde's borrowings from the Bodleian Library support the notion that he was a confirmed crammer;[23] given his determination to hide his industriousness from his friends, he was probably also a secret one. The Bodleian, the core of which is the famous seventeenth-century rectangular building in Catte Street, is the University's central library; its vast collections include a copy of virtually every book published in Britain since 1600. Wilde took out a number of periodicals containing

questions, he had to display an intimate acquaintance with social, political, military and economic developments in the classical world. For the essays in the Logic, Political Economy and Moral Philosophy sections, he needed to be familiar with the works of the British philosophers Francis Bacon, John Locke and David Hume, and the ideas of the eighteenth-century German philosopher Immanuel Kant.

[†] Wilde may well have bought a similar book in the lead up to the Moderations examination that he sat in 1876. All Honours School students at Oxford were set a 'Mods' exam roughly half-way through their course so that the dons could monitor their progress.

reviews of books that were either set texts on his syllabus or recommended as essential reading by student guides to exams. Although it seems unlikely, it is not entirely impossible that he read some of these articles instead of the texts themselves.* He also found the time for more personal reading, borrowing a volume of the *London Review* that included an appraisal of *Traits and Stories of the Irish Peasantry,*[25] a book by the Wildes' family friend, William Carleton. Wilde probably wanted to relieve the tedium and anxiety of revision by flying away for a while with the fairies.

One of the reasons why Wilde 'crammed' so furiously before Finals was that examinations had, according to some, become the be-all and end-all of Oxford intellectual life. From around 1850, dons started to prepare tutorials according to the requirements of the examinations, rather than with the idea of bestowing on their pupils an all-round culture. This, at any rate, was the view of Cardinal Newman, who denounced these developments, along with the gradual specialisation of scholarship at Oxford, in his book *The Idea of a University.* Newman urged Oxford to adopt instead the ideal of 'Liberal education', which he defined as a 'process of training, by which the intellect, instead of being formed or sacrificed to some particular purpose, some specific trade or profession, or study or science, is disciplined for its own sake, for the perception of its own proper object, and for its own highest culture'.[26]

Wilde was passionately committed to Newman's ideal. He was utterly contemptuous of 'testable' knowledge, dismissing examinations as futile exercises in which 'the foolish ask questions that the

---

* In the periodicals issued to Wilde there were, for example, articles on works by the Utilitarian English philosophers John Stuart Mill and Jeremy Bentham that had a bearing on questions in the Logic, Political Economy, and Moral Philosophy sections of Wilde's Finals exam.[24]

wise cannot answer'.[27] He criticised English schools for cramming young minds 'with a load of unconnected facts' in order to pass such tests. For Wilde, education meant the cultivation of a pupil's general culture, the awakening of their critical intellect and arousal of their aesthetic sensibility. 'We teach people how to remember, we never teach them how to grow. It has never occurred to us to try and develop in the mind a more subtle quality of apprehension and discernment.' That was why, 'considered as an instrument of thought, the English mind is coarse and undeveloped'.[28]

And yet the rot that was insidiously eating away at English education had not, Wilde believed, reached the Oxford Greats course. In his view, it still engendered and rewarded the sort of broad intellectual culture Newman extolled. It begot what Wilde would later define as 'the Oxford temper' — a mind which could play 'gracefully with ideas' rather than arrive at 'violence of opinion merely'.[29] It has been suggested that Wilde was actually defining the 'Oscar' rather than the 'Oxford' temper. Yet the spectacular array of authors, and intellectual disciplines, encompassed by Greats, and its emphasis on creating a dialogue between the past and the present *à la* Mahaffy, suggests that Wilde's praise was not exaggerated.[30] Greats remained, he declared, the 'only fine school at Oxford . . . where one can be, *simultaneously*, brilliant and unreasonable, speculative and well-informed, creative as well as critical, and write with all the passion of youth about the truths which belong to the august serenity of old age'.[31]

Greats men were still encouraged to exhibit audacious intellectual dexterity. For the oral section of the 'Mods' test Wilde took in 1876 he was given 'a delightful exam . . . not on the books [i.e. the set texts] at all but on . . . modern poetry and drama and every conceivable subject . . . epic poetry in general, *dogs*, and women . . . Whitman and the *Poetics* . . . I was up for about an hour and was quite sorry when it was over.'[32] Wilde's performance must have been a wonderful illustration of the nimble and opalescent 'Oxford temper' in action.

Wilde achieved a first at 'Mods', and then again in his Finals examination of 1878. He was one of the very few Magdalen students in the entire nineteenth century to pull off a double first, and his papers in both exams were regarded as the most brilliant of their year in the whole university.

Wilde later took immense delight in parading his classical scholarship. 'I cannot imagine,' he wrote to a newspaper which had levelled the accusation of pretentiousness against *Dorian Gray*, 'how a casual reference to Suetonius and Petronius Arbiter can be construed into evidence of a desire to impress . . . by an assumption of superior knowledge. I should fancy that the most ordinary of scholars is perfectly well acquainted with the *Lives of the Caesars* and with the *Satyricon*. The *Lives of the Caesars*, at any rate, forms part of the curriculum at Oxford for those who take the Honour School of *Literae Humaniores*; and as for the *Satyricon*, it is popular even among passmen, though I suppose they have to read it in translations.'[33]

Wilde ostentatiously, and rather snobbishly, spent the cultural capital he had accrued at Oxford here and on many other occasions.[34] The classical allusions that striate his works flaunt the honorary membership of the English upper-class elite that he had secured at the university through his intellectual and social efforts. Countless English aristocrats studied Greats at Oxford, or had, at least, acquired enough classical knowledge at their schools to confound and unnerve their social inferiors – one of the primary aims of a private education.

And yet, even as Wilde flashes his upper-class credentials, it is noteworthy that his pride is more intellectual than social. As a brilliant Honours student, he is careful to distinguish himself from 'passmen' (i.e. 'Commoners' who did not take an Honours degree), many of whom were rather dim ex-public-school boys who struggled to read classical literature in the original languages. On other occasions, Wilde extended his contempt to men, like the English aristocrat George Curzon, who toiled away arduously at Oxford only to come out with second-class degrees in Greats.[35] If Wilde was proud of being part of an elite English social club, he was even more conceited about being intellectually superior to his fellow members.*

---

* Wilde's condescending attitude to obtuse Oxonians is also displayed in his unfinished play 'A Wife's Tragedy'. A character, who is a representative Oxford 'Passman', is introduced as 'one of those . . . philistines . . . the noisy boy of the college . . . who never got through an examination . . . cared for nothing but cricket . . . [and afterwards] went out to India'.[36]

Wilde's criticism of George Curzon is especially interesting because he represented another recognisable Oxford type – the aristocratic undergraduate who sees his time at the University as a prelude to a political career. Curzon, who made countless speeches at the Oxford Union, the breeding ground of many an English politician, may well have chosen to study Greats because it was thought to be the ideal preparation for a career in the colonies (like the Oxonian in 'A Wife's Tragedy', Curzon eventually 'went out to India', becoming Viceroy there during Wilde's lifetime). Greats was believed to equip young men for life in England's far-flung empire by instilling in them exactly the sort of manly and martial virtues required to face life among the insubordinate natives. Benjamin Jowett, the Balliol don who designed the Greats course, used his influence to ensure that Classics questions appeared on the entrance exams for the Colonial and Home Offices. Wilde's disparagement of these two Oxford types emphasises his otherness.[37]

11. 'The true *liber amoris*'

URING HIS TIME in the city he regarded as the English home of Hellenism, Wilde often staged Greek symposia with his friends.[1] In his rooms, in the evenings, he would pour out 'a flood of paradoxes' and defend 'untenable' intellectual positions. 'The talk,' according to one of his companions, 'was quite unrestrained, and ranged over a vast variety of topics. Wilde said not a few foolish and extravagant things . . . We listened and applauded and protested against some of his preposterous theories.'[2] It is a scene that might have come straight out of the pages of Plato, and probably did.

As an undergraduate, and perhaps also at Portora, Wilde read Plato's dialogues in the original. The philosopher's style is fairly colloquial and would have been easy for Wilde to read, even as a schoolboy, with the help of commentaries and translations. Of these, Benjamin Jowett's 1875 English translation of the dialogues was probably the most dear to Wilde; his copy has survived.[3] He purchased the handsome five-volume edition and wrote his name ('Oscar F. O'F.W. Wilde') in pencil on the verso of the half-title page of Volume I. It is likely that he bought it soon after its publication date because, from late 1876 onwards, he tended to write only his first and last names in his books.

The Dialogues of Plato became one of Wilde's golden books. He marked and annotated most of the dialogues, and many of Jowett's introductions.[4] In doing so he read far beyond the confines of his

Greats course, for which only five of the dialogues were prescribed texts.[5] In his undergraduate notebooks he copied out numerous phrases from the volumes, sometimes using them as the starting point for his own speculations. Wilde consulted them when he came to write his mature works, in which he frequently draws on Plato for inspiration or a quotation.[6]

In the dialogues a series of conversations between the fifth-century BC Athenian philosopher Socrates – Plato's real-life intellectual master – and a number of listeners are imaginatively reconstructed. Worshipped by his disciples as a godlike genius, Socrates was dismissed by his detractors as a pretentious gadfly. His eccentric life was cut short when an Athenian court sentenced him to death after finding him guilty of propounding sophistic theories that had 'corrupted' the city's youth.

The dialogues expertly stage disputations between Socrates and one or more of his intellectual adversaries. Typically, the participants argue from differing viewpoints about the definition of an abstract concept such as Justice, Courage or Love. While Socrates' opponents generally represent commonly held opinion, he argues from the perspective of one who seeks philosophical clarity. The philosopher unsettles his interlocutor by a strategy known as 'Socratic irony' which consists of bombarding them with a series of bewildering questions.

The dialogues generally begin with a confession on Socrates' part that he knows absolutely nothing about the subject under review. They end with his adversary's acknowledgement that, given the blunt tools of thought and language available to humanity, no one can ever know anything about it. The confusion his opponents experienced would, Socrates hoped, prompt them to reflect further after the conversation's conclusion; ultimately, he wanted them to be born again, as sensitive intellectual beings. Socrates does not teach any scientific or factual knowledge; instead, his interlocutors learn how to think.

Readers of Plato's dialogues undergo the same experience of initiation and enlightenment as Socrates' adversaries. The annotations in Wilde's copy of the *Dialogues* reveal that he was inspired by Socrates' method as well as by many of his celebrated ideas. He has marked the philosopher's famous characterisation of the poet as 'a light and winged and holy thing' who is dumb 'until he has been inspired and is out of his senses';[7] there is also a line next to the famous passage in Book III of the *Republic* where Socrates denounces poets as liars who corrupt the young. Later Wilde eloquently countered these criticisms in 'The Critic as Artist' and 'The Decay of Lying', philosophic dialogues that are themselves modelled on Plato.*

Many nineteenth-century authors, such as William Mallock and Thomas Love Peacock, looked to Plato as an exemplar and as an inspiration for the dialogues they wrote. None of them came quite as close as Wilde to equalling him. One of Wilde's friends even believed that 'Plato might have been proud to sign' certain pages of Wilde's dialogues. In their eloquent and witty expression of a brilliant mind at play, Wilde had, he maintained, quite surpassed his master.[9]

Wilde mimicked Plato in his life as well as in his art. In later years he continued his Oxford custom of staging 'thoroughly Greek' evenings with his friends where they would savour the 'sweet sin of

---

* The 'Decay' draws heavily on Plato's *Phaedrus*, in which Socrates discusses rhetoric and the soul's immortality with his young friend Phaedrus. In both dialogues a wise philosophical head enlightens a callow and rather dull-witted 'straight-man' and in each a written composition is read out and discussed. The two dialogues have also been convincingly described as spirited defences of oral literary values such as exaggeration and inaccuracy.[8]

phrases' and drink 'many a sun to rest with wine and words'.[10] Naturally, Wilde assumed the star role of Socrates, while his friends variously served as appreciative audience, and intellectual foil. Wilde relished the 'intellectual friction' generated by impassioned debate – a phrase so redolent of Socrates.[11] Like the Athenian philosopher, he delighted in overwhelming his antagonists. During their dinner table discussions, the young French novelist André Gide could only stare distractedly into his plate as Wilde systematically dismantled the moral principles instilled in him by his religious upbringing. 'In his company,' Gide confessed, 'I lost the habit of thinking.' 'Since Wilde,' he told a friend, 'I only exist a little.'[12] But Gide was not really obliterated by Wilde's oracular onslaught – with time he would, as the Socratic Wilde no doubt hoped, be born again as a pagan and a homosexual.

Wilde adopted Socrates' relentless philosophic interrogation. 'Do you know the difference between art and nature?' he demanded of Gide. 'Do you know why Christ did not love His mother?' (Wilde told him it was 'because she was a virgin'.) These questions were often the prelude to a provocative philosophic paradox or a parable – rhetorical weapons again borrowed from Socrates. 'Tell me,' he asked Gide on one occasion, 'what have you done since yesterday?' On hearing the young man's rather bald account of his mundane activities, Wilde's face darkened. 'If that's really what you've done,' he said reproachfully, 'then why repeat it? You do see that it's not at all interesting . . . There are two worlds – the one that *exists* without one's speaking about it, called the *real world* . . . the other is the world of art, which one must discuss, for otherwise it would cease to exist . . . listen . . . I'm going to tell you a story.'[13] And so the master storyteller began.

Having bewildered his interlocutors with questions and paradoxical theories, Wilde seduced them with his tales. Gide was ravished by Wilde's 'little coloured' parables, just as Socrates' audience had been. In Plato's *Symposium,* the aristocrat Alcibiades, Socrates' disciple and lover, compares him to a 'flute-player more wonderful than Marsyas' because of his power of enchanting his audience: 'When I hear him,' he says, 'my heart leaps up within me, and my eyes rain tears.'[14] These words, which many of Wilde's own listeners would later echo, are marked in his copy of the *Dialogues.**

Wilde tried to realise, in his own life, various aspects of classical culture and literature. In his talk he attempted to out-Socrates Socrates by making poetry and paradox dance together, and in his amorous relations he endeavoured to revive the ancient institution of *paiderastia* (love between an older and a younger man). His fascination with that union, and with homosexual love generally, is witnessed by the readerly traces he left in his copy of the *Dialogues.*

Prior to his perusal of Jowett's Plato, Wilde had encountered the subject of Greek homosexuality in the pages of Mahaffy's *Social Life in Greece.* In Symonds's *Studies of the Greek Poets* too, he had discovered fervent and thinly veiled allusions to the topic.[18] Symonds was one of a handful of Oxford-educated scholars of homosexual persuasion, now known as the 'Oxford Hellenists', who used their commentaries on classical texts to safely explore and define their illicit passion. Wilde certainly picked up on Symonds's 'insinuendoes'. In his copy of *Studies* he marks the author's numerous references to the

---

* Wilde's copy of the *Dialogues* indeed suggests that he may have consciously tried to pick up some rhetorical tips from his Athenian master. He marks some of Socrates' fables,[15] and sometimes uses marginal crosses to chart the development of the philosopher's arguments.[16]

Wilde was also fascinated by Socrates' characteristically paradoxical queries. He marks a question the philosopher put to the boy Lysis: 'Suppose that I were to cover your auburn locks with white lead, would they be really white,' Socrates asks, 'or would they only appear to be?'[17]

relationship of the Homeric warriors Achilles and Patroklos, which is characterised as an 'intense friendship' and as a 'love that passed the love of women'.[19]

Plato's dialogues lay at the heart of the late nineteenth-century debate about Greek homosexuality. In the *Symposium*, homosexual passion is discussed frankly and with ecstatic enthusiasm at an Athenian drinking party, where the topic of love is examined by various speakers. Socrates offers an ardent and eloquent defence, describing the progression of a human soul from the love of a specific young man to the love of beauty and other abstract virtues. The philosopher ranks the passion far above its heterosexual equivalent in the spiritual hierarchy, depicting the love of women as sensual and degrading.[20]

The spiritual quality of homosexual love is emphasised throughout the *Symposium*, where it is characterised as chaste and intellectual rather than sexual – hence the modern term 'Platonic love'. Many of Plato's nineteenth-century readers strove to live up to Socrates' purely spiritual ideal of passion, with varying degrees of success. Both the *Symposium* and the *Phaedrus* celebrate the *paiderastic* union of an older and a younger man in which wisdom and experience are exchanged for energy, ardour and beauty. Other dialogues, such as *Charmides*, vividly illustrate the dynamic of the relationship. Socrates tutors Charmides – a young man who captivates him by his boyish grace – in the ways of philosophic righteousness. At a time when men could be imprisoned for life for homosexual 'offences', these dialogues must have seemed astonishing. Here was Socrates, the father of Western philosophy, a sage held up as a paragon of wisdom and virtue, declaring that it was perfectly natural for a man to fall in love with a youth, and that such a love was the portal to philosophic understanding and spiritual enlightenment.

The dialogues fell upon John Addington Symonds with the force

of a revelation. 'They confirmed,' he said, 'my congenital inclination
. . . and filled my mind with an impossible dream . . . I discovered the
true *liber amoris* at last . . . It was just as though the voice of my own
soul spoke to me through Plato.'[21] The night on which he read the
Phaedrus and the *Symposium* was, he believed, 'one of the most important of my life'. He read on through the early hours of the morning:
'the sun was shining, on the shrubs outside' before he 'shut up the
book'.[22] Symonds set about putting theory into practice by embarking
on a passionate, though entirely spiritual, friendship with a young
man.

Wilde's first perusal of Plato may have been similarly intense. His
virgin response is, alas, now beyond recovery, because the editions of
the dialogues he used at Trinity and Portora have not survived. Yet
the markings and annotations to his copy of Jowett's *Dialogues* surely
preserve an echo of that initial reaction. They strongly suggest that
Wilde was one of the many young men of the period who, in Symonds's
words, were irresistibly 'stirred, by the panegyric of paiderastic love in
the *Phaedrus* . . . the personal grace of *Charmides* . . . the mingled realism
and rapture of the *Symposium*'.[23]

Wilde placed two crosses beside the passage in *Charmides* where
Socrates declares himself 'astonished at' the 'beauty and stature' of
Charmides. He also put a line beside the philosopher's fervid
exclamation: 'O rare! I caught a sight of the inwards of [Charmides']
garment, and took flame. Then I could no longer contain myself . . .
I felt that I had been overcome by a wild-beast appetite.'[24] The
episode made an enduring impression on Wilde. 'Don't you remember,' he remarked to a friend years later, 'how the blood throbbed in
[Socrates'] veins and how he grew blind with desire?' It was, he said,
'a scene more magical than the passionate love-lines of Sappho'.[25]

In *Protagoras* Wilde underlined the passage where the eponymous
character criticises Socrates for chasing after 'the fair Alcibiades'.[26]

The intensity of their passion, which was apparently unconsummated, is vividly preserved in the pages of the *Symposium*. Wilde marked Jowett's elucidation of the famous idea of the 'Platonic Eros' in his introduction to that dialogue. In his notebooks Wilde defines this as 'the impassioned search after truth, as well as the romantic side of that friendship so necessary for philosophy . . . from the love of the beautiful object we rise to the ideal *eros*; from Charmides to the *form of the good*'.[27] Jowett's explication is far more detached, and betrays traces of uneasiness; significantly, he makes no mention of Charmides.*

Perhaps Plato revealed to Wilde much about himself that he had not known before, and gave a name, a history and a justification to a latent passion. The philosopher certainly conditioned the way Wilde viewed that passion. The description of Basil Hallward's love for Dorian in *Dorian Gray* is pure Platonism: 'The love that he bore him – for it was really love – had nothing in it that was not noble and intellectual. It was not that mere physical admiration of beauty that is born of the senses.'[30] In the extended version of Wilde's essay-story, 'The Portrait of Mr W.H.', he also characterises the relationship between Shakespeare and the actor Willie Hughes (who, he suggests, may have been the dedicatee of the Bard's sonnets) as the epitome of Platonic love, and he ascribes the Renaissance's fascination with intense male friendship to the influence of a Latin translation of the

---

* Jowett was always at pains to reassure his Victorian readers that Socrates had successfully mastered his physical desires and he characterised the philosopher's speeches as 'singular' in their 'combination of the most degrading passion with the desire for virtue and improvement'.[28] He also said that Plato's writings were full of extravagant 'figures of speech', and argued that 'what he says about the loves of men must be transferred to the loves of women before we can attach any serious meaning to his words. Had he lived in our times, he would have made the transposition himself.'[29] In reading Jowett's translations as encomia to homosexual love, Wilde was therefore reading 'against the grain'.

Symposium. That 'wonderful dialogue', he comments, 'of all the Platonic dialogues perhaps the most perfect . . . began to exercise a strange influence over men, and to colour their words and thoughts and manner of living'.[31]

Literature thus exercises a magical influence over life. Plato does not simply reveal a dormant passion to his readers; he colours their words and thoughts concerning it and affects the way they realise it in their daily existence. In 'Mr W.H.' Wilde argues that literature actually creates the feelings from which it is conventionally thought to derive – the word precedes and inspires the emotion, not the other way around. Could it be then that a dead philosopher stimulated, or perhaps even engendered, Wilde's latent attraction to other men? Was it a case of literary nurture over biological nature?

Plato certainly determined the way Wilde expressed his passion in everyday life. In characteristic fashion, he adopted a work of literature as a manual for living. In his amatory friendships with young men he sought to achieve the Platonic ideal of *paiderastic* love. Robert Ross, who was probably his first significant male love, was fifteen years his junior. As well as being Wilde's physical lover, Ross was vital to his art, acting as his muse and amanuensis. Throughout his relationship with Lord Alfred Douglas too, Wilde followed the Platonic model. He declared that their friendship ought to be chiefly dedicated to 'the creation and contemplation of beautiful things',[32] and he penned letters to the young man which could, he claimed, 'only be understood by those who have read the *Symposium* of Plato'.[33] Douglas always maintained that theirs was a predominantly, and indeed almost exclusively, 'Platonic' attachment, directly inspired by their reading of the Greek philosopher.[34]

At one of his trials Wilde was asked to define the 'Love that dare not speak its name' (a phrase coined by Douglas to describe homo-sexual love), and, by implication, his relationship with Douglas.

'The "Love that dare not speak its name",' Wilde declared, 'is . . . a great affection of an elder for a younger man . . . such as Plato made the very basis of his philosophy . . . It is beautiful, it is fine, it is the noblest form of affection. There is nothing unnatural about it. It is intellectual, and it repeatedly exists . . . when the elder man has intellect, and the younger man has all the joy, hope and glamour of life before him.'[35] Wilde's brave and brilliant extempore speech, itself so like a passage out of the *Symposium*, takes us to the heart of the matter. Plato offered Wilde far more than a convenient way of describing an inherent biological passion: he shaped, fired and may even have prompted it: Wilde's love life imitated Plato's art.*

---

* In the late Victorian period homosexual activity was commonplace in all male educational establishments such as Oxford University and public schools. In their autobiographies Symonds and Douglas remark on its prevalence among students. Wilde's physical interest in his own sex was, therefore, hardly exceptional for his time and for his class. It is interesting to note that while acquaintances remarked on some of the 'feminine' traits of Wilde's character (effeminacy and homosexuality were sometimes associated in the period),[36] it was his Irishness that excited comment in the cloisters: race, rather than any perceived sexual inclination, set Wilde apart from his peers.

So far as Wilde's mature sexuality was concerned, what distinguished him, and men such as Symonds and Douglas, from the general run of English aristocrats who had enjoyed (and in some cases, continued to enjoy) casual all male sex, was their attempt to invent a language for their passion. They differed, too, in placing homosexual love at the centre of their lives and in championing it as a political cause.

12. 'The despotism of fact'

IN THE MIDDLE of the nineteenth century Benjamin Jowett introduced elements of the philosophy of Immanuel Kant and Georg
Wilhelm Friedrich Hegel into the Oxford Greats course. The
study of German philosophy, at least in its Hegelian strain, was,
however, optional rather than compulsory in the 1870s – Kant features
on Wilde's Finals paper, but Hegel does not. The study of these
thinkers was probably left to the discretion of the tutors of individual
Oxford colleges. While Jowett's students at Balliol were encouraged to
grapple with the bewildering complexities of Kant and Hegel's writings,
it is unlikely that Wilde received the same stimulus at Magdalen, where
the teaching was neither as adventurous nor as competent.

Nevertheless, Wilde was fascinated by both philosophers, and his
attraction to them probably had roots in his Dublin past. His father's
library contained various works of German philosophy, such as the
writings of the intellectual Lessing; Speranza was familiar with other
Teutonic thinkers such as Fichte and Novalis. Like many readers of
her generation, she also fell under the spell of Arthur Schopenhauer's
vast and vertiginous *The World as Will and Idea*. She certainly knew
something of Hegel's ideas, too, as she translated a German novel
entitled *The First Temptation, or 'Eritis Sicut Deus'*, in which the protagonist
is a Hegelian philosopher.

Wilde may have read some German philosophy in his adolescence;
he certainly discussed it during his undergraduate years with his

mother.[1] As Speranza read continental philosophers, such as Schopenhauer, in their original languages, it is likely that she was also familiar with thinkers, such as the German Friedrich Nietzsche and the Dane Søren Kierkegaard, who were not yet translated (or but little translated) into English during her lifetime. This opens up the intriguing possibility that she may have introduced her son to the electrifying writings of these two philosophers, to whom he has often, and with much justice, been compared.

Writers from continental Europe often visited Merrion Square and the Wildes made frequent trips to France, Germany and Scandinavia. As Celts, the Wildes believed that they shared greater racial affinity with the peoples of mainland Europe than they did with the Anglo-Saxon English, so it was only natural that they should feel greater cultural and intellectual kinship with continentals. Many Irish intellectuals, Wilde's parents among them, were proud that English philosophy had never gained dominion over their country. That philosophy was dominated by empiricism, which is based on the belief that knowledge must be derived exclusively from sensory experience, and ought to be attained by experiment and observation rather than through the sort of abstract reasoning that characterises German philosophy. Facts, in a word, must come before theories, and scientific data before conceptual speculation.

Some of Wilde's parents' writings, and many of his own, can be described as an extravagant crusade against empiricism, and as a declaration of the superiority of philosophical ideas and the poetic imagination over mere facts. The Wildes fought passionately against what Matthew Arnold called the English 'despotism of fact', for political as well as philosophical reasons. If they admitted the truth of the English world-view there would be no intellectual vantage point from which they could criticise colonial rule in their country. Moreover, admitting the sovereignty of facts would be tantamount to acknowledging an English victory because facts are, of course, always manipulated by the governing power.* Wilde's interest in German philosophy at Oxford, and his contempt for English empiricism, are an affirmation of his Celtic identity.

Wilde was intrigued by the Kantian notion that sensory data must be processed by our minds before we can comprehend it. Kant analyses the processes that render raw facts intelligible – we filter and sort them, he says, using innate mental 'categories', such as our inbuilt grasp of the concepts of time and space. Kant thus offered a challenge to empiricism, which assumed our ability to see the external world objectively: how can we see the world 'as it really is' when we perceive it through the innate categories of our minds?

Wilde believed that the Enlightenment philosopher had brought 'speculation' from the outside world 'back to man', reinstating him, just as Socrates had done, as 'the theoretical and practical measure of all things'.[3] His fundamental message was similar to that of a poem from the *Greek Anthology*, a collection of ancient verse Wilde adored: 'Measure yourself first, and know yourself, then you can begin to measure the world.'

Hegel, in contrast, moved the focus of philosophy away from man, and set out, in Wilde's phrase, to 're-conquer the world'.[4] Yet while the early nineteenth-century thinker focused on the external universe, there was nothing empirical about his perspective. He was an Idealist who saw in human history the progressive realisation of the *Geist* – the 'mind of God' or the 'world's soul'. The *Geist* evolved over time through a constant process of contradiction and negation, which

---

* It is interesting, in this context, to read Wilde's 1889 review of J.A. Froude's novel *The Two Chiefs of Dunboy*. Froude summarises the 'Irish Problem' thus: 'The Irish disowned the facts of life, and the facts of life proved the strongest.' In his article Wilde challenges this view, partly on the grounds that Froude's 'facts' are actually fictions invented to justify English rule.[2]

would one day be resolved in a perfect synthesis.[5] Human history would then reach its apotheosis and the 'mind of God' made manifest. The notoriously obscure and abstract character of Hegel's writing makes his ideas extremely difficult to grasp. Wilde deciphered them with the aid of Jowett and Symonds, whose commentaries on the classics draw heavily on Hegel, and by reading William Wallace and T.H. Green's lucid introductory studies of the philosopher, which he purchased from Shrimpton's bookshop over the winter months of 1877–78.[6]

With the rise of modern science in the eighteenth century, empiricism had come to dominate the English intellectual landscape, as, indeed, it does to this day. Wilde believed that this philosophical outlook was largely responsible for the limited and impoverished character of England's intellectual culture, which held up, as an ideal, the 'thoroughly well-informed man' desperate to cram his mind full of 'rubbish and facts'.[7] For Wilde, as for Kant, facts were highly problematic entities; moreover, if they remained unilluminated by philosophic theories, they were meaningless. 'Facts,' as he put it, 'are the Labyrinth: ideas the guiding thread.'[8]

Wilde's anti-empiricism provided a philosophical context for his theories on art, such as his championing of fantasy over realism; it also inspired his criticism of science, whose claim to objectivity had, he thought, been undermined by Kant. Wilde believed that scientists often unconsciously projected on to facts the cultural and intellectual prejudices of their historical period. In one of his introductions to Plato's *Dialogues*, Jowett argues that such preconceptions are far more pervasive in scientific and 'commonsensical' cultures which, believing themselves to be 'resting on facts', are unaware that they are actually 'resting on ideas'.[9] Wilde glossed the passage with the word 'good'.

13. 'Such a strange influence'

IT WAS DURING Michaelmas term of 1874 that Wilde first opened *Studies in the History of the Renaissance*, a collection of art essays penned by the Oxford Classics don Walter Pater in 1873. Wilde's beautiful first edition of the book had an unusual green cloth binding and was printed in generously spaced type on 'mock-ribbed' paper, which gives a pleasant tingling sensation as you move your fingers over it.

The volume contains essays on philosophers, poets and artists of the Renaissance such as Leonardo, Botticelli and Michelangelo. Pater's relationship to the past is personal and passionate. Through years spent adoring and, as it were, *living* with the artworks and writings of the period, he absorbed its spirit. This enabled him to divine, by instinct, much about the Renaissance that was inaccessible to more scrupulous scholars.

Pater enters into a work of art imaginatively, elucidating, in a series of baroque prose poems, the impression it makes on him, and defining its special character. He calls this the 'true truth' about an artwork, next to which the facts concerning its production and history are insignificant. After gazing long and lovingly at the mysterious face of the Mona Lisa, set against the dreamy green landscape of water and stone, he writes, as if in a trance, 'The presence that rose thus so strangely beside the waters, is expressive of what in the ways of a thousand years men had come to desire. Hers is the head upon which "the ends of the world are come", and the eyelids are a little weary . . . She is older than the rocks among which she sits; like the vampire, she has been dead many times, and learned the secrets of the grave . . . and all this has been to her but as the sound of lyres and flutes . . .'[1]

Wilde hailed this passage as the quintessential piece of 'creative criticism'. Its unashamed subjectivity and its ornate, impressionistic style were, to him, causes for celebration. Pater had deepened the mystery of the painting by enriching it with a new interpretation, and his criticism could itself stand as an independent work of art. 'Who . . . cares,' he wrote, 'whether Mr Pater has put into the portrait of the Mona Lisa something that Leonardo never dreamed of?'[2]

When Pater contemplates a work of art from a more objective viewpoint he focuses, almost exclusively, on its stylistic attributes, rather than on its 'meaning' or 'message'. A work's style should, he argues, so perfectly embody the artist's 'ideas' and 'intentions' as to be indistinguishable from them. All arts thus aspire to the condition of music, because in music form and content are inseparable.

Pater suggests that art does not appeal primarily to the intellect, but rather to that instinct for form, beauty and harmony which might be called the aesthetic sense. Those endowed with this sense engage with art in an imaginative, emotional, and even physical fashion. In the conclusion to the *Renaissance* Pater describes the 'aesthetic' experience as overwhelming. Art affords us the opportunity of ecstasy, he says, coming to us without an intellectual programme or a moral purpose and 'proposing frankly to give nothing but the highest quality to [our] moments as they pass, and simply for those moments' sake'. It offers the possibility of heightened pleasure, placing us 'at the focus where the greatest number of [life's] vital forces unite in their purest energy'. The aim of existence is the enjoyment and multiplication of such intense experiences. 'To burn always,' as Pater put it, 'with this hard, gemlike flame, to maintain this ecstasy is success in life.'[3]

*

Pater's conclusion signalled his allegiance to the Aesthetic movement, a loose affiliation of artists, intellectuals and critics of various
cultures, linked by their adherence to several key doctrines regarding
art. They believed that the style of an artwork is more important
than its content, and that formal beauty is paramount. They also
held that the creation of beauty is the common aim of all the arts,
and that art is entirely separate from the 'real' world.

The origins of Aestheticism lay in the writings of Kant, who
defined art as 'purposiveness without purpose', and as something
entirely separate from the spheres of morality and action. His ideas
were refined and elaborated in the mid-nineteenth century by French
authors such as Charles Baudelaire and Théophile Gautier. In the
celebrated preface to his novel *Mademoiselle de Maupin*, Gautier declared
that all art is quite useless.

Swinburne introduced English readers to these French theories.
Art's business, he declared, 'is not to do good on [moral] grounds, but
to do good on her own ... Art for Art's sake first of all.'[4] '*Rien n'est vrai
que le beau* [nothing is true except the beautiful],' he argued. '*La beauté
est parfaite* [Beauty is perfect].'[5] Swinburne, along with Rossetti,
attempted to realise the aesthetic ideal in poetry that aimed at formal
perfection and offered the reader little in the way of a message or a
moral.

Wilde had been introduced to Kant's aesthetics at Trinity by
Mahaffy, whose own position on literature and art seems to have been
partly derived from the German philosopher: 'he took,' Wilde commented with approval, 'the deliberately artistic standpoint towards
everything.'[6]

Gautier's *Mademoiselle de Maupin* was probably among the French
novels Wilde devoured in his youth, and he knew the writings of
Rossetti and Swinburne practically by heart. He was famous at

Trinity for being their ardent disciple, and for echoing their Aesthetic views. His association with the movement was also indicated by his devotion to the works of Symonds, another 'aesthete',[7] as well as by his extravagant aesthetic attire, which included a pair of 'Umbrian' trousers that excited much laughter in the quads. Wilde was fashioning the aesthete's persona he would perfect at Oxford, where he dressed flamboyantly, ostentatiously littered his room with beautiful objects, and coined the celebrated phrase: 'I find it harder and harder every day to live up to my blue china.'[8]

Wilde had therefore been thoroughly prepared for the *Renaissance* by his earlier reading. Before he came across Pater, as he put it later, he had already gone 'more than half-way' to meeting him.[9] Yet if the don offered him little that was original in theoretical terms, his book was probably the most intellectually stimulating and stylistically seductive expression of the Aesthetic creed that Wilde had ever read.

The *Renaissance* caused a scandal on its publication in 1873. The Bishop of Oxford attacked, from the pulpit, the 'neo-pagan' character of the book's Hedonistic conclusion. Others were outraged by the sympathy the author expressed for a period of history that was a byword in Victorian England for every conceivable form of vice.*

Pater was so distressed by the vituperative criticism that he dropped his 'conclusion' from the second edition, on the grounds that 'it might possibly mislead some of the young men into whose hands it might fall'.[11] This was an accurate estimation of his book's potential influence as it became the bible of an entire generation of aesthetes. Fledgling writers, such as W.B. Yeats, discovered in it an alluring

---

* One particular 'vice' Pater hinted at proved to be especially shocking. Like Symonds, Pater was a homosexual 'Oxford Hellenist' and, in his book, he often alludes obliquely to homosexual love. In his pen portrait of the eighteenth-century German classicist Johann Winckelmann, he explicitly endorses all-male passion.[10]

epicurean creed and a daring approach to art, as well as a masterly literary style they could copy.

The *Renaissance* struck Wilde with the power of a revelation, becoming for him 'the golden book of spirit and sense, the holy writ of beauty'. More than twenty years after the event, he recalled the autumn day on which he had read the volume.[12] Such, indeed, was Wilde's love for Pater's book that, in later life, he claimed never to travel anywhere without it. 'It is possible,' he mused, 'that I may exaggerate about [it]. I certainly hope that I do; for where there is no exaggeration there is no love, and where there is no love there is no understanding.'[13]

Wilde found Pater's exhortation to seek 'not the fruit of experience, but experience itself' irresistible. He went out into the world with these words engraved on his heart, and so he lived, resolutely determined to 'eat of the fruit of all the trees in the garden of the world'. It would, indeed, be hard to think of anyone who more assiduously followed Pater's injunction to burn always with a 'hard, gemlike flame'. The don became perhaps the greatest single influence on Wilde's writings. He expounded Pater's ideas on art in his lectures and critical writings, which themselves consciously imitate the don's brand of impressionistic aesthetic criticism. As a prose stylist, Wilde's debt to his Oxford master was enormous.

Years after leaving Oxford Wilde referred to the *Renaissance* as 'that book which has had such a strange influence over my life'.[14] Interestingly, his words echo the description of the unnamed 'poisonous' French novel that famously corrupts Dorian Gray. 'It was,' Wilde wrote, 'the strangest book that [Dorian] had ever read . . . [he] could not free himself from [its] influence.'[15] Its potent effect on Wilde's protagonist is also evoked in words that may be a coded reference to Pater: 'The Renaissance knew of strange manners of poisoning . . . Dorian Gray had been poisoned by a book.'[16]

It is tempting to hear in Dorian's experience a reverberation of Wilde's first encounter with the *Renaissance*. Was Wilde, like Dorian, filled with the desire to drain the cup of life to the dregs? Did he discover in it 'the story of his own life, written before he had lived it'?[17]

Having been seduced by the book, Wilde was eager to meet its author. In 1877 he sent Pater his review of an exhibition of paintings at London's Grosvenor Gallery. It contains two flattering references to the don, and several imitations of his impressionistic criticism. There were also a number of comments that were certain to appeal to Pater's artistic and sexual taste. Wilde describes a painting of a 'boyish beauty' who is, he says, a type common 'in the Greek islands, where boys can still be found as beautiful as the Charmides of Plato'.[18] Pater responded by praising the maturity of Wilde's style and his 'quite exceptionally cultivated tastes' in a letter Wilde proudly showed off to his friends.[19]

Soon afterwards the pair met. 'When I first had the privilege of meeting Mr Walter Pater,' Wilde recalled, 'he said to me, smiling, "Why do you always write poetry? Why do you not write prose? Prose is so much more difficult."'[20] As Wilde broadly followed this advice, it may stand as a vivid emblem of the don's influence over him.*

Their relationship seemed destined to realise the Platonic *paiderastic* ideal which fascinated both of them, with the older man tutoring the

---

* Another emblem of Pater's influence on Wilde is the copy of Gustave Flaubert's *Trois contes* [Three Tales], which the don lent to his disciple in November 1877. The volume contains a story called 'Herodias', which imaginatively recreates the events leading up to the death of John the Baptist; it would be one of the most important sources for Wilde's play *Salomé*. It is fitting then that Wilde would send Pater an inscribed copy of the original French-language version of his drama.[21] The influence was not, however, all one way — during his time at Magdalen Wilde also lent Pater a number of his books.[22]

younger in the ways of intellectual refinement and literary excellence. Yet the man Wilde addressed as 'the great master' was actually rather timid and tongue-tied and so hardly suited to the role of Socrates. When the pair were together, Wilde doubtless did most of the talking. He later gave an account of a conversation with the Oxford don, where the Platonic roles of older and younger man are inverted. 'We were seated together on a bench under some trees at Oxford, watching the students bathing in the river . . . I really talked as if inspired . . . when I paused, Pater — the stiff, quiet, silent Pater — suddenly slipped from his seat and knelt down by me and kissed my hand. He got up with a white strained face. "I had to", he muttered, glancing about him fearfully, "I had to — once . . . "'[23] The anecdote sounds too good to be true, and it is hard to imagine the diffident Pater making such an effusive gesture. Yet even if it is Wilde's invention, it conveys something of his attitude to the don.

With the passing of time, the disciple became disenchanted with the master. To Wilde's disappointment Pater seemed reluctant to realise his own Hedonistic theories: 'he lived,' Wilde said, after the don's death, 'to disprove everything that he has written.'[24] How ironic that Wilde should have been so altered by the work of a man who kept life at a safe distance.*

* Wilde's relationship with Pater and his writings has often been contrasted with his relationship to the art critic and Slade Professor of Fine Arts at Oxford, John Ruskin (1819–1900). Wilde religiously attended Ruskin's lectures and enjoyed many 'walks and talks' with the professor which he would remember as 'the dearest memories of my Oxford days.'[25] Yet significant differences emerged in their attitude to art. While Ruskin embraced the term 'aesthetic' in its broadest sense, he never equated it with amorality in art, nor did he wish to separate art from society and politics. 'The keystone to his aesthetic system' was, as Wilde put it, 'ethical always'.[26] Wilde acknowledged the influence of the man he addressed reverently as a 'poet', 'priest' and 'prophet', but ultimately rejected his brand of Aestheticism as too moral and didactic: 'He would judge of a picture,' Wilde said, 'by the amount of noble moral ideas it expresses; but . . . the rule of art is not the rule of morals.'[27]

PART II

The
Library

'Hermes with the Infant Dionysus' by Praxiteles.

14. 'Spirit of Beauty! tarry still awhile'

WHEN WILDE CAME down from Oxford to London in early 1879 he was the complete intellectual article. The books that he brought with him to the English capital — Aeschylus' *Agamemnon*, the *Dialogues* of Plato, and the works of his mentors, Mahaffy and Pater — had shaped his vision of the world. These volumes took their place on the shelves of the apartments he rented in London between 1879–85, no doubt with many other golden books from his youth. A number of his parents' works, such as his father's *Irish Popular Superstitions* and *Lough Corrib*, would have been there, along with the novels of Balzac and Disraeli. These personal classics, which had formed Wilde's personality, also formed the core of his adult library.

Wilde took his books with him when he moved between his various London residences. His addresses sound so aristocratic that they must have inspired great confidence in the tradesmen he dealt with. There was Keats House, Chelsea, which Wilde himself christened after his favourite rhymer; 9 Charles Street, Grosvenor Square; and Thames House, Salisbury Street, just off the Strand. His apartments were, however, actually rather inexpensive and bohemian in character, and he shared them with friends. Descriptions of their interiors remind us of his undergraduate rooms at Magdalen. He adorned them with Pre-Raphaelite paintings and countless ornaments, and always had a plentiful supply of tobacco and alcohol on hand to serve the hordes of actresses, poets and painters who dropped in to catch up with all the gossip.

Some of Wilde's books would have been set out on shelves; others were probably left in untidy piles on the floor. Disorder seems to have been the keynote of his bachelor libraries: one friend was horrified to find a precious volume among a lot of rubbish.[1]

In the years 1879–85, Wilde's life altered rapidly and radically. In imitation, perhaps, of his hero Lucien de Rubempré, he attempted to cause a sensation in literary and social circles with his volume of verse *Poems* (1881) and his dandified attire. Like Disraeli, he kept himself in the public eye and in the papers, with his witty epigrams and his extravagant public gestures, which included (or so he made people believe) walking down Piccadilly with a lily in his hand.

Such strategies succeeded in turning Wilde into a media celebrity, famous for being famous as much as for his oracular proclamations on art. These pronouncements did, however, establish him as the popular spokesman of the Aesthetic movement. In 1882 he embarked on a lecture tour of America, during which he attempted to convert the country to the Aesthetic creed. He encouraged people to surround themselves with objects of beauty and to dress exquisitely, and he advocated the foundation of local art schools. On his return to England he lectured on art in the provinces. The press coverage his lectures received, not all of which was flattering, turned him into a household name.

After the failure of his two dramas, *Vera* (1880) and *The Duchess of Padua* (1883), to reach the stage, Wilde settled down into a fairly conventional routine of lecturing, book reviewing in the national press, and domesticity. In 1883 he fell in love with a Dublin girl called Constance Lloyd whom he described as a 'grave, slight, violet-eyed little Artemis, with great coils of heavy brown hair'[2] (see plate 5). The following year he married her. Given Wilde's undergraduate fascination with homosexuality, and the possibility that, even at this early date, his interest in it was not purely theoretical, this may seem surprising. There can be little doubt, however, that he was genuinely enamoured of Constance, so it is likely that Wilde was attracted to both women and men at this time. Only later would his passion for his own sex dominate his emotional life.

Constance gave birth to two boys whom Wilde cherished: Cyril was born in 1885 and Vyvyan in the following year. At the beginning of 1885, the Wildes moved into 16 (now 34) Tite Street, Chelsea, which became known as the 'House Beautiful' because it exemplified many of Wilde's Aesthetic theories regarding design and decoration (see plate 7). The interior was devised by the renowned theatre designer and architect E.W. Godwin; Wilde was involved at every stage of the enterprise. Apart from his childhood house at Merrion Square, this would be Wilde's only 'home' as he was fairly nomadic during every other phase of his life. Within the house, three rooms were exclusively his: the bedroom on the top floor, the smoking room on the first, and the library on the ground floor.

The white front door of No. 16 opened on to a grey-white hall with a bright yellow ceiling. A white silk curtain hung down in front of the staircase that went up to the first floor. The library was immediately to the right of the hall, at the front of the house, overlooking Tite Street. Its bay windows are so close to the street that it is easy to see into the room from the pavement. Alfred Douglas would refer to the room as 'little'. By any standards other than a lord's, however, the library was sizeable, occupying half of the ground floor (the rest of the floor was taken up by the dining-room). The library's ceiling was as high as those of most late Victorian houses, and there was a dado rail at five feet six inches up the wall. The room faced east, in accordance with the view of the Roman architect Vitruvius, who held that libraries ought to make the most of the morning sunshine for reading and warmth – advice that many Victorian architects followed.[3]

Originally the walls were 'to be distemper dark blue' with the upper part of the walls above the wooden rail, along with the cornice and ceiling, painted a pale gold colour, and the rail itself in golden brown.[4] These specifications were altered during the initial stages of the work and the room became a harmony of yellow and red, with buttercup yellow walls and shiny lacquered red-brown woodwork.

Wilde seems to have been responsible for the transformation from golden brown to red: 'Don't you think,' he asked his architect, 'a vermillion band in the front room . . . would do?'[5] He may also have been behind the decision to paint the walls yellow, which was, for him, the happiest of colours. 'You have yellow walls!' he exclaimed on a visit to a friend's house, 'so have I – yellow is the colour of joy.'[6]

The words that Wilde inscribed, in red, blue and gilt above the library's doorway were highly appropriate for the works he would compose there. The inscription read:

> Spirit of Beauty! tarry still awhile,
>> They are not dead, thine ancient votaries,
> Some few there are to whom thy radiant smile
>> Is better than a thousand victories.

These lines, from Wilde's poem 'The Garden of Eros', articulate that sincere devotion to beauty that colours so many of his works. In consciously drawing on another writer – Shelley, who coined the phrase 'Spirit of Beauty' – they are also typical of the echo-filled and highly allusive writings that Wilde penned in the room. Above the inscription there was a series of painted sunflowers and flame-coloured aureoles.[7]

In the spring and summer time, the morning sun poured into the room from the large bay window, reflecting the shiny gilt lettering on the spines of Wilde's books. Like his mother, however, Wilde was not fond of excessive light, and there were times when he blocked out the sun's rays by pulling a glass bead hanging across the window or by placing in front of it a large wooden screen decorated in a Moorish pattern. According to Wilde's son Vyvyan, screens were used in many of the rooms at Tite Street, making the interiors dark, exotic and 'mysterious'.

Wilde may have preferred to have artificial light in the library. He maintained that the 'soft light' given off by lamps and wax candles was 'the best to read by' and 'very much prettier and healthier than gas'.[8] The idea of concentrating light in libraries by the use of circular mirrors also appealed to him, so it is probable that various glasses were strategically positioned around the room. Wilde loved the way artificial light played upon the interrupted surfaces of a ceiling, so it is unlikely that his library's ceiling was smooth. An additional play of light was provided in winter by the flames of a coal fire, which was framed by an ornate russet oak fireplace, situated on the wall opposite the door. (It was removed from the house during renovation in the 1950s and given to Magdalen College, where it was installed in an undergraduate room very close to Wilde's former residence on the Kitchen Staircase[9] – see plate 6).

An eight by seven foot Persian carpet dominated the floor. A large piece of old oriental embroidery hung on one of the walls and a black sheepskin rug lay in front of the fire. An antique sofa covered in moreen probably faced the fireplace; there were also three beautiful chairs: a Chippendale mahogany corner chair, an antique Italian ivory inlaid elbow-chair and a large easy chair with two horsehair cushions. Perhaps Wilde selected one of them to read in according to the book, or to his mood.

Curiously, given Wilde's aversion to conventional Victorian interior decoration, the general impression is one of typical nineteenth-century heaviness, profusion and clutter. The room contained, among other things, an antique carved oak chest, a four-tier enamelled red 'whatnot', several antique brass lamps and brackets, a Chinese lantern, two Japanese masks, a bronze flower, a bronze lobster, an antique pier glass and a nest of Japanese baskets.[10] Most of Wilde's friends described the library as 'Eastern', 'Turkish' or 'Moorish' in character, on account of all the hangings, lanterns, baskets and ottomans.

The library of a nineteenth-century aesthete had to be beautiful, both for its own sake and also because it was the room in which literary beauty was solemnly worshipped. Wilde shuddered with revulsion at

Wilde, aged 27, reclining with a book.

the idea of taking up 'a volume of Keats . . . in a library furnished as most are' — that is, with appalling taste. You would, he said, have to make an enormous spiritual jump, before achieving 'the proper frame of mind to appreciate his poetry'.[11]

The aesthete regarded his library as a chapel dedicated to beauty, in which the rarest and choicest of art works, both literary and visual, could be assembled in perfect harmony. That is why Dorian Gray's library contains, among other exquisite items, Venetian satin covers, tables of dark wood encrusted with nacre, pearl-coloured octagonal stands and an ebony Florentine cabinet. Thomas Griffiths Wainewright, the art critic and poisoner who was the subject of Wilde's essay 'Pen, Pencil, and Poison', filled his library with artistic objects from every culture and epoch. Wilde imagines the arch-aesthete lying there in the midst of his Greek vases, colourful gems, exquisitely bound books and antique bronzes, entranced by the magic and mystery of beautiful things.

Wilde once said that he required Chippendale near him in order to write. The jest may well have been serious, because, as noted, his library contained a chair in that style.[12] The Japanese embroidered silk gown he kept there may also have acted as a literary inspiration, reminding him, perhaps, of the legendary cowl that Balzac had worn during his furious fits of composition. Wilde evidently believed that his surroundings directly influenced the style of his writing: he once asked a friend to bring him some Queen Anne furniture to help him write a mock Restoration drama.[13]

Wilde was certainly inspired to write by the most precious item of furniture in the library — a writing-desk formerly owned by the historian, philosopher and essayist, Thomas Carlyle. Wilde's mother was a friend and admirer of the 'Sage of Chelsea', and it is likely that she had encouraged her son to read him as a boy. Wilde's letters display an intimate knowledge of Carlyle's *oeuvre*, and he knew many of his favourite Carlylean passages by heart. Speranza introduced her son to Carlyle on a visit to the author's Chelsea home in 1879 and, on that occasion, Wilde may have caught a glimpse of the desk that would become the centrepiece of his library. It is not known how or when Wilde acquired it, but he probably picked it up from the antique dealer who sold some of Carlyle's effects after his death in 1881. Wilde worshipped the desk as a relic of one of his literary heroes; he also believed that it possessed talismanic qualities. As Carlyle was a prodigiously industrious author, even by Victorian standards, Wilde hoped that it would be a fetish against idleness, one of his great temptations, and prompt him to put 'black upon white . . . black upon white'.[14]

The library was the ideal theatrical backdrop to Wilde's writing, creating just the right mood for his daily literary performance. In the morning, having first dressed with extreme care, he would descend the stairs and enter the beautiful room. After donning, perhaps, his Balzacian gown, he lit a cigarette and sat down at Carlyle's desk. He was now ready to begin his work, or rather his 'play' as he liked to call it.

The writing-desk was probably placed in front of the window.[15] Made of mahogany, it had a rising slope and a drawer in which Wilde must have placed the expensive notebooks he used to write in. On top, his paperknife and Indian brass inkstand were on permanent display.[16] As Wilde was a chain smoker, he made room on the desk for his 'silver match box frames', and the large biscuit tin full of cigarettes that he carried with him around the house. The porcelain bowl that served as an ashtray would also have found a place there. Wilde famously called the cigarette 'the perfect type of perfect pleasure. It is exquisite, and it leaves one unsatisfied. What more can one want?' Smoking was a pleasure he took very seriously indeed. He purchased as many as 300 expensive gold-tipped cigarettes at a time from high-class tobacconists, and even had them make up a special batch with his own name written on them.[17]

A waste-paper basket stood beside the desk. Into this Wilde consigned 'discarded manuscripts . . . and gaily-coloured [cigarette] boxes'.[18] It was also the final resting place of reviews of his own writings: 'two hundred and sixteen criticisms of *Dorian Gray*,' he claimed, ' . . . have passed from my library table into the wastepaper basket.'[19]

The scent of tobacco dominated the room, pervading the books and the furniture; it was balanced by the dusty, musty odour of the volumes themselves, as well as by the flowers that Wilde placed all around. He liked to arrange roses and violets in bunches; single lilies and narcissi stood in Venetian glasses. The faint smell of alcohol would also have been perceptible: decanters containing Wilde's favourite drinks of claret, hock and brandy were set out on a side-board, along with champagne tumblers and goblets for his yellow and purple wine.

Only a few pictures hung on the walls, but that is hardly surprising given the amount of space taken up by the bookshelves. There was a painting by the nineteenth-century French artist, Adolphe Monticelli, a picture by the Pre-Raphaelite artist, Simeon Solomon, Aubrey Beardsley's drawing of the actress Mrs Patrick Campbell and a Japanese painting of children at play.

The most striking work in the room was a cast of the famous bust of the god Hermes, which had been fashioned by the ancient Greek sculptor Praxiteles (see p. 108). Wilde thought that Greek sculptures created a pure and noble atmosphere in the rooms they adorned and that casts of men were particularly suited to libraries.[20] He may even have believed that his cast of Hermes would magically influence his writing. Just as the Greeks had 'set in the bride's chamber the statue

Aubrey Beardsley's portrait of Mrs Patrick Campbell, which hung in Wilde's library.

of Hermes . . . that she might bear children as lovely as the work of art she looked at' in the moment of conception, so too may Wilde have hoped to conceive lovely literary children in the presence of his cast.[21]

The bust was part of Praxiteles' celebrated masterpiece, Hermes with the Infant Dionysus, in which the god is depicted carrying the child deity. Wilde placed this archetypal icon of classical male beauty on a red-lacquered tripod near his writing-chair. It was probably to the right of the ground floor window, within touching distance of the desk. The plaster of the cast did not, alas, 'retain the beauty and transparency of the original', which was, according to Wilde, 'like ivory lit by the sun'. Viewing it on his visit to Greece in 1877, he had been convinced that 'the spirit of the god still dwelt within the marble'.[22]

Hermes was the Olympian god of orators, wits and poets, and the inventor of the lyre. He was also the deity of liars and thieves. In most legends he is depicted as a cheeky trickster, who becomes embroiled in scrapes out of a love of mischief and extricates himself from them through marvellous eloquence, a prodigious gift for telling stories and a genius for playing the lyre. This was the god whose shadow was cast across Wilde's writing-desk.

15. 'Holy of Holies'

IMMEDIATELY AFTER MOVING into Tite Street Wilde instructed his builder, Mr Sharpe, to make several alterations to the library, one of which was to 'provide and fix [a] new brass keyhole to [the] new bookcase'.[1] This was perhaps the large bookcase Wilde placed to the right of the fireplace, in which he locked away his precious copies of the 'Greek Classics'.[2] In the room there was also an 'enamelled red open bookcase' and a 'walnut wood revolving bookcase'.[3]

Victorian bookcases were designed to hold larger quarto and folio-sized books at the bottom, along with periodicals, prints and papers. The spaces between the shelves became progressively smaller as they went up, so that the top shelf held the smallest books. As it was considered important to have all books within easy reach, Wilde's bookcases would not have been particularly high. They were probably placed a little away from the wall, and well clear of the water pipes, in order to keep the books at just the right temperature.

Wilde owned around two thousand volumes. If this seems a meagre estimate for a man as ostentatiously over-educated as Wilde, we should remember that he was a writer, rather than a collector or a scholar, and that his was a working library. The figure was, in any case, hardly inconsiderable by Victorian standards. Both Edward Fitzgerald, the celebrated Victorian translator of the Persian poet Omar Khayyám, and Sir William Wilde, amassed around only eight hundred volumes over the course of lives significantly longer than Wilde's.

Wilde probably grouped some of his books by genre, language and subject. His French novels and his volumes of Shakespeare criticism were certainly placed together. Given the design of typical Victorian bookcases, however, the size of the books is likely to have been the most important factor in determining their position.

The volumes Wilde happened to be reading at a particular time were probably piled up on the floor around a divan or on top of his writing-desk. If he shared the typical Victorian gentleman's horror of having his books handled by servants, he would have tidied them up himself at the end of each working day; otherwise he may have given strict instructions that they were to be left untouched.[4]

Wilde liked the colour of interiors to be harmonious. 'Colours resemble musical notes,' he declared, 'a single false colour or false note destroys the whole.' Most nineteenth-century libraries were offensive to his fastidious aesthetic sensibility because of the discordant notes provided by the motley colours of the volumes. Unlike the books of previous centuries, Victorian publications were, he complained, 'bound in all manner of gaudy colours' and modern bookbinding was, in consequence, 'one of the greatest drawbacks to the beauty of many libraries'.[5] Richer, or perhaps more dedicated, bibliophiles overcame the problem by having all their books beautifully rebound in buckram or morocco.[6] Wilde thought the idea expensive and impractical – 'you can't,' he said, 'have all your books rebound.' 'The only thing left,' he concluded, 'is to have curtains to hide them out of sight.'[7] Wilde does not seem to have followed his own precept, however, as visitors to his library remarked on the visibility and prominence of his books. On entering the room one journalist was struck by the abundance of 'books, periodicals, manuscripts . . . on all sides'.[8]

The books on Wilde's shelves offered to his eye a carnival of incongruous colours. The nineteenth-century English novels he possessed came in orange, yellow, cobalt blue and garish green. Their bulky Victorian bindings produced a harsh counterpoint to the dainty, and sometimes deceptively chaste-looking, white covers of the slim volumes of verse he owned. The books were also of vastly varying sizes. His *Cyclopaedia of Costume* was a gargantuan red folio volume. In contrast, some of his books of poetry, such as the blue anthology *Book-Song*, were of tiny duodecimo size.

Variety was also the salient characteristic of the cityscape that met Wilde's eyes whenever he raised them from his work. Although he often blocked out the view from the window, given his curiosity and artistic interest in modern life, there must have been times when he drew back the screen to gaze out at Tite Street. He would have often seen there the horse-drawn omnibus that stopped right in front of the house, as well as countless hansom cabs passing by. He must, too, have frequently viewed dockers on their way to and from work on the Thames, at the bottom of Tite Street, and children heading off to play in the nearby Royal Hospital Gardens.

Chelsea was far more bohemian then than it is now. In those distant days, journalists, clergymen, artists, and even writers could afford to live there.[9] Right behind Tite Street ran the ironically named Paradise Row – 'one of the most forbidding of Chelsea's slums with wretched, filthy back-yards, from which the sounds of brawling rose nightly'.[10] When the fighting got out of hand 'a procession would form and walk up [the Row], along Cheyne Place and down to Tite Street to the casualty ward of the Victoria Hospital for Children', directly opposite the Wildes' home.[11]

Rich and poor, old and young, artists and lawyers, the healthy and the sick: this was the pageant of London life that paraded before Wilde's library window. No wonder he was reluctant to simplify or moralise about the world in the works he penned there. He preferred instead to express life's bewildering and invigorating diversity and complexity in inherently ambiguous and indeterminate forms such as the dialogue and the drama.

Variety was also the keynote of the natural world outside Wilde's window. The light of dawn cascaded into the room when he drew back the screen in the mornings, suddenly illuminating the resplendent colours of the spines of his books. Sunset was reflected in the windows of the buildings opposite, an effect Wilde captured in *Dorian Gray*. Dorian looks out from his library and sees that 'the sunset had smitten into scarlet gold the upper windows of the houses opposite. The panes glowed like plates of heated metal. The sky above was like a faded rose.'[12] For once the arch-anti-realist may have gone directly to life for inspiration.

Wilde also followed the progress of the seasons from his desk. In the spring he was moved to rapture by the sight of the lilac blossoms and his beloved laburnum, which hung its dusty gold over the black cast-iron railings of Tite Street.[13] In the tree-lined garden of the children's hospital opposite his window he saw the leaves turn from lush green to burning red in the autumn, and the flowers retire beneath the earth to sleep with the coming of the winter.

The sound of the fighting in Paradise Row was clearly audible in the house.[14] Noise also came from the Thames wharves. The din created by the dockers was indeed so loud that Carlyle, who had lived only a few streets away from Wilde, constructed a library at the top of his house in order to escape it. Even there, he continually complained about the racket. To make matters worse, Wilde's library was situated directly above the kitchen and the servants' quarters, and muffled sounds would have reached him from below. Reverberations also filtered down from the first-floor drawing-rooms whenever Wilde's boys played there; he heard them on the staircase too, where they often engaged in sword fights.

Vyvyan described the library as his father's 'Holy of Holies . . . in the vicinity of which no noise was to be made'; it had, he said, to be 'passed on tiptoe'.[15] When their father was inside, the boys were never permitted to enter 'except by special invitation'; when he was absent it still had 'a sort of "A" certificate to it, in that we were forbidden to enter it unless accompanied by an adult'.[16] Perhaps Wilde even went so far as to request his manservant, Arthur, to put on felt slippers whenever he walked near the room, just as he had asked his servant at Oxford to wear them because of his horror of creaking floorboards.

Many Victorian gentlemen regarded their library as 'a kind of shrine remote from the interruption of servants, wife and children'.[17] If this idea seems a little stuffy for Wilde, it should be remembered that in the mid-1890s he rented a room away from his home 'in order to have the opportunity of thinking and writing without the interruptions inseparable from my own household'.[18] The library was the one room where a gentleman might 'be at home with himself'.[19] It was a museum dedicated to his personal history, containing books purchased in every period of his life, and a permanent exhibition of his taste. 'A library,' as a famous contemporary bibliophile put it, 'should be [a man's] portrait.'[20] The library was, too, a sort of secular equivalent of the Catholic confessional. Here a man sat alone, meditating on his life, chronicling his thoughts in the diary or the letters he penned there.

Wilde imbibed some of these conventional nineteenth-century attitudes. The library served him as a retreat from the rest of the house; it was also a symbol of his personal history as its contents bore witness to the various stages of his life and literary career. Likewise, Wilde clearly subscribed to the notion that a book collection is expressive of character – throughout his works he conveys a great deal about the temperament of his fictional creations by giving us a peek at their bookshelves.

16. 'The falser is the truer'

SOME TIME IN the 1880s Wilde made the acquaintance of Alfred Nutt, head of the London publishing house and bookshop David Nutt, which had been established by his father. Nutt, then in his thirties, was highly influential in the Celtic revival movement and a renowned folklorist, becoming president of the Folk-Lore Society in the 1890s. These twin intellectual passions may explain why he was drawn to Wilde's fairy tales, which resound with so many folkloristic and Celtic echoes. Nutt published five of them in the 1888 collection *The Happy Prince and Other Tales*, a volume written, in Wilde's words, 'partly for children, and partly for those who have kept the childlike faculties of wonder and joy'.[1]

In the year of the volume's publication, Wilde became one of Nutt's regular clients. An invoice made out to Wilde from David Nutt's details seventy or so purchases he made between 1888 and 1895.* Nutt specialised in foreign books, keeping a plentiful stock of continental language titles, and English translations of world literature. Wilde acquired from him some of the volumes of French fiction that comprised around a quarter of his library — easily the best-represented genre in his collection.

Between 1889 and 1890 Wilde bought Balzac's tale, *L'Enfant maudit*

---

* The invoice is among Wilde's bankruptcy papers at the Public Record Office. Nutt was one of the creditors who demanded payment soon after Wilde's arrest.[2]

[The Cursed Child] and Flaubert's *Correspondence*, along with numerous copies of the latter's *Trois Contes* [Three Tales] which he presumably presented to friends. Flaubert was the 'sinless master' from whom Wilde learned how to write fictional prose; like Keats, he was also a sort of imaginary literary friend for Wilde, who often passed favourable comment on his writings. 'Flaubert has just told me,' Wilde would announce to an acquaintance, 'that he was lost in admiration when I recited him [my] wonderful lines.'[3] Wilde preferred the more fantastic and experimental titles in Flaubert's *oeuvre* to his fictional surveys of nineteenth-century society. While *Madame Bovary* was of course a work of genius, nothing in the whole world was as beautiful as *Salammbô*, Flaubert's vast novel set in ancient Carthage.[4] Wilde was especially fond of the proto-surrealistic masterpiece, *La Tentation de Saint-Antoine* [The Temptation of Saint Anthony], and at one time considered translating that 'amazing book'. He consulted Nutt as to the viability of the venture, but, alas, nothing came of it.[5]

Wilde purchased works by the great nineteenth-century French intellectual Ernest Renan. That author's *Life of Jesus*, in which Christ is depicted as an entirely human, but utterly mesmerising, personality, was a golden book of Wilde's youth; in age, he called it 'that gracious fifth Gospel, the Gospel according to Saint Thomas'. He picked up *L'Avenir de la science* [The Future of Science], another of Renan's books, from Nutt in 1890. In it, Renan argues that science can teach us far less about human psychology, or how to live contented and ethical lives, than art or religion. It was a view that must have appealed to Wilde who strongly objected to science's attempts 'to make the material include the spiritual', and who found it ridiculous that scientists endeavoured to trace the origin of an 'emotion' to 'a secretion of sugar'.[6]

Nutt's invoice charts Wilde's adventures in other European literatures. He bought *Fioretti di S. Francesco* [The Little Flowers of St

Francis], a medieval collection of colourful anecdotes concerning the saint's life and miracles, as well as Dante's three-volume *Opere minore* [Minor Works], which includes the *Convito*, an arcane treatise on philosophy written in poetry and prose. It is possible that Wilde toiled his way through these demanding medieval Italian texts, but it is more likely that they were bought for his wife Constance, who was far more proficient in Italian than he was. His linguistic competence would probably have been up to the challenge of Gabriele d'Annunzio's novel *Episcopo*, which he bought on 22 February 1895. This first-person narrative of a modest clerk who murders his wife's lover is written in simple colloquial Italian. The purchase is intriguing because scholars have often compared Wilde to his contemporary D'Annunzio, Italy's most famous, but also famously humourless, aesthete.

Purchases of Tolstoy's *Polikúshka*, and *The Pursuit of Happiness* offer us a sample of Wilde's taste in Russian literature. He adored the epic 'grandeur' of Tolstoy's fiction: he can 'crowd', Wilde commented, 'without over-crowding, the great canvas on which he works'.[7] Wilde read both Tolstoy novels in French translation. He may have done so because English versions were unavailable, but it is just as likely to have been a matter of preference. Wilde certainly chose the French version of Turgenev's novel *The Virgin Soil* over the widely available English translation. He bought that particular volume not from Nutt but from Franz Thimm's, another bookshop specialising in foreign titles, which he frequented.[8]

To Wilde, Turgenev was 'by far the finest artist . . . of the three great Russian novelists of our time . . . He has that spirit of exquisite selection, that delicate choice of detail, which is the essence of style [and] his work is entirely free from any personal intention'; these qualities placed him above Tolstoy and Dostoevsky in Wilde's pantheon. Not that Wilde was unimpressed by the latter: Dostoevsky was, in his view, a genius for the 'fierce intensity of passion and concentration of impulse' of his fiction and for his 'power of dealing with the deepest mysteries of psychology and the most hidden springs of life'.[9]

Wilde travelled to realms far further afield than Europe. The Nutt invoice suggests that his book collection was as cosmopolitan as the furniture in his library. He adored 'Oriental' poets, such as Omar Khayyám, for their ability to blend 'philosophy and sensuousness . . . simple parable or fable and obscure mystic utterance'. Wilde especially loved to read 'wise Omar' in Fitzgerald's poetical translation but also enjoyed the 'strange purple and fresh amethyst' of Justin McCarthy's 1889 prose version.[10] In November 1894 he purchased an anthology of Persian poetry called *Flowers from a Persian Garden*, which had been done into English prose by W.A. Clouston. In the same month he also bought E. Arnold's *Indian Poetry*, which contains an English rendition of an Indian version of the Old Testament 'Song of Songs'.

Like many of his contemporaries, Wilde was profoundly fascinated by all things Japanese. He possessed Sir Rutherford Alcock's large illustrated volume *Art and Art Industries in Japan*, a survey of the history of Japanese art, as well as a number of novels set in Japan, such as Edward Greey's *The Wonderful City of Tokio*. These titles may attest to the seriousness of Wilde's youthful intention to lecture in the land of the rising sun. He had dreamed of drinking 'amber tea out of a blue cup' there, while gazing 'at a landscape without perspective'.[11]

Wilde retained the energy and inquisitiveness of an undergraduate throughout his life by continuing his Oxford studies into adulthood. He owned George Lacy's *Liberty and Law*, which sets out to refute various economists of the *laissez-faire* school; it is exactly the sort of volume he had pored over at college in the later 1870s. The same could be said of his copies of the *Origin of Species*, Darwin's famous statement of the theory of evolution, and *First Principles*, in which Herbert Spencer argued that individualism should be the basis of both ethics and a free society. Both books significantly influenced Wilde's intellectual outlook; for him Darwin was the greatest nineteenth-century 'critic of the book of nature'.[12]

Wilde's abiding fascination with the classics is evinced by the presence of a scholarly edition of Aristotle's *Poetics* on his shelves.[13] He regarded this seminal definition of Greek tragedy as a 'perfect little work of aesthetic criticism',[14] perhaps because Aristotle is careful to distinguish literature from life: 'Poetry is not,' as Wilde's edition summarised the Greek philosopher's position, 'a metrical version of medicine, physics or history. It must be judged by its own laws, its own fundamental standards.'[15]

Wilde seems to have adopted Socrates' motto 'the unexamined life is not worth living'; as an adult, he continued to wrestle with the philosophical questions that had absorbed him during his youth. One Socratic question that occupied him was: what is the best state for man to live under? His library attests to a profound interest in politics, which will come as no surprise to anyone who has read his essay 'The Soul of Man under Socialism'. Wilde adumbrates a socialist, or rather anarchist, utopia of the future in which poverty will be eradicated by the abolition of private property and a redistribution of wealth, and all ugly and useful chores will be carried out by machines. The working classes, no longer alienated by the capitalist system, will be free to develop their personalities by exploring art and literature and thus realise the perfection that lies dormant within them.

Wilde's preoccupation with politics and social issues is evidenced by his copies of the early plays of his acquaintance George Bernard Shaw.[16] His fellow Dubliner presented capitalist English society, and its bastion and dominant class, the bourgeoisie, as rapacious, cruel and morally rotten. Wilde admired Shaw's incisive mind: 'England is the land of intellectual fogs,' he told his 'Celtic' brother, 'but you have done much to clear the air.'[17] Somewhat surprisingly, he also praised Shaw's 'superb confidence in the dramatic value of the mere facts of life' and the 'horrible flesh and blood' of his dramatic creatures.[18] Yet despite Wilde's high regard for Shaw's works, they were never on intimate terms. Wilde described Shaw as 'an excellent man: he has no enemies; and none of his friends like him'.[19]

Wilde owned several novels dealing with the 'condition of England' question, such as Israel Zangwill's *Children of the Ghetto*, a graphic evocation of poverty set in the blind alleys of Spitalfields.[20] He also possessed non-fictional surveys of social deprivation such as General William Booth's *In Darkest England and the Way Out*. The founder of the Salvation Army gives an account of London poverty along with its possible remedies, one of which is mass emigration to the colonies. Wilde may well have read the volume during the composition of 'The Soul of Man'.[21]

Wilde was a committed supporter of the Irish 'Home Rule' campaign which was spearheaded by the Irish parliamentary leader Charles Stewart Parnell. In his library there was a set of reports of the proceedings of the 1888–89 Parnell Commission, which cleared the MP of the charge of advocating violence;[22] Wilde had attended the proceedings. He was also present at a dinner of 'The Eighty Club' on 8 May 1888 at which Parnell made an eloquent appeal for Irish autonomy. According to the published copy of the speech which stood on Wilde's shelves, Parnell sat down to 'loud and prolonged cheers, the audience all rising to their feet and waving their napkins over their heads'.[23] Wilde was interested in other aspects of the 'Irish Question'. He owned a pamphlet entitled *The Land League*, which contains a powerful oration by Michael Davitt, founder and leader of the Land League movement. Davitt, with whom Wilde corresponded, promotes pacific political agitation for Irish tenant rights and peasant ownership of the land.[24]

Wilde's early fascination with Celtic myths and legends endured. In his childhood he had learned 'to gaze with wondering eyes into "the younger day" and to find the path "to the shores of old Romance"'.[25] Irish folk stories and Ossianic legends had pointed the way. In adulthood, he re-traced his steps to those shores using, as his guide, *The Vision of MacConglinne*.[26] The medieval 'Irish wonder tale', which Wilde read in a parallel Gaelic-English text edition, tells the colourful story of MacConglinne, a wandering Bard who suffers terrible injustices at the hands of a vindictive clergy. Through the abundant resources of his own wit, and the intervention of an angel, he vanquishes his enemies and is restored to his place at the right hand of his king.

Nutt, who was an amateur of Celtic literature, may well have recommended *MacConglinne* to his customer. It is almost certain that Nutt sent Wilde a copy of the engaging scholarly volume *Studies of the Legend of the Holy Grail*,[27] which he himself had written. Wilde received it on 28 July 1888, just after its publication. The *Holy Grail* posits the theory that the Arthurian legends derive from ancient oral Celtic poetry. In its pages, Nutt draws many fascinating parallels between the two traditions, describing, for example, Tír na nÓg as the 'Irish Avalon'.

Wilde is likely to have been intrigued by Nutt's thesis because he was a lover of Arthurian literature. In the celebrated legends, tales of romance concerning Launcelot's love for Queen Guinevere are blended with stories of chivalry featuring the Knights of King Arthur's Round Table. Wilde probably first encountered them in childhood. His father and mother were evidently enamoured of Arthurian literature, bestowing on their daughter the name 'Isola', which is Gaelic for Isolde.

In 1889 Wilde purchased from Nutt a massive scholarly edition of

Sir Thomas Malory's *Le Morte D'Arthur*, the most famous version of the legends.[28] This hefty and expensive book is certainly not for the Arthurian novice or for the faint-hearted, as it reproduces the tortuous archaic English text of William Caxton's 1485 edition. 'Nowe turne we unto Sir Tristram' reads a typical line, 'that whanne he was come home and wyste la bele Isoud was gone.' It requires genuine passion, along with an abundant store of patience, to wade through over 500 pages of this prose. The experience does not seem to have dampened Wilde's enthusiasm, however, as he would re-read Malory's book a decade later.

Wilde was deeply versed in the mythology, folk tales and early epics of a number of cultures. He regarded them as fascinating works of literature, which the modern fiction writer might turn to, with profit, for inspiration. Indeed 'most of the good stories of our time' were, he believed, 'really folklore, myth survivals, echoes of the past'.[29] His library contained an autographed copy of D.G. Brinton's *The Myths of the New World*,[30] a book on the symbolism and mythology of the native Americans. He also owned an English edition of the *Kalevala*, a collection of traditional folk songs and ballads from Finland, which he reviewed in 1889. It was, he thought, animated with a 'wonderful passion for nature', and he delighted in its vivid representation of a world where 'in everything, visible and invisible, there is . . . a divine presence'.[31] Here speaks the man who was brought up in Tír na nOg.

Wilde praised those who attempted to revive 'the spirit of old romance', by breathing new life into ancient folklore.[32] He loved Tennyson's *Idylls of the King*, that remarkable modern contribution to the great cathedral of Arthurian literature, and he owned an inscribed copy of William Morris's *The Roots of the Mountain*, a prose romance set in central Europe before the Roman conquest. Wilde delighted in another book by the indefatigable poet, painter, designer and publisher, which shared the same flavour and historical context. He enthusiastically described Morris's prose and verse, *A Tale of the House of the Wolfings and All the Kindreds of the Mark*, as a 'return by a self-conscious effort to the conditions of an earlier and a fresher age . . . a kind of Saga . . . [or] folk-epic . . . nobly imaginative in its method and purely artistic in its aim'.[33]

Wilde lauded Morris's *Tale of the House of the Wolfings* as a wonderful corrective to the realistic trend of much nineteenth-century fiction. 'In days of uncouth realism and unimaginative imitation,' it was, he said, 'a high pleasure to welcome work of this kind'.[34] Wilde's fondness for epic poems and folk tales must be seen in this context. These ancient works, along with nineteenth-century pastiches, are informed by a vision of the world in which man is not yet alienated from nature, or from the inner world of his hopes, dreams and fears. It is a passionate vision, deeply infused with the colours of the imagination and the emotions, and expressed in a consciously artificial style that aims at beauty rather than an accurate transcription of the 'primary' world. Such writings are, of course, the diametric opposite of Victorian realist fiction, which attempted to render 'reality' with scientific precision and objectivity, often at the expense of beautiful form.

Wilde's loathing of realism was philosophical in origin. Along with anti-empiricist philosophers such as Kant, he believed that objectivity was an illusion. 'People,' as one of his characters puts it, 'only discover in [nature] what they bring to her.'[35] Wilde's attitude was also political. He detested realism, as Pater perceptively pointed out, because he associated it with 'the *bourgeois*, our middle-class'.[36] In Wilde's view, realistic novels, while purporting to be objective and 'documentary', actually confirmed and propagated the values of that class.

Wilde's antipathy to realism was of a piece with his belief that literature should shake up the reader's vision of the world. 'Art,' as he put it in 'The Soul of Man', 'is a disturbing and disintegrating force. Therein lies its immense value.'[37] It is also a corollary of his conviction that deliberately artificial works of art, which appeal to the reader's unconscious and emotions as well as to their reason, achieve a greater resonance and therefore a greater 'realism' than naturalistic productions: 'how much *truer*,' in his words, 'Imagination is than Observation.'[38]

Consequently a work such as the *Iliad*, with its beauty, internal coherence and emotional and intellectual scope, strikes a far deeper chord in readers than any factual account of military deeds. That is why Wilde claimed that 'Achilles is even now more actual and real than Wellington'.[39] By the same token, Wilde thought his idiosyncratic dramatic versions of historical tales, such as his play *Salomé*, were truer than the more 'accurate' accounts of historians. Their scientific studies offered 'the truth of a Professor', but Wilde preferred 'the other truth, my own, which is that of a dream. Between two truths, the falser is the truer.'[40]*

---

* 'The Decay of Lying' is Wilde's anti-realist manifesto. In the dialogue he pours scorn on naturalistic writers such as Émile Zola, and praises authors such as William Thackeray for colouring their fiction with the imagination, and casting it in a beautiful and artificial form. Wilde also criticises 'non-fiction writers who place far too great an emphasis on 'facts', holding up, as an ideal, authors who, in contrast, keep facts 'in their proper subordinate position, or else entirely' exclude them 'on the general ground of dullness'. He gives particular praise to 'the works of Herodotus, who, in spite of the shallow and ungenerous attempt of modern sciolists to verify his history, may justly be called the "Father of Lies" . . . the published speeches of Cicero and the biographies of Suetonius; . . . Tacitus at his best; . . . Pliny's *Natural History*; . . . Hanno's *Periplus*; . . . all the early chronicles; . . . the *Lives of the Saints*; . . . Froissart; . . . Sir Thomas Malory; . . . Marco Polo; . . . Olaus Magnus and Aldrovandus and Conrad Lycosthenes; . . . Benvenuto Cellini; . . . Casanova; . . . Defoe's *History of the Plague Year*; . . . Boswell's *Life of Johnson*; . . . Napoleon's dispatches; and . . . the works of our own Carlyle'.[41] This catalogue is enumerated by Vivian, the protagonist of the dialogue, but it is almost certain that the author is speaking through him. Wilde nominated some of these titles when he compiled his list of 'Books to Read' for the *Pall Mall Gazette* (see Appendix I, pp. 317–8).

17. 'More than usually revolting sentimentality'

IT IS HARDLY surprising that there was a voice training primer on the bookshelves at Tite Street, as Wilde is known to have carefully styled for himself a smooth and seductive voice that struck listeners as at once natural and artificial. Nor is it at all peculiar that he possessed a copy of Izaak Walton's *Compleat Angler*, and several other books on angling, because he had been a keen fisherman in the west of Ireland during his youth.[1]

Our virtual tour of Wilde's multi-coloured bookshelves does, however, offer a few surprises. What are we to make of the presence of a book on violin-making, or his history of the study of music in Germany or his guide to the art of mixing American cocktails?[2] These volumes were presented to Wilde by their authors, the last perhaps in recognition of the extraordinary drinking feats he performed during his 1882 lecture tour of America, when he would often drink his fellow party guests under the table. As Wilde kept a plentiful supply of spirits in his library, he may have attempted to concoct some of the book's two hundred recipes.

Wilde is not known to have mastered, or even to have essayed, another intricate art represented in his collection – he owned a copy of a book on theatrical dancing.[3] His copy of *The Orchid Grower's Manual* may, however, reveal a genuine interest in the art of cultivating that fragrant flower.[4] Wilde was famous for having green fingers – quite literally, for he was the inventor of that 'magnificent flower', the green carnation.[5] The presence of the manual on his shelves puts one of his lesser-known epigrams in a new, and rather literal light. 'I have never sown wild oats,' he wrote 'but I have planted a few orchids.'[6]

Wilde was exceptionally superstitious: he believed in ghosts, attended seances and frequently visited fortune tellers. Nevertheless, the appearance of Madame Blavatsky's *The Key to Theosophy* among his books comes as something of a surprise, if only because his interest in that spiritualist philosophy has hitherto been unknown.[7] The *Key* is a handbook of the Theosophical movement's central beliefs, which include reincarnation and the notion that all humans have dormant psychic and spiritual powers. It is a heady concoction of Plato, Buddhism and the ideas of Renaissance alchemists such as Paracelsus. It may have been the alchemical element of Theosophy that particularly attracted Wilde: his library also contained Franz Hartmann's *Paracelsus*, an anthology of that philosopher's writings.[8] The magus's musings on magic, sorcery, astrology and theosophy give eloquent expression to his belief in the invisible spiritual powers present in the material world and in the godlike power of the human imagination.

Perhaps, like the theosophist W.B. Yeats, who also owned Hartmann's book, Wilde found in these teachings an antidote to the materialistic vision of nineteenth-century science. Hartmann suggests that this is precisely why Paracelsus' writings remain evergreen: 'We think we know a great deal more than Socrates and Aristotle,' he writes, 'because we have learned a few superficial things'; yet 'if we know more about steam-engines . . . they knew more about the powers that move the world.'[9]

Yet, despite his possible interest in these and other arguments, Wilde is very unlikely to have been seduced by spiritualist philosophy, on account of its emphasis on the vague and the ethereal. 'Who,' he asked, 'would exchange the curve of a single rose leaf for that formless intangible being that Plato rates so high?' Such things are 'far less than the meanest of the . . . arts.'[10]

We like to think of Wilde as the most un-Victorian of men so it is rather astonishing to find on his bookshelves so many volumes that embody and celebrate the values of that era. It is impossible to know why Wilde bought certain books, or to recover, in the absence of annotations, something of the spirit in which he read them. Yet the sheer number of quintessentially Victorian volumes makes it fairly unlikely that they were 'ironic' purchases bought to laugh over with friends.

Wilde owned at least one issue of the *Boy's Own Annual*, which he presumably read to his two young sons.[11] With its sensational and moralistic tales of heroism set in the distant corners of the British Empire, and its sentimental doggerel written for boarding-school boys who pined for home, it is typical of Victorian boys' literature. Even more surprisingly, Wilde's library contained an intensely earnest book of practical and moral advice for young boys entitled *The Sunny Days of Youth: A Book for Boys and Young Men*.[12] Boys are urged to read the Bible and Shakespeare in order to learn the virtues of civility, industry and manliness – the quality which, above all others, they should strive to acquire. A companion volume to *Sunny Days* entitled *The Five Talents of Woman: A Book for Girls and Women* also stood on Wilde's shelves.[13] The girl reader is offered counsel on ways to lure a potential husband, 'by means not unworthy of her'. She is then instructed on how to fulfil to perfection, and 'by the grace of God', the role of 'a helpful wife'.[14] As Wilde was married to an activist for women's rights, and was himself something of a proto-feminist, his possession of this book seems inexplicable.

Wilde owned numerous three-volume novels, the popular literary genre so dear to the Victorian middle class, despite the fact that he took a mischievous delight in ridiculing it throughout his writings. Of one example of the genre he declared, 'The book can be read without any trouble and was probably written without any trouble also'; another inspired the epigram 'the nineteenth century may be a prosaic age . . . [but] we fear that, if we are to judge by the general run of novels, it is not an age of prose'.[15] The form had, he suggested, only produced masterpieces of the '*genre ennuyeux*, the one form of literature that the English people seems thoroughly to enjoy'.[16]

Miss Prism, Cecily Cardew's governess in *The Importance of Being Earnest* (1899), is the authoress of what Lady Bracknell describes as a 'three-volume novel of more than usually revolting sentimentality'. Prism offers a spirited defence of her literary efforts and the genre as a whole. After upbraiding her pupil for speaking disrespectfully of 'all the three-volume novels that Mudie sends us', she extols such novels for their faithfulness to the cardinal principle of fiction – 'The good end . . . happily, the bad unhappily. That is what fiction means.'[17] Mudie's was an enormously successful Victorian circulating library that specialised in the triple-decker. Established in the middle of the century by a nonconformist, it was famous for its respectability, sending out to its subscribers only those novels that passed its rigorous censors.

Margaret Maliphant, Eugenia and *Hazel Fane* were among the many three-volume novels on Wilde's shelves.[18] They are shoddily written, slushy and didactic productions eminently worthy of Miss Prism's pen. Their style, however, is positively Greek and graceful, compared to that of S.R. Crockett's *The Lilac Sunbonnet*, another novel Wilde owned.[19] A typical line of that justly forgotten book reads: 'In the young man's heart there was no answering gladness, though in sooth she was an exceeding handsome maid.'[20] Perhaps these books were presented to Wilde by their authors, or he may have written reviews of them that have remained untraced. It is almost impossible to imagine him perusing them for pleasure – the guiding principle of so much of his reading. Another principle that strongly influenced Wilde's choice of books was their appearance. Here, too, his triple-deckers are a shocking anomaly. Their heavy and gaudy formats must have been offensive to such a fastidious connoisseur of beautiful covers and bindings. A typical three-volume novel in Wilde's collection has a cloth cover the colour of mud, and is adorned with a hideous design of a thistle done in scarlet.[21]

Their heavy bindings and florid decorations made three-volume novels relatively expensive at 31 shillings 6 pence. From the middle of the century, cheaper novels were issued by publishers such as Cassell and Routledge, in an attempt to loosen the triple-decker's hold on the fiction market. These books were sold from new outlets such as W.H. Smith's, which opened its first railway bookstall at Euston station in the 1850s. Wilde sometimes affected to despise these cheap editions, and was at great pains to ensure that the format of his own books immediately distinguished them from such tradesman-like productions. 'I don't want a "railway bookstall" book,' he told one of his publishers. 'I should like [something] dainty . . . and nice'.[22]

None of these reservations prevented Wilde from purchasing a number of cheap mass-market literary productions for his own library. He owned Cassell's *Illustrated Shakespeare*, a particularly plain and economical edition of the plays, complete with adverts for Cazeline oil and Thompson's Kalydor soap in its end leaves. He possessed a number of volumes from John Morley's cheap biographical series *English Men of Letters*, and from Bohn's Standard Library of Modern Classics, as well as several Tauchnitz British Authors paperbacks.[23] In the endpapers of his copy of George Meredith's novel *One of Our Conquerors* there is the label of W.H. Smith's, whose bookstalls no self-respecting bibliophile would have been seen dead in.[24]

Wilde devoured the cheap popular literature of his day. He enjoyed the magazine stories of Frank Harris, and relished W.H. Pollock's horror tales; he thrilled to the terrifying stories of the German writer E.T.A. Hoffmann and to the spine-chilling fiction of that 'Lord of Romance', Edgar Allan Poe.[25] Wilde gorged himself on popular genres such as the 'mesmeric' and the 'magic picture' novel, too, appropriating countless scenes and motifs from them for his own works.[26] None of these predilections are, however, at all out of character: as a youth, Wilde had adored the gossipy and sensational productions of Maturin and Disraeli, so it is clear that he had a genuine partiality for good, honest literary trash.

Perhaps then, it was not entirely with his tongue in his cheek that Wilde once told a friend that he wished he had written *The Dolly Dialogues* more than any other book.[27] On other occasions, when Wilde had considered this issue, he had nominated Pater or Swinburne; this time he selected Anthony Hope's best-selling novella about the pretty young society girl Dolly Foster. The book is almost entirely made up of delightfully inconsequential chit-chat: 'I met him,' Dolly says, apropos of a young man, 'three years ago. He was – oh, quite unpresentable. Everything he shouldn't be. A tee-totaller, you know, and he didn't smoke. Oh, and he wore his hair long, and his trousers short.'[28] Dolly's conversation is reminiscent of the exquisitely trivial talk of the dowagers in many of Wilde's own social comedies.

Like a good Victorian too, Wilde appears to have enjoyed a healthy helping of melodrama now and again. A three-volume novel he owned called *Alison* is comprised of painfully stilted society dialogue interspersed with the most gushing passages imaginable. 'But life is strong,' the author reassures us at the denouement, in which the hero and heroine are silhouetted against the sunset: 'hope is strong too – but love is strongest of all . . . and love and life for a moment stood transfigured in the golden glory.'[29]

*

In *Dorian Gray* the eponymous hero takes down 'a volume at hazard' from his bookshelves: it is the 'Japanese-paper edition' of Gautier's famous verse collection *Émaux et Camées* [Enamels and Cameos] issued by Charpentier in a binding 'of citron green leather, with a design of gilt trellis-work and dotted pomegranates'.[30] Had Wilde imitated his fictional creation by selecting a book at random from his library, he is just as likely to have discovered a triple-decker in his hand.

On Wilde's shelves you would have probably found a book by Carlyle within speaking distance of a mawkish Victorian novel, and a dainty edition of Pater shaking with fear next to *Melmoth the Wanderer*. What was true of the collection as a whole was also true of individual items: Wilde adored works from the 'streaky bacon' school of writing. He owned several books by the American novelist Bret Harte, who appealed to him precisely because he offered a rich and heterogeneous literary feast: 'Wit, pathos, humour, realism, exaggeration, and romance,' wrote Wilde of one of Harte's novels, 'are in this marvellous story all blended together, and out of the very clash and chaos of these things comes life itself.'[31]

Wilde's motley taste in literature is of a piece with his temperament. A born actor, he had an unparalleled ability to enter entirely into a role or an emotion, only to discard it for another a few seconds later. Wilde's library was truly his portrait.

18. 'The vulgar beast'

D AVID NUTT'S WAS at No. 270 the Strand, in the very heart of bookish Victorian London, a city which then boasted over four hundred independent book dealers. Just off the Strand was Holywell Street, popularly known as 'Booksellers' Row'. After his visits to Nutt's, Wilde may have browsed the multi-coloured shelves of the Holywell Street dealers. Perhaps he was tempted to enter J. Poole & Co., at No. 39, which specialised in classical texts, or H.R. Hill & Sons, at No. 1, which stocked books on science and art.[1] He certainly frequented Paternoster Row, near St Paul's, another warren of London bookshops.[2]

Sometimes Wilde engaged a dealer in a bookish conversation.[3] Perhaps it was in this manner that he struck up his acquaintance with Alfred Nutt or his friendship with the dealer and publisher Arthur Humphreys. A generous and intellectually precocious man, Humphreys had, at the age of only twenty-six, become a partner in the famous bookshop, Hatchard's, which then, as now, occupied 187 Piccadilly.*

---

* Humphreys and Wilde often exchanged book gifts. The dealer sent Wilde an inscribed copy of *Love's Garland: A Book of Posy Gift Mottoes and Old Rhymes* (London, 1894), a reprint of a collection of seventeenth-century courtly poems that Humphreys himself issued in a beautiful miniature volume. Wilde reciprocated with a copy of his poem *Ravenna*, which he inscribed 'Oscar Wilde in London, 4 July 94'. When the book was auctioned in the 1920s a pink needlework cover with pomegranate designs and the initials 'AH' and 'CW' was found inside. It must have been sewn by Constance Wilde, who was very close to Humphreys, and may even have been his lover.[4]

Mayfair was another nest of bookshops Wilde explored. He certainly knew Bernard Quaritch's shop at 15 Piccadilly and the Bodley Head outlet in Vigo Street, just north of the Albany; he also frequented Franz Thimm's at 24 Brook Street, Grosvenor Square.

Nutt frequently posted books to Wilde;[5] on occasion, he also had Humphreys send him books. 'Would you kindly send Cyril,' Wilde asked him, 'a copy of Butcher and Lang's translation of [the] *Odyssey* – from me . . . I am very anxious he should read the best book for boys, and those who keep the wonder and joy of boyhood, ever written.'[6] The price of the *Odyssey* was charged to Wilde's Hatchard's account, which, by the time of his bankruptcy in 1895, amounted to £60 17s. 11d.[7] – an enormous sum if we consider that the average price of books Wilde purchased from Nutt was only six shillings. Wilde must have bought around two hundred and fifty books from Hatchard's – over a tenth of his entire library.

Humphreys published *Oscariana* (1895), the first collection of Wilde's epigrams, which had been selected by Constance. A contract for the volume was signed on 18 August 1894 at Hatchard's, with Alfred Douglas as one of the witnesses.[8] The pair dropped in again on 13 February 1895, to buy a copy of Aristotle's *Poetics*. We can imagine Wilde and Douglas wandering contentedly around the lavishly furnished Piccadilly shop, with its plush leather seats, large display cabinets and its imposing wooden Doric columns.

Wilde is also likely to have been a habitué of several Soho bookshops. His friend Leonard Smithers sold rare editions, literary curios and erotica, first at 174 Wardour Street, and later at 3 Soho Square. Wilde often scoured the shelves of the Librairie Parisienne in Coventry Street, near Leicester Square, in the company of friends; browsing for books was evidently a pleasure he liked to share.[9]

As his library contained a number of book dealers' catalogues, it seems likely that Wilde ordered volumes from some of them.[10] In a letter to Bernard Quaritch he thanked the dealer for sending him his latest list of choice items but added that he was not rich enough to rob him of his 'treasures'.[11]

Some Victorian gentlemen fainted with joy at the sight of their favourite volumes; others compared their libraries to their mothers, lovers or wives.[12] In the 1890s, anthologies of rapturous poems in praise of books were published; one of these, edited by Gleeson White, was called *Book-Song*.[13] Wilde himself contributed to the collection, but his poem is by no means as impassioned as some of its companion pieces, which are breathless love lyrics written to libraries.

Gleeson White, who knew Wilde, is fairly representative of the 1890s bibliophile. The author of some of the verses in *Book-Song*, and a collector of valuable volumes, White pasted his personalised bookplate into each of his tomes and carefully noted the circumstances in which it had been bought.[14] Edmund Gosse likewise adorned his volumes with a specially designed bookplate; he also had many of his favourite books rebound in expensive bindings, on the principle that 'a Jewel deserves a jewel-case'.[15] In contrast, Wilde never commissioned a personalised bookplate, and he is known to have rebound only a couple of his books.

Indeed, when it came to his collection, Wilde was often guilty of extreme negligence. Surviving copies of his books are generally in an extremely poor condition: their spines are often fragile and their corners knocked and bumped. Their pages have frequently been cut in such a rough manner that Wilde may have lazily used his finger instead of a paperknife. Friends sometimes remarked on his disregard for his volumes: one was appalled to find a rare copy of La Rochefoucauld's *Maxims* at the bottom of his cupboard.[16] Other Wildean offences against books included placing flowers between their pages[17] and leaving volumes in other people's houses.[18]

Wilde showed no compunction about writing in books either,

annotating them copiously and inscribing them. This latter habit struck horror into the hearts of arch-bibliomanes. Charles Ricketts, the 'subtle and fantastic' artist,[19] who designed the gorgeous edition of Wilde's poem *The Sphinx* (1894), shuddered when he opened up his presentation copy of the book — Wilde had desecrated the title-page with an inscription. Ricketts ripped out the offending page, and cursed 'the vulgar beast' to his face.[20]

Wilde's most heinous crime against books was perpetrated in 1886 when he prepared a lecture on the poet Thomas Chatterton. Only about a quarter of his lecture notes are made up of his own observations. The remainder consist of paragraphs, and sometimes entire pages, that he cut out from two Chatterton biographies in his library: Daniel Wilson's *Chatterton: A Biographical Study* and David Masson's *Chatterton: A Story of the Year 1770*.[21] Wilde pasted these extracts into his lecture notes, linking them with a brief commentary.

Wilde's sabotage was the work of a readerly Jack the Ripper. Such vandalism is not, however, without precedent among writers. It was a common practice among scholars in pre-modern times, and even lingered on into the nineteenth century. Edward Fitzgerald excised from the books in his library all of the passages that failed to give him pleasure. Similarly, Darwin is said to have torn out, from each of his books, every page that bore no relevance to his own work.[22] Like Darwin, Wilde was evidently an author-reader, regarding certain books chiefly as sources for his own writings.

Perhaps a pair of scissors permanently rested on Wilde's library desk next to his cigarettes. In preparing his other works he may have habitually sliced and slashed his way through books. To be fair, though, the Chatterton lecture notes are the only surviving evidence of Wilde's malpractice, which is further mitigated by the consideration that he did not have a photocopier at his disposal.

19. 'The *look* of a book'

TRUTH IN WILDE'S life, to adapt his famous saying, is one whose contradictory is also true.[1] Despite the litany of scarlet sins he committed against books, he cherished and venerated them. He spoke of his golden books with the reverence usually reserved for sacred texts, and he described his library fondly, giving special mention to its 'collection of presentation volumes from almost every poet of my time . . . its beautifully bound editions of my father's and mother's works; its wonderful array of college and school prizes; its *éditions de luxe*'.[2]

The presentation volumes Wilde received, from authors such as Whitman and Morris, were evidently among the most treasured items in his collection. They were memorials of acquaintance as well as a testimony to the respect these writers felt for Wilde's work. The reference to the 'beautifully bound editions' of his parents' works, and to 'college and school prizes', also shows the importance of personal association for him.

The editions of Wilde's own works that stood on his library shelves can, too, be classed as personal mementoes of immense sentimental value. Among these was a unique copy of *Intentions*, Wilde's 1891 anthology of dialogues and critical writings, that had been rebound for him as a birthday present by Ada Leverson. Leverson, whom Wilde addressed as 'The Sphinx', was the 'wilful and wonderful' author of witty journalistic sketches and one of Wilde's closest and most faithful friends.[3] Her gift, among the loveliest books Wilde owned, has a deep green cover, echoing the olive of the original edition. It is decorated with a delicate gilt design of roses and poppies; next to these, also traced in gilt, are the title and Wilde's initials. Wilde described the present as 'more green than the original even . . . I read it as a new work, with wonder and joy.' He was equally effusive about its contents, declaring, with endearing candour, 'I simply love that book.'[4]

Wilde adored volumes which had another sort of personal association attached to them: he delighted in books that had been owned, or inscribed, by his literary heroes. He possessed a copy of Tennyson's poems formerly belonging to Carlyle, and a volume on the classics that hailed from the library of the Irish Nationalist leader Daniel O'Connell.[5] Wilde may have coveted books inscribed or annotated by his other heroes. He certainly 'wondered' at the sight of a rare book which belonged to an acquaintance – a copy of Dante's *Divine Comedy* 'in which Keats had written . . . marvellous notes on Milton'. Yet, probably due to lack of funds, he did not own any such items himself and had to content himself instead with his unadorned first editions of Keats's *Endymion* and *Lamia, Isabella, The Eve of Saint Agnes, and Other Poems*.[6]*

Wilde was particularly fond of his *éditions de luxe* – books that were published in rare and luxurious formats. On his shelves there was a host of elegant volumes of French poetry, such as *Mimes*, written by his friend Marcel Schwob (Wilde's copy was one of twenty printed on Japanese paper).[7] Exquisite volumes of English verse were also on display. John Gray's *Silverpoints* was one of the highlights of his

---

* Wilde owned numerous editions of Keats's writings, and multiple copies of the same works by other favourite authors such as Shakespeare and Poe. He probably used one edition as his 'reading' or 'working' copy, while cherishing the more valuable volume as a sumptuous material object or as a holy relic of its creator.

collection. Wilde adopted the handsome young man (whom he addressed as 'Dorian') as his protégé and lover, and agreed to underwrite his book's production costs. Yet, in the event, when the pair fell out, another of Gray's *paiderastic* patrons paid for its publication. *Silverpoints* is the apotheosis of aesthetic publishing; Wilde described it as 'dainty' – one of the highest terms of praise for a book in the period – and urged the publisher of one of his own books to use it as a model.[8]

Wilde had an especial passion for two books of poetry in his library: Rossetti's *Poems* and the verse drama *The Tragic Mary*, penned by his friends Katharine Bradley and Edith Cooper (Bradley's niece), who wrote under the alias Michael Field.[9] He lauded the volumes as 'the two most beautiful books of the century'.[10] Wilde also owned countless handsome prose volumes, such as Morris's Kelmscott Press edition of Meinhold's *Sidonia the Sorceress*, in Speranza's marvellous translation. It is a masterpiece of ravishing binding and type.[11]

Wilde could not, by the standards of his time, be called an out-and-out bibliomaniac, yet he was a member of a particular order of that society – that of the dandies of books. Book dandies can be distinguished from conventional bibliophiles by their interest in the book as a harmonious aesthetic object. They regarded volumes as delicious symphonies of text, illustration and binding; their Holy Grail was a book in which these elements formed a perfect unity. To them, books were beautiful works of art in themselves, rather than mere repositories of the text.

Wilde always emphasised the importance of literary style over a work's subject or meaning, so it was natural for him to extend his interest to the decorative details of the book itself. His passion for 'the book beautiful' is of a piece with his conviction that, in art, form and content should be one and indivisible; it is consistent, too, with the immense value he placed on appearances. 'It is only shallow people,' he wrote, 'who do not judge by appearances. The true mystery of the world is the visible, not the invisible.'[12]

Wilde invariably judged a book by its cover. 'The public,' he said, 'is largely influenced by the *look* of a book. So are we all. It is the only artistic thing about the public.'[13] A volume's format and type were also of paramount importance: 'I do not approve of the shape of the *Pseudonym Library*,' he remarked of a series of miniature duodecimo sized large-print volumes. 'It is unjust to a good style to print it on a tiny page. Imagine turning Pater over rapidly. It is violence.'[14] In his book reviews Wilde was equally fastidious. When covering a batch of books he sometimes made a point of discussing the most beautiful volume first and he frequently urged publishers to produce 'decorative ornament that will go with type and printing, and give to each page a harmony and unity of effect'.[15]

The most eloquent testimonies to Wilde's obsession with the 'apparel of books'[16] are the first editions of his own works, in which he attempted to embody his ideal of 'the book beautiful'. He offered criticisms and suggestions to his publishers at every stage of a book's production, advising them on the cover ('I always *began* [a work] with the cover,' he remarked)[17] as well as on the binding, paper and type. 'The type,' he wrote to the publisher of one of his volumes, 'seems crisp and clean. I suppose it is as *black* as one can get? Perhaps a shade *thicker* would be well.'[18] Wilde became incensed when publishers failed to follow his instructions or to meet his high standards: 'Why, oh! why,' he wrote to the publisher of the American edition of *The Happy Prince*, 'did you not keep to my large margin [i.e. that of the English edition] – I assure you that there are subtle scientific relations between margin and style, and my stories read quite differently in your edition.'[19]

Wilde's strenuous efforts paid dividends. His first editions are gorgeous material objects and landmarks in the late Victorian revival of printing. The first edition of *Dorian Gray*, designed by Charles Ricketts, is a particularly elegant volume. Golden marigolds are scattered across a cover the colour of cigarette ash; the title and author's name are engraved in gilt on the ivory white spine. In its beguiling beauty it reminds us of one of the seductive and poisonous books mentioned in the novel itself – perhaps a deliberate ploy on Wilde's part to blur the distinction between the worlds of fact and fiction.

The first edition of *A House of Pomegranates* (1891), again designed by Ricketts, has an opulent cover adorned with fanciful gilt shapes. Wilde was fond of these purely decorative figures which found no 'imitative parallel . . . in that chaos that is termed nature'.[20] The most exquisite of all Wilde's first editions is that of *The Sphinx* which is bound in vellum and gold from a design by Ricketts (see plate 9). That artist, who illustrated and decorated the book throughout, chose the revolutionary three-colour type of black, green and red for the text. The book is so beautiful that, read in any other format, the poem seems to lose half of its power. It was issued in an ordinary edition of two hundred copies, and a limited large paper edition of just twenty-five.[21]

Wilde endeavoured to make his name synonymous in the public mind with exquisite books. In 1882, at the very outset of his literary career, he was photographed twice with a luxurious limited edition copy of his *Poems* in his hand (see p. 114). Printed on Dutch hand-made paper, the volume was bound in vellum; its cover has a gilt design that the author himself traced from a Chinese jar (see plate 8).[22]

Wilde attempted to project the image of himself as a dandy of books through his writings. They contain many long and loving descriptions of delicate and delightful volumes. Dorian Gray has no fewer than 'nine large-paper copies of the first edition' of his favourite novel, 'bound in different colours, so that they might suit his various moods'.[23] Wilde's hero also takes pleasure in 'an elaborately illustrated edition of *Manon Lescaut*'.[24]

Dorian is not the only dandified bibliomane to appear in Wilde's writings. The 'subtle connoisseur' Thomas Griffiths Wainewright was, Wilde tells us, a lover of 'bookbindings, and early editions, and wide-margined proofs'.[25] In the dialogue 'The Critic as Artist' Gilbert boasts of owning a copy of Baudelaire's verse collection *Les Fleurs du mal* [The Flowers of Evil] that is 'bound in . . . Nile-green skin . . . powdered with gilded nenuphars and smoothed with hard ivory'.[26]

Although Wilde was an authentic dandy of books, he was also that rare thing — a dandy with a sense of humour. In this respect he differed from that archetypal fictional biblio-dandy of the period, Duc Jean Des Esseintes. The fantastically fastidious duke, the hero of J-K. Huysmans's *À Rebours* [Against Nature], has his favourite titles printed to his own bizarre specifications and he handles his books with the solemn reverence of an altar boy carrying the accoutrements of the mass.

Wilde laughed at the fussiness and excessive refinement of his own attitude to books. He enjoyed the joke of a friend who, knowing his fondness for wide margins, advised him to publish a volume that was *all* margin. He also parodied his own love of limited editions by declaring his intention to bring out *The Sphinx* in an edition of just three copies: 'one for myself, one for the British Museum, and one for Heaven. I have some doubts,' he added, 'about the British Museum'.[27]

20. 'Sensuous and intellectual'

R EADING WAS AN extremely sensual experience for Wilde. He hoped that readers would feel a *shudder* at the denouement of his play *Salomé*, in which John the Baptist is beheaded: 'it is', he said, 'only the shudder that counts.'[1] He delighted in the 'frisson'[2] books afforded him, and enjoyed works which stirred 'the blood while one reads like the sound of a trumpet . . . producing a physical as well as a spiritual delight, [that] exults the senses no less than the soul'.[3]

The look of a book could inspire rapture in Wilde: he wept tears of ecstatic joy at the sight of one particularly beautiful cover[4] and his writings contain several eulogies to exquisitely decorated antiquarian books.[5] He was a great connoisseur of contemporary book illustration, having a particular fondness for the designs of Charles Ricketts and Aubrey Beardsley. Wilde praised Beardsley, whose illustrations to the English edition of *Salome* (1894) have attained iconic status, as a master of 'fantastic grace, and the charm of the unreal'.[6]

Beautiful volumes doubtless appealed to Wilde's sense of touch. It is easy to imagine him stroking a spine and smoothing his fingers over hand-made paper, or across a cover of rich uneven material, to savour the pleasant sensation. Like *À Rebours*'s Des Esseintes, who was titillated by books fastened with black and pink cords, Wilde may even have derived an erotic pleasure from handling certain volumes. He found a volume of verse 'cased in creamy vellum and tied with ribbons of yellow silk' so alluring that he called it a 'Circe of a . . . binding', a reference to the seductive sorceress of Homer's *Odyssey*.[7]

Wilde's sensitive nose must have been charmed by the fragrant scent of newly cut pages or by the maturer, oaky smell of the older tomes on his bookshelves. We are, after all, speaking of a man who was an amateur of perfumes, and who, in *Dorian Gray*, described reading as an intense olfactory experience. 'The heavy odour of incense,' he wrote of Dorian's favourite novel, 'seemed to cling about its pages and to trouble the brain.'

That line is followed with a paean to the novel's style, which makes an irresistible appeal to Dorian's sense of hearing. 'The mere cadence of the sentences, the subtle monotony of their music . . . produced in the mind of the lad . . . a malady of dreaming'.[8] Wilde is probably referring to silent reading here; the effect of reading aloud was equally intense for Dorian. He is described 'leaning back with half-closed eyes . . . saying over and over' two lines from a volume of Gautier's verse that lies open before him, and luxuriating in the images they evoke.[9] Wilde often read poetry aloud in the company of friends, and it is highly probable that he recited verse when he was alone. The delight he took in savouring the sound of his favourite words is well documented; besides, he could hardly have memorised so much poetry had he *not* read it aloud, repeating the lines to himself until he had caught the secret of their cadence.

Wilde regarded books as 'talking books' rather than as silent objects. When referring to them he often used metaphors relating to conversation: 'as Renan *tells* us' he writes, or 'as Mommsen *says*'. He describes books as 'speaking' to the reader, or even chattering away amongst themselves on the bookshelves. The limited Japanese vellum edition of *Earnest* was rather particular about who it conversed with: 'it is not,' Wilde commented, 'on speaking terms with the popular edition: it refuses to recognise [its] poor relation . . . Such is the pride of birth.'[10]

If Wilde was unable to hear a distinct authorial voice when he read a book, he was disappointed. He censured his old master Mahaffy for not writing as well as he talked.[11] He complained, too, that 'since the introduction of printing . . . there has been a tendency . . . to appeal more and more to the eye and less and less to the ear' — the 'sense' which literature 'should seek to please, and by whose canons of pleasure it should abide always'. He advocated a return to Greek literary values: 'the test' for Greeks, he says, 'was always the spoken word in its musical and metrical relations. The voice was the medium, and the ear the critic.'[12]

Even Wilde's sense of taste demanded satisfaction from books. He frequently employed gastro-literary metaphors: Balzac's fictions were as rich and heavy as truffles,[13] while many English novels were utterly 'indigestible' on account of the excessive amount of padding they contained. '"The proof of the padding",' as he put it, '"is in the eating," and certainly English fiction has been very heavy — heavy with the best intentions.'[14] Wilde also put his metaphors where his mouth was by actually eating books. He habitually tore off the top corner of a page as he read it, then rolled the paper up into a ball and put it in his mouth.[15] Surviving copies of his books confirm that he was the most voracious of bookworms. The publisher's catalogue at the end of his copy of Aristotle's *Ethics* has been ripped to shreds, apparently by a ravenous reader. On page 333 of the copy of Elizabeth Barrett Browning's *Aurora Leigh* he purchased for a friend, the top corner has been torn away. Wilde perused the book before presenting it to his acquaintance and, as it was a gift, he must have struggled to contain himself; after over three hundred pages, however, hunger evidently got the better of him.[16]

Wilde's imaginative and intellectual response to a book may have been so intense that reading made him peckish. In the middle of some of his undergraduate notes he has drawn a doodle of a large and delicious looking brioche.[17] Equally evocative is the jam stain clearly visible on page 30 of his copy of W.H. Mallock's *The New Republic*[18] – vivid testimony to the fact that Wilde gorged himself on books and food simultaneously. Sometimes he also drank while reading: one of his books is stained with purple wine.[19] Once again, this gives a literal inflection to a Wildean metaphor for reading: 'I have been turning over the leaves,' Wilde said of one book, 'tasting as one tastes wine.'[20]

In dining on his books Wilde was perhaps consciously imitating St John of the biblical Book of Revelation, who famously ate a scroll given to him by an angel in order to fully absorb God's word. This idea chimes nicely with Wilde's belief that books must become a vital part of the reader's existential experience. He was convinced, too, that reading was as essential as eating, if not more so: 'A man can live for three days without bread,' he would say, translating Baudelaire's famous maxim, 'but no man can live for one day without poetry.'[21]

Books made a powerful appeal to Wilde's aesthetic 'sixth sense'.[22] Occasionally described as a sort of aggregate of the five physical senses, the 'aesthetic' sense was more often distinguished from them. It was also, in Wilde's view, 'separate from the reason and of nobler import', and 'separate from the soul and of equal value'.[23] Those endowed with a refined aesthetic sense instinctively appreciate the form, beauty and harmony of works of art. As the 'off-spring of a fervid and emotional race', Wilde was, he claimed, the natural heir to the Celtic 'ardour for art' and beauty.[24] And, indeed, beauty was always to him the wonder of wonders. No one, it was said, adored it so intensely; one friend remarked that Wilde 'looked so deeply at the Light of Beauty that he saw only that; it dazzled and blinded him.'[25] 'There is not a single colour hidden away in the chalice of a flower,'

Wilde claimed, 'or the curve of a shell, to which, by some subtle sympathy with the very soul of things, my nature does not answer. Like Gautier I have always been one of those *pour qui le monde visible existe* [for whom the visible world exists].'[26]

The 'aesthetic experience' was sometimes peaceful for Wilde. 'The harmony that resides in the delicate proportions of lines and masses,' he wrote apropos of a beautiful painting, 'becomes mirrored in the mind. The repetitions of pattern give us rest.'[27] More often he characterises it as a species of ravishment. A 'cry of pleasure' breaks from the lips of Wilde's 'Young King' when he comes into contact with artistic beauty.[28] Such artistic rapture was, Wilde thought, 'the most sensuous and most intellectual pleasure in the whole world'.[29] The experience of 'beauty, mere beauty' could fill his eyes with tears. When he narrated his fairy tale 'The Selfish Giant' to his two young boys Wilde wept. On being asked why, he told his sons that really beautiful things always made him cry.[30] He found the following lines from Keats's 'Ode on a Grecian Urn' overwhelmingly poignant, too, no doubt on account of their harmonious euphony and assonance:

> What little town by river or sea shore,
>   Or mountain-built with peaceful citadel,
> Is emptied of this folk, this pious morn?[31]

Yet beauty could inspire joyous laughter as well as tears: he was so thrilled by lovely words such as 'vermilion' and 'marjoram' that he giggled with pleasure when he uttered them.

Wilde had such an acute horror of ugliness that he could not bear to remain long in a room that was unattractively furnished or in the company of the unbeautiful. He would abandon a novel if he came across a line that offended his sensibility. He abhorred the phrase 'the Birds were singing on every twig and on every twig-let', which he read in a novel written by an acquaintance. 'When an artist,' he said, 'comes on a sentence like that . . . it is impossible for him to go on reading.'[32] His reaction was the same whenever he encountered the word 'magenta' in a book.*

Other elements of Wilde's reading experience were more cerebral. Pater believed that art and literature engender a 'quickened multiplied consciousness'; Kant remarked on the pleasurable 'free-play' of the understanding they inspire. Keats spoke of 'negative capability' – a state of mind in which unfamiliar, multiple, and sometimes even conflicting ideas and viewpoints could be entertained simultaneously. Wilde the reader must often have enjoyed this blessed mental state. The true critic will, he said, 'ever be curious' of 'fresh points of view . . . For what is mind but motion in the intellectual sphere?'[36] And what, we might ask, is better for setting the mind in motion than reading? He spoke enthusiastically, too, of the inestimable joy of seeing issues from every angle or 'in the round'.[37]

Wilde also thought that books could smash into a million pieces

---

* Sometimes Wilde looked beyond the ecstatic moment of aesthetic bliss and tried to gauge the long-term effects of the experience. He believed that a discerning critical and artistic 'taste' would be formed by frequent exposure to beautiful things. At times, he even favoured the Platonic notion that constant contact with beauty would lead a person to instinctively shun ugliness and evil (words that were often synonymous in the Wilde lexicon). Yet the moral degradation of Dorian Gray, who tries in vain to make himself 'perfect through the worship of beauty', flatly contradicts this view.[33]

Nevertheless, Wilde subscribed wholeheartedly to Aristotle's idea that the artistic experience might purify the reader and initiate them 'into noble feelings of which he might else have known nothing'.[34] Initiation, as opposed to direct moral instruction, accurately captures Wilde's conception of art's enduring effect. 'The good we get from art,' he said, 'is not what we learn from it; it is what we become through it. Its real influence will be giving the mind that enthusiasm which is the secret of Hellenism, accustoming it to demand from art all that art can do in rearranging the facts of common life for us', and teaching us 'to love the things of the imagination for their own sake'.[35]

the unified and monolithic ego of the reader – which he believed to be an illusion – setting free their authentic protean selves. Drawing on Darwin's principle of heredity – the idea that genetic characteristics are passed down from one generation to another – Wilde argued that each individual carried within them the accumulated experience of the entire human race. Far from being a 'single spiritual entity . . . personal and individual,'[38] man was 'a being with myriad lives and myriad sensations, a complex multiform creature that bore within itself strange legacies of thought and passion'.[39] Consequently, 'no form of thought is alien' to man, 'no emotional impulse obscure'.[40]

That is why, according to Wilde, when we read King Lear's wild and whirling speeches, or Juliet's nocturnal soliloquies, we *become* the characters – their experience is there, buried deep within us. We can effortlessly 'see the dawn through Shelley's eyes' and feel 'the weak rage and noble sorrows of [Hamlet] the Dane'. 'Do you think,' Wilde asked, 'that it is imagination that enables us to live these countless lives? Yes, it is . . . and the imagination is the result of heredity. It is simply concentrated race-experience.'[41]

This idea throws an interesting light on the eclectic character of Wilde's book collection. Its heterogeneity attests, perhaps, to Wilde's desire to fully explore his ancient Darwinian soul and to express all the myriad sides of his protean personality. The library was a stage on which he acted out his various fantasies, and experienced again his 'previous lives'. In the room, no particular life, and no single aspect of Wilde's personality, would have been privileged; everything was equally important and everything was equally true.

While reading, Wilde would have been in constant motion, lifting objects to his mouth, such as food, paper, pens, drinks and cigarettes. According to his friend, the author and caricaturist Max Beerbohm, Wilde had 'the vitality of twenty men'.[42] We can imagine him hastily turning the pages of the volume in front of him and rapidly scribbling lines in his notebooks as he did so. And, when the tension and restlessness became acute, Wilde would have risen from his chair or divan and paced around his library. He must have frequently walked across to the bookshelves to check a reference, or over to the fire to dispose of a half-smoked cigarette.

This image of intense energy contrasts strongly with the impression of indolence Wilde tried to convey.[43] When he received guests in the library he would 'throw himself on a sofa', rather like his own creations, Lord Henry Wotton and Dorian Gray, who hurl themselves on library furniture with such alarming regularity throughout Wilde's novel.

Yet despite his languid pose, Wilde generally got into a book, as one friend put it, and then out of it, quicker than anyone alive.[44] He was an inveterate dipper, declaring that it was 'perfectly easy in half an hour, to say whether a book is worth anything . . . Ten minutes are really sufficient, if one has the instinct for form. One tastes it, and that is quite enough — more than enough, I should imagine.'[45] Wilde could grasp the narrative architecture of a novel almost at a glance. It was perhaps, in part, with this purpose in mind that he habitually turned to the back of a work of fiction to 'begin at the end'.[46] Reading the last page first was, too, 'the only way to stimulate the curiosity that books, with their regular openings, always fail to rouse. Have you ever overheard a conversation in the street,' he said to a journalist, 'caught the . . . end of it, and wished you might know more? If you overhear your books in that way, you will go back to the first chapter.'[47] When Wilde started with the denouement he also felt 'on pleasant terms of equality with the author',[48] and gained the ideal vantage point for judging their skill in working out a story.

Wilde was one of the speediest of speed-readers. 'He turned the pages [of a novel] fast to begin with,' a friend remembered, 'then faster and faster, and a little slower towards the end of the book. But he could not have been more than three minutes.'[49] It is hard to believe that Wilde literally took three minutes to peruse an entire volume, but others confirm this report, and embellish it with the astonishing detail that he often chattered away on other subjects while he read.[50] Wilde claimed that he could read both of the open pages of a book simultaneously. Recent experiments with speed-readers seem to refute this assertion, but only a fool would side with modern science against Oscar Wilde. Although the gift of lightning speed-reading is uncommon, Wilde was certainly not unique. The Victorian historian Macaulay could take in an entire page at a glance; the Romantic Lake poet Robert Southey needed only a matter of minutes to find 'everything in a book it was likely he would ever want'.[51]

Southey's phrase reveals one of the secrets of speed-reading: knowing exactly what you are looking for before you open a book. Nothing could contrast more sharply with the practice of passive readers who meet a volume on its own terms. Such readers enter a book entirely, in both an imaginative and an emotional sense; they carefully consider all of its arguments, and from every point of view. Wilde was the antithesis of this.

Wilde's friends often put his speed-reading to the test. One acquaintance remembered him spending only a few minutes with a novel before closing it with a smile. He then proceeded to answer questions on the book without a single error. '"Can you tell us, Oscar",' he was asked, '"where Wilfred fell from the clouds?" "He dropped in on his uncle and aunt at Cheltenham",'[52] came the instant reply. Wilde's answers also demonstrated his ability to memorise excerpts from the dialogue verbatim, and to recall, in some detail, many of the characters and scenes. He had first performed this party trick at Portora school, where, 'for a wager', he would 'read a three-volume novel in half an hour so closely as to be able to give an accurate résumé of the plot' or, 'by one hour's reading, . . . to give a fair narrative of the incidental scenes and the most pertinent dialogue'.[53]

Wilde's memory became as legendary as his speed-reading. Among friends, he would spout reams of verse; at the Sheldonian Theatre, he recited from memory all 330 lines of his poem *Ravenna*, when it earned for him Oxford University's prestigious Newdigate Prize. Even more astoundingly, Wilde knew a great deal of prose by heart. He regurgitated passages of Carlyle's *The French Revolution*, and declaimed line after line from the novels of Meredith. One friend described him reeling off sentences from Flaubert which seemed to 'unfold just like jewel-studded brocades'.[54] This facility was doubtless nurtured by his upbringing in a distinctly oral literary culture, which encouraged the development of powerful memories among its members.

Wilde's gift for aural recollection was complemented by a potent photographic memory. On one occasion, an acquaintance quoted a line from Pater in his company but was at a loss to recall its source. 'It is in *Appreciations*,' Wilde informed them without a moment's hesitation, 'in the essay on "Style", page 7 – left-hand side, – at the bottom.'[55]

21. 'Smoke and talk'

IN 1888 WILDE invited his fellow Dubliner W.B. Yeats to Christmas dinner at Tite Street. Yeats was twenty-three at the time, and trying to establish himself as a poet and critic in London; Wilde was thirty-four, and a reviewer, poet and lecturer of some renown. The young poet was overwhelmed by the opulence of Wilde's 'House Beautiful', and by his host's conversation. 'I never before heard,' he said, 'a man talking in perfect sentences, as if he had written them all overnight with labour and yet all spontaneous.'[1]

Not that Wilde monopolised the conversation. At one point, he asked Yeats to entertain his eldest son Cyril with an Irish fairy tale. Wilde believed that it was the sacred duty of a father to narrate stories to his children, and he knew that Yeats was a *seanchaí* of genius; on one occasion he even went so far as to compare his gift for storytelling to that of Homer. 'Once upon a time,' Yeats began, 'there was a giant.' Cyril was so frightened that he screamed and ran out of the room. Wilde looked grave and disapproving. Yeats had been guilty of lacking sensitivity to the tastes and temperament of his audience – an unpardonable sin in a *seanchaí*.[2]

After dinner, Wilde cast the young poet in the less demanding role of audience. We may imagine him leading Yeats out of the dining-room, through the hall into the library, and offering the young poet a comfortable chair and a drink. Wilde then proceeded to read out his dialogue 'The Decay of Lying', welcoming Yeats's interruptions along the way. After he had uttered the phrase, apropos of Hamlet, 'The world has become sad because a puppet was once melancholy', Yeats halted him and asked 'Why do you change "sad" to "melancholy"?' 'I wanted a full sound at the close,' Wilde explained.[3]

In reciting the dialogue Wilde was returning it to its oral origins. He had conceived it over the course of a dinner with another friend.[4] He was also mirroring the 'Decay' itself. In the dialogue a flamboyant writer called Vivian reads out the proofs of an article he is composing entitled 'The Decay of Lying: A Protest', to his slower-witted friend Cyril – Wilde mischievously named the characters after his two boys. Cyril, the 'straight-man' of the piece, interrupts Vivian's recitation with questions and comments, just as Yeats did. To add to the pleasant confusion of life and art, the setting for the 'Decay' is also a library.

In both Wilde's art and his biography, the library appears as a word-splashed, phrase-filled place. In the 'Decay' (and in the dialogue 'The Critic as Artist' which also has a library as its backdrop) the words of the interlocutors fly in and out of the multi-coloured volumes on the shelves, around the desks and the beautiful ornaments, just as they did in Wilde's own book-lined room. In his library Wilde not only conducted scripted symposia in which he read from his own writings; he and his friends also enjoyed many extempore discussions of artistic and philosophical matters, during which they relished what Wilde called the 'delightful wickedness' of delectable words.[5] These 'Athenian' conversations, some of which were committed to paper by Wilde's friends, were very similar to the talk contained in his written dialogues.[6]

The library, along with the smoking room on the first floor, was the place where Wilde received visitors. When the young poet Theodore Wratislaw was ushered into the august presence there,

Wilde could not resist showing off one of his very favourite volumes – a beribboned bible that had been rebound for him in morocco leather. For the occasion, he may have recycled his famous epigram on the Bible: 'When I think of all the harm that book has done, I despair of ever writing anything to equal it.' Wilde was not above repeating his aphorisms, especially when beautiful poets were present. He certainly seems to have played the great author that day, perhaps in a bid to seduce Wratislaw. With a wave of his hand he pointed to a pile of bills on his desk and declared insouciantly 'I shall not open them.'[7] Another fledgling poet who was granted an audience in Wilde's library looked, according to Swinburne, like 'Shelley with a chin'. Richard Le Gallienne, the unfortunate possessor of the jutting jaw, was asked, during their meeting, how old he was. 'Twenty-three!' Le Gallienne replied. 'Twenty-three' Wilde commented with a deep sigh. 'It is a kind of genius to be twenty-three!'[8]

If the master was absent or dressing, his guest would be shown into the library by Wilde's manservant, Arthur. After Wilde made his no doubt theatrical entrance they would enjoy together the best of conversation and the best of cigarettes. When their talk had finished, the visitor would be taken up to the first floor to meet Wilde's wife and his two boys.

If Wilde's guests became intimates, they were granted an almost permanent right of entry to the library, even when the master was writing. Alfred Douglas claimed that Wilde always liked to have him nearby when he worked. 'Bosie', as Wilde liked to address him, probably sat beside Wilde when he penned the social comedies *A Woman of No Importance* and *The Importance of Being Earnest* between 1893 and 1894. At the head of an early draft of another play, *An Ideal Husband* (1899), Wilde has written: 'June 19. 93. Bosie Present'.[9] As both Wilde and Douglas were restless and extremely garrulous creatures, it is impossible to imagine them being still or silent for long. Wilde may have talked away while he wrote, just as he sometimes conversed when he read. He probably recited to Douglas the funniest lines as he composed them, and invited his lover to make comments and suggestions.

To many Victorian authors, the library was 'essentially a private retreat'[10] – the typical 'man of letters' sat alone 'quietly in his study'.[11] We think of the famous painting of Dickens at his library desk, with only the children of his fancy for company, or of Anthony Trollope, who locked himself up in the silence of his library until he had composed his daily quota of words.

Thomas Carlyle abhorred disruptions. In the little study that had been constructed at the top of his Chelsea house the author was, in his own words, 'lifted above the noise of the world, peremptory to let no mortal enter upon his privacy'.[12] Interestingly, just like Carlyle, and perhaps in conscious imitation of him, Wilde had originally intended to use a small room on the top floor of the Tite Street house as his writer's study. In eventually settling on the noisier, and more accessible, ground-floor library as his work place, Wilde was effectively renouncing the austere Victorian ideal of silent, solitary labour.

Our earlier characterisation of Wilde's library as an aesthete's temple of peace and as a gentleman's hermitage, must, therefore, be qualified. Pater, who described his library as a 'sort of cloistral refuge from a certain vulgarity in the actual world',[13] would have been most uncomfortable in the room. Wilde seemed to welcome interruptions from the world, at least when they came from friends. At the beginning of the 'Decay' Cyril suddenly enters the library to disrupt Vivian at his literary devotions. 'My dear Vivian,' he exclaims, 'don't coop yourself up all day . . . Let us . . . smoke and talk.'[14] These were probably fond and familiar words for Wilde.

22. 'Mirror of perfect friendship'

WILDE'S COPY OF *Players of the Period*, Arthur Goddard's survey of contemporary actors, is inscribed by Goddard 'To Oscar Wilde'. After these words Wilde has written 'who gave it to his friend Dorian Jesmond on Oct 4. 91'.[1] Similarly, Wilde's copy of Meredith's novel *One of Our Conquerors* contains the inscription 'Offered to Maud Beerbohm-Tree. By Oscar Wilde. Edinburgh. October 1892'.[2]

Wilde liberally distributed books among his friends. Often he presented them with beautiful volumes on principle, the principle being that 'If one gives away a book, it should be a charming book – so charming, that one regrets having given it.'[3] To Wilde, books were the perfect symbols and seals of friendship. Many of his inscriptions include phrases such as 'with many pleasant memories of friendship'[4] or 'in memory of an old and noble friendship'.[5*]

It was as 'a memento of friendship'[7] that Wilde gave a copy of Matthew Arnold's *Selected Poems* to his friend 'Miss Nellie' (Helena Sickert), inscribing it 'from her friend Oscar Wilde October 2 1879'.[8] Miss Nellie, who would become famous as a writer and lecturer on women's liberation, was fifteen at the time, and she looked up to Wilde as a mentor. He delighted her with his jokes and fantastic tales,

---

* Like many Victorians, Wilde also referred to his favourite volumes as his 'friends'. He coupled friends and books, too, when he spoke of his metaphorical '*livre d'or* [golden book] – my little book where I write the names of my friends'.[6]

'pouring out' for her pleasure 'stories and descriptions whose extravagance piled up and up till they toppled over in a wave of laughter'.[9] He also encouraged Miss Nellie's early adventures in literature: *Selected Poems* was the very first volume of verse she owned.

Wilde marked nine of his favourite poems in the book by placing bright blue silk threads at the page where they commenced.* By identifying these verses, Wilde ensured that he would be present, in Miss Nellie's mind, when she perused the volume. Likewise, when he later sent her a copy of his own *Poems* he guaranteed that he would be in her thoughts, as she turned the pages, by asking her to guess his favourite piece in the collection.[11]

Wilde's alliance with Robert Ross was eminently bookish. When they first met in 1886, Ross was a sixteen-year-old with, in Wilde's phrase, 'the face of Puck and the heart of an angel'. He was 'charming, and as clever as can be, with excellent taste'.[12] They fell for each other, and Ross became, or so he later claimed, the first man to 'seduce' Wilde. Prior to that date Wilde had, according to Ross, formed alliances with men that had been platonic rather than physical in nature. A recent biography attempts to discredit the idea that Wilde was quite so virginal,[13] and it is perhaps unlikely, given the prevalence of homosexual activity at Oxford. Wilde's friendship with Ross was, however, probably his first long and emotionally significant homosexual relationship; it may also represent his earliest attempt at following the *paiderastic* model.

The affair ushered in an entirely new phase of Wilde's writing

---

* Wilde selected, for Miss Nellie's delectation, famous poems such as 'The Scholar-Gipsy', 'Sohrab and Rustum', 'Shakespeare', 'Dover Beach' and 'Lines Written in Kensington Gardens', along with 'To a Friend', 'To a Republican Friend, 1848', 'To a Gipsy Child by the Sea-shore', 'The Forsaken Merman', 'Immortality', 'The Good Shepherd with the Kid' and 'Rugby Chapel'.[10]

Robbie Ross in his early twenties.

career, during which young Robbie, as Wilde liked to call him, seems to have acted as his muse, as well as his general assistant and intellectual sparring partner.[14] Wilde had, before 1886, gained some renown with his poems, reviews and lectures, but he was by no means a famous author; with Ross's help, that was set to change. Over the next four years Wilde discovered his brilliant and distinctive genius, penning works which, for the first time, express the full force of his iridescent humour and agile 'Oxford temper', and which ostentatiously display his elegant handling of language.

'The Decay of Lying' was born out of a dinner with Robbie – 'Idea, title, treatment, mode, everything.'[15] 'The Portrait of Mr W.H.', too, was 'half' Ross's, and 'would not have been written' without him.[16] Later on, Robbie would supply Wilde, for inclusion in one of his social comedies, some epigrams that he had taken down from his conversation.[17] He would also offer Wilde countless judicious suggestions on early manuscript drafts of his works.[18]

To judge by Wilde's letters to his young acolyte, their talk would often have consisted of amusing book chat. 'Rossetti's letters are dreadful,' he writes in one, 'Obviously forgeries by his brother.' '[Huysmans's] En Route is most over-rated,' he comments in another 'It is sheer journalism. It never makes one hear a note of the music it describes.'[19] It is highly appropriate then that some of Wilde's book gifts to Ross bear allusive literary inscriptions.

One of the first books Ross received was the copy of The Happy Prince which is inscribed to 'R. Tristram Ross'.[20] In other books Wilde presented to his disciple he refers to him as 'R.T. Ross'. Ross's middle name was Baldwin, so this is another example of Wilde's bestowing a nickname on a friend. We can only suppose Tristram to be a reference to the star-crossed Arthurian knight who loved the Lady Isolde with such tragic consequences (Baldwin was the name of another of Arthur's men).

Wilde may also have been alluding to modern adaptations of the Tristram legend by Arnold and Swinburne, 'Tristram and Iseult' and Tristram of Lyonesse.[21] In these poems Tristram is forced to choose between two Isoldes, one of whom represents physical passion, the other a pure and selfless love. This would chime with Wilde's frequent jokes about the austerer side of Robbie's nature (he was a devout Catholic), which was often at war with his sensual urges.*

---

* Wilde encapsulated Ross's deeply divided self in another nickname he conferred on his friend – 'Saint Robert of Phillimore' (Upper Phillimore Gardens, Kensington, being the street where Ross lived). St Robert of Phillimore, according to Wilde, was no beacon of piety, but a 'saint known in Hagiographia for his extraordinary power, not in resisting, but in supplying temptations to others. This he did in the solitude of great cities, to which he retired at the comparatively early age of eight.' This is probably an allusion to Ross's seduction of Wilde.[22]

Another inscription to Ross is equally literary and esoteric. 'To the mirror of perfect friendship: Robbie',[23] Wilde wrote in his copy of *Earnest*. This phrase directly echoes Socrates' celebration of *paiderastic* love in the *Phaedrus*.[24] And what better way of commemorating a relationship that, in so many respects, approximated closely to the Platonic model? Like a pair of bookends, the copies of *The Happy Prince* (1888) and *Earnest* (1899) that Wilde presented to Ross stand at the beginning and the end of an acquaintance filled with books and book talk.

It was equally fitting that two other great loves in Wilde's life should be memorialised by book gifts. Wilde's wife Constance was extremely well read. Cultural and intellectual sympathy played a significant role in their courtship and marriage. Wilde wooed her by talking divinely about literature and art and by asking her opinion of his writings; he showered book gifts on Constance, too, adorning her copy of *Poems* with the marvellous phrase 'To a poem from a poet', and dating it 6 July 1883.[25]

After their marriage, the couple read works of German literature together in the original. It is likely that Constance helped her husband through the masterpieces of Italian literature, for which she had a passionate interest. She kept copies of Dante, Petrarch and Tasso, Italian poets of the Middle Ages and the Renaissance, in her bedroom on the top floor of Tite Street. There she arranged them in her beautiful Chippendale bookcases or put them among her favourite volumes on the carved book-rest right next to her bed. Her copy of Keats's poems would certainly have stood there; it was the golden book of her life, accompanying her on her travels and lying beside her when she died.[26]

To the right of Constance's bedroom door a special bookcase was set aside for her copies of her husband's works. It also held the first

Inscription in Robbie Ross's copy of Earnest. *The 'little play' was dedicated to Ross.*

editions Wilde gave their two sons.* This lover's library included Constance's copy of Wilde's *Poems*, as well as a *Happy Prince* inscribed 'To Constance with her husband's love' on 25 July 1888.[27] Her copy of *Dorian Gray*, which bore the words 'Constance from Oscar with his love. May 91',[28] would have been there also.

A short while after that date, in a copy of *Lord Arthur Savile's Crime and Other Stories* (1891), his collection of society tales, Wilde wrote 'Constance from Oscar, July. '91'. As was his custom, Wilde appears to have drawn the recipient's attention to certain passages in the text by marking them in pencil. In the tale from which the collection takes

---

* Wilde loved presenting books to his sons, lavishing on them copies of Rudyard Kipling's children's stories, Stevenson's tales of adventure and the science fiction of Jules Verne.

its name, a line appears in the margin next to the following sentences: 'Actors are so fortunate. They can choose whether they will appear in tragedy or comedy . . . But in real life it is different. Most men and women are forced to perform parts for which they have no qualifications.'[29]

This makes poignant reading. It seems to express a terrible truth about the Wildes' marriage. Constance was eminently qualified for the role of writer's companion (she assisted Wilde ably both as a sympathetic critic and hostess) but fortune had assigned her an additional part for which few nineteenth-century women would have been adequately prepared – the doting wife of a man attracted to other men. After the first three or four years of their marriage that passion began to dominate Wilde's sexual and sentimental life, and there was probably little room left in them for Constance. His affair with Robbie Ross may have sounded the death knell for their romance, which had been genuine and passionate before 1886. Wilde's inscriptions suggest that he retained thereafter a deep affection for Constance, but she would cease to be the person in whose absence he felt 'incomplete'.[30] While Wilde's homosexual urges were paramount in the demise of their relationship, his upbringing by a spectacularly bohemian mother, and his intense devotion to art – next to which all other loves in his life were 'as marsh-water to red wine'[31] – hardly suited him to the role of dutiful husband. 'I [was] really very fond of my wife,' Wilde confessed later, '[but] bored to death with married life.'[32]

Wilde's veneration for his mother also found expression in book gifts. In 1879 Speranza had followed her younger son to London, settling in Oakley Street, Chelsea with Willie, Wilde's older brother. She set herself up as an authoress and society hostess. Her son shone brightly in her legendary salons, talking, in his adoring mother's words, 'like Plato, divinely'.[33] These took place on Wednesday and

Saturday afternoons, behind drawn curtains and under dim lighting. In the gloom Speranza hoped that no one would see the furrows on her face or the disorder of her rooms.[34]

On his frequent visits to Oakley Street, Wilde brought his mother book offerings (he would often bring money as well, paying her bills whenever he was in funds). He presented Speranza with a copy of *Erechtheus*, Swinburne's pastiche of Greek tragedy, writing in it 'J.F.W. [Jane Francesca Wilde, Speranza's full name] very affectionately from Oscar'.[35] Wilde was even more demonstrative when he inscribed her copies of his own works. In *Intentions* he wrote: 'From your affectionate son the author, with his love'. The inscription in his second social comedy *A Woman of No Importance* (1894) reads, 'To my dear mother: with my love'.[36] Speranza always commented on her son's mature writings, just as she had criticised his youthful efforts. The prose of his fairy tales was, she declared, superior to Pater's: 'I used to hope you would equal [him],' she wrote after perusing the collection *A House of Pomegranates*: '*now* I think you are far beyond and above Pater.'[37]

Some Wildean inscriptions contain amusing nonsense. Several employ the curious phrase 'To——, in admiration and astonishment'.[38] In the copy of *The Sphinx* he gave to the artist William Rothenstein, Wilde wrote ' . . . from his friend and admirer the author. In June: a June of rain and roses. Time: Sometime B.C.'[39] Another inscription, scrawled in the French poet Louis Fabulet's copy of *The Ballad of Reading Gaol* (1898), was written in a more poetical vein: 'In remembrance of a charming evening when the wine was red, and the moon was silver'.[40] Some of Wilde's inscriptions were indeed so poetical that they were eventually published as poems in their own right. The translator of Persian poetry, Justin McCarthy, was presented with a copy of *The Happy Prince*

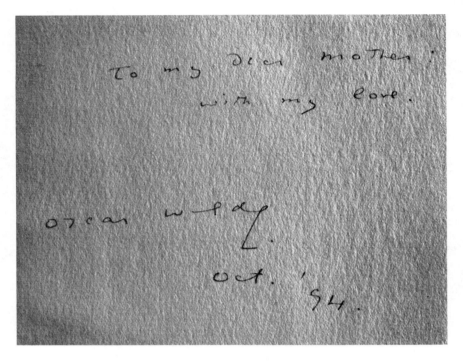

Inscription in Speranza's copy of A Woman of No Importance.

containing the following lines, which later appeared in an anthology of verse.[41]

> Go – little Book,
>   To him who – on a lute with horns of pearl –
> Sang of the wonder of the Golden Girl –
>   And bid him look
> Into thy pages – Haply it may be
> That he may find some comeliness in thee.[42]

Other inscriptions were acts of homage to Wilde's literary masters. In a copy of his *Poems* he wrote 'From the author to Mathew Arnold in affectionate admiration',[43] unfortunately misspelling Arnold's Christian name. He sent the same volume to Swinburne, Morris and the poet Robert Browning, thus declaring, at once, both his discipleship and his genius. He was also soliciting entry into their select literary fellowship. His eventual admittance into their circle is attested by the inscribed volumes Morris and Swinburne presented to Wilde in their turn, along with those he received from the French bards Victor Hugo, Stéphane Mallarmé and Paul Verlaine, and the American poet Whitman.[44]

Some of the books presented to Wilde bear interesting inscriptions. In a volume of verse from the 1890s Scotch poet John Davidson he is extravagantly hailed as 'King Oscar'.[45] In another inscription, Marcel Schwob addressed Wilde with almost equal reverence, as 'The Prince with the splendid mask'.[46]

The most famous inscription written to Wilde adorns his copy of Rennell Rodd's verse collection, *Songs of the South*. Rodd, an aesthetic poet from Balliol College, and Wilde's close friend, presented the book to Wilde soon after its publication in 1880. The inscription includes a poem in Italian and it has always been assumed that it was composed by Rodd himself. It is, however, a quotation from 'Postuma', a poem by the nineteenth-century Italian poet Lorenzo Stecchetti.[47] In light of Wilde's later life, the lines, translated by Richard Ellmann, make very curious reading indeed:

> At thy martyrdom the greedy and cruel
> Crowd to which thou speakest will assemble;
> All will come to see thee on thy cross,
> And not one will have pity on thee.[48]

23. 'Touched by other lips'

ON THE EVENING of 24 November 1886, Wilde gave a lecture on the poet Thomas Chatterton at Birkbeck College, London. It was a freezing night and there was one of those legendary Victorian pea-soupers. When Wilde emerged out of the thick fog into the hall at Birkbeck he found, to his amazement, an audience of eight hundred people gathered there. He assumed they had come out of a genuine interest in Chatterton, but they may also have been drawn by the chance to hear him.[1] After his lecture tour of America in 1882, and his subsequent tour of England, Wilde had become renowned as a public speaker.

Wilde was in love with Chatterton's legend and writings; so 'ardent' a 'Chattertonian' was he that he made a pilgrimage to Bristol, the poet's native town, just prior to his lecture, to imbibe the 'ancient spirit of the place' that had so moved his hero.[2] Through his immersion in the literature of the Middle Ages and the Renaissance, and an exquisite sensitivity to the spirit of the past, Chatterton had composed, in the 1760s, pastiches of medieval poetry and then passed them off as the original work of a fifteenth-century monk Thomas Rowley. So marvellous were his poems and so expert the medieval charactery in which he inscribed them that he convinced scholars of their authenticity. Only much later, after Chatterton's early death at the age of seventeen in a London garret ('the most tremendous tragedy in history,' according to Wilde)[3] would his works be widely dismissed as plagiarisms and forgeries.

In his lecture Wilde seems to be outlining a writerly ideal, and fashioning for himself a model of authorship. Chatterton, he says, began by saturating himself in the literature of the Middle Ages, then he became proficient in imitating its finest exponents. Having completed his apprenticeship he proceeded to pen his 'own' works. He effortlessly absorbed the language of his contemporaries too: he could scribble off, by the yard, 'polished lines like Pope, satire like Churchill . . . [and emotive verse like] Gray, Collins, Macpherson'. Chatterton assimilated the language of others and then abandoned himself to its ebbs and flows, surfing on the waves of words that rose and fell within him.

Wilde characterised the 'marvellous boy' of English literature as an author 'of the type of Shakespeare and Homer: a dramatist [who] claimed for the artist freedom of mood'. The poet's forgeries and imitations were motivated by 'the desire for artistic self-effacement'[4] rather than by kleptomania or creative sterility. They were also inspired by the delight Chatterton took in playing with the poetic postures and styles of his literary precursors. Rather than expressing a unified and 'authentic' self in a single and sincere voice, Chatterton's poetry was a polyphonic wall of sound.

When Wilde composed his works he surrounded himself with books. A friend remembered him writing a poem 'with a botanical work in front of him from which he . . . [selected] the names of flowers most pleasing to the ear to plant in his garden of verse'.[5] Aubrey Beardsley's caricature of Wilde, 'Oscar Wilde at Work', shows the author at his desk surrounded by mountains of books.

As if to signal his dependence on his sources, books make cameo appearances throughout Wilde's *oeuvre*: 'The Critic as Artist' begins when Gilbert asks the laughing Ernest what he has found so funny in

Aubrey Beardsley's caricature 'Oscar Wilde At Work'.

the volume he is reading. And then there is the bookishness of Wilde's works themselves, which are saturated with references to writers and their books. Wilde marshals the names of so many authors and volumes in his dialogues that they sometimes read like the catalogue of a library – of Wilde's library, to be precise. At one point in 'The Portrait of Mr W.H.' the narrator describes himself taking down several books from his library shelves and poring over them. This is doubtless a mirror image of Wilde himself in the act of writing his essay-story, when he must have repeatedly gone over to his shelves in search of the many quotations that appear in the piece.

The image of Wilde prowling round his library in search of quotations and inspiration might, along with Beardsley's caricature, stand as an emblem of his authorship. Wilde's idea of composition was essentially pre-Romantic: like a writer of the Renaissance or of the classical period, he believed that books, not life, ought to be the chief inspiration for literature. The author's task was to adapt and conflate, in novel and exciting ways, the books they read, rather than create original works that expressed their 'authentic' self or related their personal experiences.

Wilde used the terms 'originality' and 'original genius' in a pejorative sense. The Brontës were far too original to be great, he said; they were always at the 'mercy of genius'. Wilde meant that, denied an education in the great literary works of the Western canon, the sisters had been forced to draw exclusively upon reserves of subjective thought and experience. Yet more than that was required to create a work of art. 'It is not,' Wilde declared, 'everyone who says "I, I" who can enter into the kingdom of art.'[6] True literary geniuses were indeed never original. Shakespeare was the greatest of all authors precisely because he worked within an existing literary tradition, taking fragments of his reading and shaping them into song.[7]

Wilde looked back to the era before the early nineteenth century, when the Romantics had made egotism all the rage, to a time when literature was seen as the inspired and dextrous work of the craftsman-like reader-writer. Artisan authors – for whom Chatterton was the patron saint – began their apprenticeship by imitating the best literary models: imitation and admiration being, in Wilde's words, 'the portal to all great things'.[8] * For Wilde, imitation had nothing to do with plagiarism or lack of originality, for no one could ever be truly original. Every author was 'the child of someone else', in so far as all writers copied, consciously or otherwise, from their pre-decessors. True originality could 'be found rather in the use made of a model than in the rejection of all models';[10] and great poets were those capable of drawing new music from reeds that had been 'touched by other lips'.[11]

Wilde's own poetry is a chorus of echoes. In one poem he adopts the vigorous tone and imagery of the seventeenth-century poet John Milton, in another he plays gently on the lyre of Keats. The reader is continually dazzled by the range of Wilde's reading and the repertoire of styles and tones at his command. The poems are essentially dramatic performances; examples of what Wilde called 'literary acting'. He impersonates his favourite authors just as, in conversation, he sometimes mimicked his friends.[12] On one occasion, Wilde characterised the Jacobean dramatist Ben Jonson as 'a beast [who] fed off books',[13] because of his gift for digesting the words of his literary heroes and regurgitating them in his own writing. He might have been describing

---

* Translation was helpful for the fledgling writer too, as Wilde knew from personal experience. Some of his first poetical efforts were superb English renditions of classical texts; at university, he dazzled his peers with his Greek compositions. In these exercises he was asked to mimic the styles of ancient authors. In some undergraduate notes he thus translates passages of Shakespeare and Wordsworth into a variety of Greek verse modelled on Euripides.[9]

himself. And it is here, perhaps, that the true significance of Wilde's habit of eating books is revealed – he gobbled them up to nourish his own writings.

Wilde's works display a literary sensibility keenly susceptible to the influence of others: on one occasion, he even claimed to have 'been influenced by all the books' he had read.[14] He admired Pater's gift for mimicry, praising his ability to echo, in his critical prose, 'the colour and accent and tone' of whichever writer he happened to be analysing.[15] In his own reviews, Wilde himself sometimes exhibits a similar facility.

Wilde's unfinished undergraduate essay 'The Women of Homer' is in part an appraisal of Symonds's *Studies of the Greek Poets* (Second Series), and in part a general introduction to the heroines of the *Iliad* and the *Odyssey*.[16] In it, Wilde attempts to out-Symonds Symonds by copying his idiosyncratic brand of impressionistic criticism and his lush poetic style. 'And so', Wilde writes, ' . . . following the cunning Circe and the enchantress Calypso . . . we come face to face with Nausicaa . . . it is like leaving a hot conservatory for the fresh spring air, or a crowded gaslit room for the soft breezes and silver glories of the night.' These musical, metaphoric lines might have come straight out of *Studies*. In fact, they probably did. They resoundingly echo Symonds's own comments on Nausicaa: 'Odysseus,' he says, then 'passes . . . into the company of this real woman. It is like coming from a land of dreams into a dewy garden when the sun has risen.'[17]

In the course of *Dorian Gray*, Wilde imitates and parodies exponents of countless genres such as the Gothic novel and dandy literature, as well as several varieties of popular Victorian fiction such as the 'magic picture novel' and the 'mesmeric novel'. The catalogue of sources and inspirations for Wilde's novel is constantly being augmented by scholars: it includes books as diverse as Disraeli's *Vivian*

Grey, Stevenson's *Dr Jekyll and Mr Hyde*, Balzac's *Le Peau du chagrin* [The Wild Ass's Skin] and the volumes of Irish folk tales collected by Wilde's parents.*

Before embarking on a new work Wilde required a literary model to follow. Thus the plays of the 'Belgian Shakespeare', Maurice Maeterlinck, provided the prototype for his *Salomé*. Wilde always needed to immerse himself in the style and the language of a genre before he worked in it.

Books by other authors created the appropriate mood in which Wilde could compose, warming him up, as it were, before his writerly performance; he told one acquaintance that he began each working day by reading a few pages from Flaubert's *Temptation of Saint Anthony*.[18] Like Chatterton, Wilde first absorbed a language then gave himself up to its ebbs and flows, allowing its internal movements and momentum to lead him forward. A friend, for whom Wilde invented one of his spoken stories, witnessed him in this blessed, trance-like state of inspiration: 'On and on' Wilde went, 'the pure diction, the delicate imagery . . . ' flowing out of lips that curved into a smile. 'Was this prose,' the listener wondered, 'or was this poetry in a new measure? A sense of his mastery of the strange instrument held me in a stillness of delight.'[19]

During a debate at the Oxford Union in 1881, the undergraduate Oliver Elton famously denounced Wilde's *Poems* as a catalogue of literary thefts from Byron, Donne, Sidney, Swinburne, Morris,

---

* This list displays the promiscuity of a taste that encompassed popular fiction as well as high art. An essential part of Wilde's genius may have been his ability to find inspiration in the 'lowest' as well as in the highest cultural sources, and in his gift for creating literary worlds in which these elements coexist in harmony, or at least in a delirious state of 'streaky bacon' contrast. In this sense, Wilde's works are microcosms of his dazzlingly miscellaneous library at Tite Street.

Shakespeare and other poets.[20] The artist James Abbott McNeill Whistler echoed the accusation when he condemned Wilde as a shameless literary thief who only had 'the courage of the opinions of others'. Beardsley repeats the charge in his caricature 'Oscar Wilde at Work', which mischievously hints that Wilde borrowed brazenly from his favourite books.

Perhaps Wilde's critics simply failed to understand his ancient conception of authorship. Their opinions belong, after all, to the post-Romantic period in which self-expression, originality and sincerity were often used as the touchstones of literary criticism. And yet their indictments cannot be dismissed so easily, because Wilde certainly did steal from other writers, and not only out of a desire to imitate or to echo them.[21]

On occasion, Wilde was the most playful of plagiarists. He included Whistler's accusation that he only had the 'courage of the opinions of others' in one of his critical dialogues, without mentioning his source. When Whistler read the piece he took the bait and once again charged the author with plagiarism, this time using the quotation as evidence. Wilde's so-called plagiarisms are also often deliberate allusions. When he echoes Pater in the early chapters of *Dorian Gray*, he clearly intends the reader to recognise the references. Dorian is seduced by Lord Henry's hedonistic creed, which he borrows wholesale from the notorious conclusion to the *Renaissance*. Invoking the Oxford don creates a thematic resonance, bringing to the reader's mind a whole series of Pater's phrases and ideas. Wilde was gratified when his readers identified such intentional echoes, pronouncing himself 'charmed' when an acquaintance recognised his allusions to Flaubert.[22]

Some of Wilde's plagiarisms were probably unconscious. His famous comparison of dining with male prostitutes to 'feasting with panthers'[23] has been traced back to the line 'I supped with Lions and

Panthers' from Balzac's *Lost Illusions*. But was Wilde aware of his source?

And yet, and yet . . . Wilde did sometimes stoop to downright plagiarism, especially in his early works, incorporating the phrases of other writers into his writings, sometimes verbatim, without an acknowledgement of any kind. The poem *Ravenna* is a cento made up of his own poetry and lines taken from other authors. His talk on Chatterton, too, vividly demonstrates his magpie method of composition. In preparing it Wilde literally cut out and then pasted into his lecture notes excerpts from two Chatterton biographers. He crosses out the occasional line or substitutes a word to improve the style of these extracts; in his talk he presumably read them out as though they were his own invention.

There were, however, extenuating circumstances. Wilde did not envisage the reissue of *Ravenna* in the sort of anthology that has made its plagiarisms palpable. His lectures too, were oral works, which cannot be subjected to conventional criteria of plagiarism; nor did he ever intend publishing them. None of these mitigating factors apply, however, to the notorious Chapter 11 of *Dorian Gray*, in which Wilde copied out verbatim phrases from works on embroidery and jewellery, in his grand tour of his hero's eclectic artistic taste.[24]

Wilde defended his plagiarisms with customary nonchalance and wit. 'It is only the unimaginative who ever invents,' he remarked. 'The true artist is known by what he annexes, and he annexes everything.' 'Of course I plagiarise,' he confessed to a friend. 'It is the privilege of the appreciative man. I never read Flaubert's *Tentation de St Antoine* without signing my name at the end of it . . . All the "Best Hundred Books" bear my signature in this manner.'[25] Wilde held that plagiarism only existed where the imitator failed to surpass his source in brilliance: 'When I see a monstrous tulip with *four* wonderful petals in someone else's garden,' he explained, 'I am impelled to grow a monstrous tulip with *five* wonderful petals, but that is no reason why someone should grow a tulip with only *three* petals.'[26]

Wilde's plagiarism illustrates the intimate connection between his reading and his writing. Without books to feed on, and without their silent physical companionship, perhaps he would never have penned a line. He may even have regarded his volumes as amulets which he needed close by him in order to compose. On one occasion he asked a friend to bring him a copy of Thackeray's *The History of Henry Esmond* while he was writing a play set in the same historical period as the novel.[27] Presumably he thought it would help him with the style of his drama, but the book may have acted as a talisman as well as a tool.

A literary tradition, Wilde believed, was based on a sort of communism of ideas and motifs.[28] 'Never say you have "adapted" anything . . . ' he advised a writer. 'Appropriate what is already yours – for to publish anything is to make it public property.'[29] Chatterton was, in his view, fully entitled to filch lines from his predecessors, just as Coleridge was justified in stealing from Chatterton, and Scott from Coleridge, and so on down the entire roll call of nineteenth-century poets which ended, of course, with Wilde himself.[30] To Wilde, a literary tradition was a confraternity of cutpurses, and the only way to gain admission was by breaking and entering.

Wilde was gratified when his own writings inspired other authors. He was 'cheered' when he read Max Beerbohm's tale *The Happy Hypocrite*, which uses *Dorian Gray* as a model. Before reading it, Wilde had, 'always been disappointed that my story had suggested no other work of art in others. For whenever a beautiful flower grows in a meadow or lawn, some other flower, so like it that it is differently beautiful, is sure to grow beside it, all flowers and all works of art having a curious sympathy for each other.'[31]

24. 'Unseen ideal'

O N AN AUTUMN day in 1890 Wilde took down a copy of *The Happy Prince* from his library bookshelves and wrote inside it: 'Clyde Fitch from his friend Oscar Wilde. Faëry-Stories for one who lives in Faëry-Land'.[1] Fitch, a starry-eyed twenty-five-year-old, with whom Wilde enjoyed making 'merry over a flagon of purple wine' and inventing 'tales with which to charm the world', had just embarked on what would be a triumphant career as a dramatist in his native America.[2] He was also one of the many amorous conquests Wilde made after his affair with Robbie Ross in 1886.

Book gifts played a crucial part in Wilde's seduction campaigns. He besieged the men he courted with inscribed copies of his first editions; he also bestowed books on his lovers to sustain or memorialise their relationships. *The Happy Prince* was one of several volumes Wilde presented to Clyde Fitch. Soon after their first meeting in the summer of 1889, Wilde had given him a copy of 'The Portrait of Mr W.H.' In 1891, Fitch would receive *Dorian Gray* adorned with the inscription: 'To Clyde, to whom the world has given both laurels & love, from his friend who wrote this book'.[3]

Wilde was convinced of the magical power of the word: 'Do you wish to love?' Gilbert asks in 'The Critic as Artist'. 'Use *Love's Litany*, and the words will create the yearning from which the world fancies that they spring.'[4] He must have hoped that his presents would act like love potions or charms on the young men he courted, perhaps revealing a latent passion to them, or exciting a fresh desire. At the very least, they would further Wilde's Socratic ravishment of his acolytes. In Fitch's case, Wilde's love potions proved to be very potent indeed. After reading 'The Portrait of Mr W.H.', which describes Shakespeare's passionate attachment to the young actor Willie Hughes, Fitch declared his undying 'adoration' for the 'great genius' who had penned it. 'Oh! Oscar!' Fitch enthused. 'The story is *great* — and — fine! *I* believe in Willie Hughes . . . Invent me a language of love. *You* could do it. Bewilderedly, All yours, Clyde.'[5]

Fitch was particularly susceptible to Wilde's gifts because he was a fledgling author. With the *succès de scandale* of the original magazine publication of the decadent 'Dorian Gray' in 1890, and the 1892 performance of *Lady Windermere's Fan* (1893), Wilde's first, and enormously successful, social comedy, he achieved his lifelong ambition of becoming both famous and a little infamous. Disciples such as Fitch applauded Wilde's triumphs and were flattered by the attention he lavished upon them. Perhaps they also hoped Wilde would further their careers — which, in many cases, he did. In the company of his devotees, who would address him as 'Shakespeare' or 'the divinity', Wilde played the role of the 'great genius'.[6] Inscribing and presenting books was an essential part of his act.

Edward Shelley, another young man with literary ambitions, worked in the offices of Wilde's publisher John Lane. Wilde struck up a conversation with him on a visit there, and was delighted to discover that the rather highly strung seventeen-year-old adored his works. Over the ensuing months Wilde bombarded Shelley with inscribed copies of his first editions, along with tickets to see his plays, until, finally, the boy succumbed. Wilde seems to have been genuinely concerned about the education of the working-class Shelley. He offered the young man £100 to enable him to return to his studies and bought many books for him. Wilde mischievously inscribed one of these – John Oliver Hobbes's novel *The Sinner's Comedy* – with the words 'From the author, August 1892, to dear Edward Shelley'.[7] This was probably a joke at the expense of Hobbes, who had tried, with qualified success, to imitate Wilde's witty epigrammatic manner in the novel.[8]

Book gifts were significant in Wilde's pursuit of Lord Alfred Douglas. His Lordship, who had been born in 1870, was the third son of the Marquess of Queensberry, an irascible and unstable man who had a frosty, and sometimes violent, relationship with his family. Lady Queensberry loathed her husband and divorced him in 1887; she bestowed all of her love on her boys, whom she utterly spoilt. Alfred addressed her as 'my own darling'; like Wilde, she often called him 'Bosie', a nickname derived from his childhood sobriquet 'Boysie'. The name was apt because Douglas remained, to the end of his days, a spectacularly egotistical boy. When he was in the mood, however, he could turn on his considerable charm and display the charisma characteristic of narcissists. Wilde accurately described him as a 'wilful, fascinating, irritating, destructive, delightful personality'.[9]

At Winchester school, Douglas had given free rein to his sexual attraction to other boys, having no doubts or qualms about his instincts. As a schoolboy he also demonstrated his gift for writing technically virtuoso verse. By the time Wilde met him, Douglas had left Winchester for Magdalen College, Oxford where, like Wilde, he studied Greats. There, however, the comparisons between them end. While Wilde had walked away with the highest first in his entire year, the indolent Douglas did not even turn up for his Finals exam. As a lord, he may have considered such tests irrelevant to his future; or perhaps, being woefully under-prepared, he simply lost his nerve. When Magdalen reprimanded him for his absence, he sent himself down (i.e. expelled himself) in a rage; soon afterwards he told the president that posterity would regard the college's harsh attitude towards him as the greatest blot on its history. It was a typical gesture in its belligerence, haughtiness and theatricality.

Douglas's ignominious exit from Oxford lay some time in the future, however, when he first met Wilde at Tite Street in July 1891. The appointment had been arranged by Lionel Johnson, who was also there in attendance. Johnson, an Oxford friend of Douglas's, was no more than five feet tall, and had dark slicked-back hair, which accentuated the pale oval face that seemed at once infantile and prematurely aged. Wilde always thought Johnson looked like a baby dressed up in adult clothes, quipping, on one occasion, as Johnson left a bar, that he was about to hail a passing perambulator. Douglas, in contrast, was a svelte, yet athletic five foot nine blond, with striking looks that can be described as a combination of classical Greek and English aristocracy graceful. Douglas liked to characterise himself as a 'boyish' beauty, and would continue to do so well into middle age. Temperamentally too, Douglas and his friend were quite a contrast: Johnson was a complex and brooding introvert, Douglas an out and out extrovert given to hysterical public ebullitions of feeling.

When the Pierrot-like homunculus and the upper-class Adonis walked up the four steps to the white front door of No. 16 and rang the bell, it was opened by Wilde's manservant, who showed them into the library. Surrounded by beautiful volumes, Douglas and Johnson's conversation might have turned to books, and to one book in particular, which was represented on the shelves in multiple copies: *Dorian Gray*, an inscribed copy of which Wilde had sent to Johnson on its publication two months earlier.

Johnson admired the novel so much that he composed an extravagant poem in Latin 'In Honour of Dorian and His Creator'. Evidently Johnson read between the lines that describe Dorian's passionate relationships with other men, as he writes, in his eulogy, about the 'strange loves' the hero so 'avidly' explores: 'Here are the apples of Sodom the very hearts of vices, and tender sins'.[10] Johnson doubtless mentioned such 'purple' matters (to use a phrase for 'homosexual' current in Wilde's circle) when he lent Douglas his copy of *Dorian Gray*. Bosie, in turn, was captivated by the book and became eager to meet its author.[11] The young aristocrat's afternoon audience with Wilde was thus directly inspired by the novel; his expectations of the meeting would, too, have been powerfully shaped by it. Perhaps Douglas dreamed of stirring in Wilde the desire to play Lord Henry to his Dorian. He seems to have always yearned for a loving and Socratic father figure who might substitute his natural father, whom he abhorred. He would certainly have fancied himself as a double for the beautiful and aristocratic Dorian.*

As Wilde put the final touches to the costume he had selected for the occasion, he too may have wondered whether life was about to imitate his art. In arranging the meeting, Johnson would surely have expatiated on Douglas's beauty and told Wilde of his ardent devotion to *Dorian Gray*. His profile of the young Magdalen man may have even dared Wilde to hope that he would finally encounter what Basil Hallward, Dorian's artist friend, calls 'the visible incarnation of that unseen ideal whose memory haunts us artists like an exquisite dream'.[13] Wilde certainly identified with the intense, and rather melancholy, painter. 'Lord Henry,' he said, is 'what the world thinks me . . . Basil Hallward is what I think I am'.[14] Basil discovers his artistic

---

* If Douglas did harbour such hopes as he sat in the Tite Street library on that June afternoon, the portents would have struck him as auspicious. He was, as he doubtless realised, acting out a scene from Chapter 4 of the novel in which Dorian waits for Lord Henry in the beautiful little library of his Mayfair house. Dorian passes the time by examining the room's Persian rugs and ornate furniture, and by casting his eye over Lord Henry's *éditions de luxe*. Life, yet again imitated art, as Douglas would have whiled away the time in exactly the same fashion.[12]

ideal in Dorian, who becomes his muse and the mainspring of his art.

If Douglas and Wilde's expectations of the meeting did indeed derive from the novel, then neither would be disappointed. When he entered the library, Wilde was instantaneously infatuated at the sight of a young man every bit as beautiful, and as ostentatiously aristocratic, as his fictional hero. Basil is momentarily petrified when he first sets eyes on Dorian; a ravished Lord Henry compares the boy to Adonis and Narcissus after seeing his painted image. Wilde would, in time, liken Douglas to both of these Greek deities, so it is possible that they came into his mind as the young poet rose from the divan to greet him. He certainly saw Douglas as the embodiment of the godlike figure which represented love, the poetic muse, and all that was desirable to him.

Incarnations of that archetypal deity had tripped through the pages of Wilde's golden books. He was Charmides, the youth who had made the venerable Socrates burn with desire; he was Willie Hughes, the boy actor whose graceful form had risen up to embrace Wilde when he had turned the pages of Shakespeare's sonnets.* And he was Pico della Mirandola, the marvellous boy of the Italian Renaissance, whose first meeting with the ageing philosopher Marsilio Ficino had,

---

* Willie Hughes would enter Douglas's life in an uncanny, and thoroughly Wildean, way. In his book *The True History of Shakespeare's Sonnets* (London, 1933) Bosie defended and elaborated Wilde's theory that the dedicatee of Shakespeare's sonnets was the boy-actor, Willie Hughes. Soon after the book's publication, Douglas actually unearthed the first factual evidence confirming the historical existence of a sixteenth-century boy from Canterbury called William Hughes, who may have been an associate of Christopher Marlowe, Shakespeare's rival playwright. Wilde himself had been unable to discover any empirical confirmation of his theory, which he had based, as he puts it in his essay-story, 'not so much on demonstrable proof of formal evidence, but on a kind of spiritual and artistic' intuition. How extraordinary that Douglas, Wilde's own Willie Hughes, should happen upon that evidence. It all sounds too good to be true, but true it all is: life again imitated Wilde's art.[15]

according to a passage in Pater's *Renaissance* that Wilde loved, opened an entirely new phase of Ficino's writing career. 'When Pico,' as Wilde paraphrased Pater's words, 'stood before Ficino in all the grace and comeliness of his wonderful youth, the aged scholar seemed to see in him the realisation of the Greek ideal.'[16]

And now, a young poet from Oxford stood before him as the manifestation of his 'unseen ideal' and the fulfilment of all these literary prophecies. The magical first impression Douglas made on Wilde endured to the end of their encounter. Inspired to verbal brilliance by the young man's beauty, Wilde enchanted Douglas with his talk; eagerly, the young man agreed to another meeting. Before leaving Tite Street the guests were taken up to the drawing-room to meet Constance, Cyril and Vyvyan.

25. 'Mysterious by this love'

T HE FIRST MEETING of Wilde and Douglas in July 1891 was prompted, informed and framed by Wilde's art. It was, in every sense of the word, written. This is no doubt partly why it made such a profound impact on Wilde, who could only see life through art's crystal. It is entirely appropriate that, at their second encounter, which took place a couple of weeks later at the Savile Club, Wilde presented Douglas with a copy of the large paper edition *Dorian Gray*, inscribing it with the words 'Alfred Douglas from his friend who wrote this book. July 91. Oscar'.[1] The gift set the tone of what would be an extremely bookish love affair; it also ensured that its progress would be strongly influenced by Wilde's novel.

Douglas carried the book back to Magdalen where he read it through fourteen times running. Its effect on him was overwhelming; he later described it as an extraordinarily powerful weapon of seduction. Bosie also explicitly compared *Dorian Gray* to the novel Lord Henry gives to Dorian, when he claimed that he had been 'poisoned' by it.[2]* It is not difficult to see why he drew the parallel. As Dorian reads the 'poisonous' novel, 'the sins of the world' pass 'in a dumb show before him'. 'Things that he had dimly dreamed of were

---

* Douglas said that he knew of the cases of over a hundred young men whom Wilde had conquered through the agency of his novel's black magic.[3]

suddenly made real to him. Things of which he had never dreamed were gradually revealed.'[4] It is hard to imagine *Dorian Gray* revealing any sins of which the extremely experienced Douglas had never dreamed. Yet the book, containing as it did Lord Henry's eloquent exhortations to Dorian to burn always with a hard, gem-like flame, may well have confirmed and encouraged Douglas's choice of the primrose path of pleasure in life. It is also possible that he saw, in its hedonistic hero, a prefiguring type of himself.

It would be six months before Wilde's relentless campaign bore fruit, at least so far as sex was concerned. Not that sex, at least between Douglas and Wilde themselves, would play a vital part in a relationship that they both characterised as spiritual and Platonic (their mutual sexual attraction was rather limited, and found expression chiefly in their hunting in tandem for other lovers). As part of his bid to impress the young man, Wilde presented to Bosie, in those early months of their affair, all of the books he had written up to 1891, from *Poems* (1881) to *Lord Arthur Savile's Crime* (1891). He adorned them with effusive and poetical inscriptions, one of which read 'Pomegranates for a pomegranate flower'.[5]

The inscriptions Wilde penned to Douglas thereafter chart the progress of their relationship. In June 1892 he gave Bosie the exquisitely designed limited edition of his *Poems* (1892) designed by Charles Ricketts. Opposite the title-page he wrote 'From Oscar to the Gilt-mailed Boy. At Oxford, in the heart of June'.[6] That volume was followed two months later by a copy of *Intentions* in which Wilde inscribed the words 'Bosie from his friend the author. August 92. In memory of the higher philosophy'.[7] Wilde was referring to Plato's *Symposium* where homosexual love is described by Socrates as more spiritual and intellectual, and therefore 'higher', than the 'sensual' love of men and women. It is fitting that he should have written the phrase in a volume which contains 'The Decay of Lying' and 'The Critic as

Artist', Platonic dialogues in which a young man is initiated into a new understanding of art and the world by an older, wiser head.

About a year after Wilde presented Douglas with *Intentions* the pair became inseparable. From June 1893, when Douglas came down to London from Magdalen without taking his degree, they saw each other practically every day. So frequently did Bosie appear in public with Wilde that he was referred to, in a newspaper, as Wilde's 'shadow'. Wilde continued to shower books on his young lover, but the words he wrote in them became less passionate and poetic: 'For Alfred Bruce Douglas,' Wilde wrote in Bosie's copy of *Lady Windermere's Fan*, 'from the author, London, Nov '93'.[8] They were now an established couple who could express their affection in other ways.*

The latter-day Socrates also heaped upon his young Alcibiades countless volumes written by other authors. Douglas received a copy of the works of Andrew Marvell from his lover; Wilde also presented him with John Fletcher's Jacobean play *The Faithful Shepherdess*. Bosie's copy of the poems of the eighteenth-century author James Thomson contains markings that appear to be in Wilde's hand; perhaps, as was his custom, Wilde wished to indicate his favourite lines for his friend's delectation.[10]

---

* Douglas's copies of the other books Wilde published between 1893 and 1895 bear equally laconic inscriptions. One of these is particularly interesting for reasons that have nothing to do with its wording. In a copy of the original French-language edition of *Salomé* the words 'Bosie from Oscar' have been scrawled near the printed dedication, which read 'À mon Ami PIÉRRÉ LOUŸS'. Curiously, the inscription is not in Wilde's hand, but in an unconvincing imitation of it. It seems to be the work of Douglas himself — it is certainly very similar to the handwriting displayed opposite the title-page, where Bosie has written his own name. The words 'Bosie from Oscar' may express Douglas's envy at being over-looked for the dedication in favour of Louÿs, a French poet of Wilde's acquaintance. This was, after all, the first new work Wilde had published since he and Bosie had become an item.[9]

Wilde passed on to Douglas his copy of *Ghazels from the Divan of Hafiz* in the hope that 'the honey of [the] verse' might 'charm' him.[11] *Ghazels* is an English prose anthology of the fourteenth-century Persian verse of Hafiz, in which the beauty of 'youths' and the pleasures of wine and love are celebrated. It is the ideal present for an absent lover: 'Without your love, I am alive without life,' reads one poem. 'Better than eternal life is union with the beloved,' Hafiz declares in another.[12]

While the pair were staying together at Brighton in 1894, Douglas caught influenza. Wilde lavished food and books on the invalid, and tended him throughout his sickness. As a result of nursing Douglas, Wilde himself came down with influenza and was confined to his bed. Bosie, however, proved to be far less solicitous than Wilde had been. When Wilde begged him to procure a volume from the local bookseller, Douglas did not even take the trouble to go there, covering up his negligence with the lie that the shop's assistant had promised to bring the book round to their hotel. After a day or so, when Wilde complained about Bosie's behaviour, the young man exploded into an Aeschylean rage that petrified Wilde.[13]

This episode throws light on the less agreeable side of their relationship, which was punctuated by countless lovers' tiffs. Some of these were extremely trivial; others were the sort of spectacular melodramatic performances one would expect from two intensely theatrical participants. Looking back on their affair Wilde would complain bitterly of his lover's petulance and ferocity. The masochist in Wilde, however, probably enjoyed Bosie's tantrums at the time.

Their friendship was, as the poet W.H. Auden remarked, a classic union of the under-loved and the over-loved. The under-loved, starved of affection in childhood (in Bosie's case, from his father), cannot believe that his partner really cares for him and so feels constantly compelled to put his lover to the test. The over-loved, on the other hand, welcomes this inherently problematic and unstable state of affairs, because he is bored and unconvinced by the love that has always been showered upon him.[14] This was the psychological dynamic of Douglas and Wilde's dramatic affair, which Wilde would later characterise as a tragic romance, forgetting that they also acted out countless comic scenes.[15*]

A large part of their fun was derived from book talk. To the end of his days the younger man would fondly recall their long and stimulating discussions about authors such as Dickens, Meredith, Stevenson, Tennyson, Kipling and Swinburne.[16] In the run up to Douglas's Oxford exams, Wilde helped his lover revise, by discussing Plato's dialogues with him. Bosie's friend and tutor, Campbell Dodgson, participated in these debates. During them Wilde would implore Dodgson 'with arms outspread and tears in his eyes to let [his] soul alone and cultivate [his] body'.[17] It was an utterly Athenian scene.

In the halcyon days of their relationship, Douglas bought Wilde a silver cigarette case which might stand as a memorial of their love. He had a quotation from the seventeenth-century metaphysical poet John Donne inscribed on it:

> The phoenix riddle hath more wit
> By us; we two being one, are it;
> So, to one neutral thing both sexes fit.
> We die and rise the same, and prove
> Mysterious by this love.[18]

Four hundred years of scholarship have failed to unpack these lines, which are from the poem 'The Canonisation'. That may be because

* The tensions of the Wilde–Douglas relationship must, however, also be seen in a broader social context. As homosexuals, they were outlaws, and, as such, denied the possibility of enjoying a stable and peaceful relationship by society.

they were not meant to be understood at the purely rational level of 'meaning'. They intimate, through jangling rhymes and subtle symbols, an idea of harmony between a pair of lovers, a mystical union of opposites which is at once sexual and spiritual, sacred and profane, male and female. Donne's lines provide the ideal epigraph to a complex and ambiguous alliance, which was a potent blend of sensual and spiritual elements, and in which love was sometimes mixed with hate.

26. 'The heavy odours of the hothouse'

WHEN ALFRED DOUGLAS entered Wilde's library in the summer of 1891, he brought with him the perfume and the promise of sex. He would also bring sex into the room in a literary sense. Between 1892 and 1893 Bosie presented Wilde with various issues of *The Spirit Lamp*, an undergraduate magazine which he edited during his time at Magdalen.[1] The poems and articles published in its pages celebrated homosexual passion, with a frankness that was exceptional for the period. The editor solicited works by homosexual authors such as Lionel Johnson, John Addington Symonds, and the notorious aristocrat Lord Henry Somerset, who had been forced to flee England when his amorous relationship with a young man became public knowledge. Bosie also persuaded Wilde to furnish the magazine with a sonnet and two prose poems.

The poets in the group contributed to a genre of verse which had been known since the 1880s as 'Uranian poetry'.* Uranian poets forged an allusive poetic language with which they could freely discuss their passion. They also tried to give a positive definition to a love that

---

* The term 'Uranian' was coined by the German sexologist Karl Ulrichs, who took it from Plato's *Symposium*. In that dialogue heavenly and earthly love are personified through the two Aphrodites of Greek mythology: Aphrodite, daughter of Uranus, whose love was pure and spiritual, and Aphrodite, the daughter of Dione, whose passion was sensual. Homosexual love is characterised as spiritual and therefore 'Uranian', in contrast to the more 'earthly' love enjoyed by heterosexuals.

remained 'nameless', and undefined outside the pejorative designation conferred on it by the law and medical science.

Wilde's relationship with the editor of *The Spirit Lamp* brought him into the heart of the Uranian fold. His interest in Uranian verse, however, predates his meeting with Bosie by several years. His library contained several representative works of the genre from the 1880s and early 1890s by poets such as Marc-André Raffalovich, a wealthy Russian based in London, whose verse, Wilde said, exuded 'the heavy odours of the hothouse'. Wilde also owned inscribed copies of *Erotidia* and *Bertha: A Story of Love*, poetry collections by the young Oxonian Charles Sayle.[2] These volumes are fervent declarations of Uranian faith. The former contains the lines

> write again in a bold, round hand:—
> 'He loved boys and thieves and sailors . . . '

In *Bertha* Sayle writes:

> There is no sin, nor any need of cure
> For we are Nature's children — and she, sure
> It is, is wholly pure and sanctified.

Wilde was impressed by this volume, recommending it to a young man he was courting.[3] His reference to *Bertha* was probably a way of testing the young man's attitude to homosexual love: once again, a book played a crucial role in his seduction strategy.

Wilde's interest in Uranian poetry goes all the way back to his Oxford days. He owned *A Vision of Love Revealed in Sleep*, a book by the Pre-Raphaelite painter, Simeon Solomon. He must have purchased the volume some time before 1877, when he mentioned it in an article.[4] Solomon's homosexuality was notorious by that date. In 1873, he had been arrested in a public convenience on London's Oxford Street for 'indecent exposure' and 'intent to commit sodomy'. Although he eventually escaped imprisonment and fled to France he was ruined by the scandal. Ostracised by elite artistic and social circles, his life would end in poverty, insanity and a premature death.

Wilde must have been familiar with at least some of Solomon's tragic biography when he purchased his allegorical prose poem. In *A Vision*, love is described as a beautiful boy 'half-seated, half-lying' on a throne. Like some Caravaggio cherub his lips are 'parted with desire' as he is 'borne gently upward' into the air, 'naked, and glowing exceedingly'.[5]

Wilde was intimately acquainted with the authors to whom the Uranian poets turned for inspiration. One of the poems in Sayle's *Bertha* has an epigraph from Whitman, beginning with the line:

As I lay with my head in your lap, Camerado[6]

It was taken from the 'Calamus' section of the original 1855 edition of *Leaves of Grass*, a collection which, with its colloquial language and sprawling free verse form, had revolutionised American poetry. In the 'Calamus' poems Whitman enthusiastically celebrated 'comradeship' between men. Edward Carpenter, the socialist and campaigner for homosexual rights, described the poems as powerful agents of revelation which opened a 'new era' in the lives of many young homosexuals in the late Victorian period.[7]

Wilde visited Whitman on two occasions during his 1882 lecture tour of America. 'I have come to you,' he declared, by way of introducing himself, 'as to one with whom I have been acquainted almost from the cradle' — a reference to the fact that his mother had read *Leaves* to him as a child.[8] Wilde brought with him, as an offering, a copy of his play *Vera* which he inscribed 'to a beautiful poet, a sincere republican and a charming friend'.[9] The two men drank Whitman's home-made elderberry wine and chatted away about poetry and homosexuality. Wilde boasted to a friend of having left one of their meetings with the great man's kiss on his lips.[10]

Wilde was familiar, too, with the ancient precursors of the Uranian poets and delighted in a number of Renaissance productions that were animated by homosexual passion, such as the philosopher Michel de Montaigne's essay 'On Friendship' and the poems of Richard Barnfield. He owned a copy of Symonds's edition of the *Sonnets of Michael Angelo Buonarroti*,[11] which contained translations of some of the sculptor's famous love sonnets to Tommaso Cavalieri. On its publication in 1878, Wilde was one of only twelve recipients of inscribed copies of the book, which suggests that Symonds knew of the young Oxonian's interest in homosexual love.[12]

Wilde was probably versed in all of the classical literature that touched on homosexual passion.[13] He was well read in the erotic literature of the ancients, much of which has a specifically homosexual flavour. Some of his undergraduate notes display a detailed knowledge of the finer linguistic points of homoerotic comic verse. He translates into English the Greek terms for 'small pole or penis', 'priapism' and 'paiderastia'.[14]* The homoerotic literature of the Romans also fascinated Wilde. His letters contain numerous references to Petronius Arbiter's racy first-century 'novel' *Satyricon*.

---

* In some fragmentary notes on his 1877 trip to Greece, Wilde makes an intriguing allusion to the ancient literature of the Greek islands. He claims that it is far 'more impassioned and erotic' than the literature of the mainland, attributing this difference to the superior beauty of the boys who populate the islands. 'Two youths of about twenty' he encountered in Corfu were, he says, far more 'sensuous' and richly 'coloured' than normal Greek boys. Wilde probably had the homoerotic literature of poets such as Sappho (whom he called 'the marvellous singer of Lesbos') and Anacreon in mind, when he made this observation.[15]

Petronius's unfinished narrative charts the desultory odyssey of two youths, Ascyltus and Encolpius, who travel around Italy and further afield in the company of their boy lover Giton. Giton is an extremely feisty flirt who, at one point in the rambling tale, threatens to cut off his genitals if his lovers persist in arguing. As Wilde would compare one of Douglas's amorous conquests to Giton, it is just possible that he witnessed a similar scene.[16]

In the latter half of the nineteenth century, scientific and sociological discussions of homosexuality began to appear in books and pamphlets. In his seminal study of 1886, *Psychopathia Sexualis*, the German sexologist Richard Krafft-Ebing outlines the 'typical' characteristics of 'congenital inverts' (his term for homosexuals). They often display, he says, an artistic temperament, and are frequently prone to paranoia, temporary insanity and pathological emotional states; his general conclusion is that homosexuality is an innate disease.

Wilde seems to have read *Psychopathia Sexualis* in the early 1890s,[17] but it is hard to imagine him having much sympathy with the German's thesis. He may well have been thinking of Krafft-Ebing when, after his imprisonment, he bemoaned the fact that his personality and sexual habits had become 'problems' of interest to German psychologists.[18]

For his part, John Addington Symonds was appalled by the prevailing medical definition of homosexuality. He eschewed the scientific approach in favour of a historical and sociological exploration of the subject, believing that this would offer greater intellectual scope and provide him with far more powerful ammunition in his struggle against intolerance. Symonds waged that war in his landmark 1883 pamphlet *A Problem in Greek Ethics*, which argues that, far from being a 'disease', homosexuality was the norm in Greek society. In contradiction of the German sexologist Karl Ulrich, who had characterised homosexuals as an effeminate 'third' sex, Symonds maintained that homosexuals were typically 'manly' and 'martial' in character.[19] It was an idea that he had previously rehearsed in *Studies of the Greek Poets* (First Series). Wilde glossed the relevant passage in his copy of the volume with the word 'good'.[20]

Symonds continued his attempt to free homosexuals from the prison of scientific classification in the pages of *A Problem in Modern Ethics*, which was published in 1891. He argues that, though homosexual passion is universal, both the expression and the understanding of it are specific to different cultures; historical context rather than biology, is all.

Wilde must have been familiar with Symonds's pamphlets. Both were published in private editions of only a few copies, but their first readers reprinted them. The reprints were then circulated among the faithful and sent to a number of prominent social figures with the author's blessing. It is inconceivable that Wilde, who regularly corresponded with the author, failed to see these 'Problem' polemics.

Wilde was also aware of Edward Carpenter's pleas for homosexual rights. In *Towards Democracy*, a long and mystical prose poem published, in various sections, between 1883 and 1902, Carpenter made an impassioned appeal for tolerance. He suggested that Whitman's ideal of 'comradeship' between men of diverse backgrounds could undermine the English class system – an idea for which Wilde may have expressed some sympathy.[21] Wilde enjoyed the same author's *Civilisation: its Cause and its Cure*, telling a friend that the book was so 'charming' and 'suggestive' that he read it 'constantly'.[22] Carpenter argues there that 'male friendship carried over into the region of love' was the 'ideal passion of the Greek period'.[23]

*

Many of the books mentioned in this chapter are likely to have found a place on the bookshelves of Wilde's close friend George Ives. Ives was in his mid-twenties when Wilde encountered him at an Authors' Club dinner in 1892; 'why,' Wilde asked, striking up a conversation with the young man, 'are you here among the bald and the bearded?'[24] Ives was at the epicentre of London Uranian society, and an indefatigable campaigner for homosexual rights. He amassed, in his bachelor apartments at E4 The Albany, Piccadilly, London (the original address of Jack Worthing in *Earnest*), an enormous literary collection of books, articles and press cuttings relating to homosexuality. As the author of several volumes of Uranian poetry, Ives must have possessed countless works of that genre. He also collected scientific studies of homosexual passion such as *Die homogene Liebe* (1895–1900) and A. Moll's *Les Perversions de l'instinct genital* (1893).[25] In addition, his collection included copies of the writings of his friend, Edward Carpenter.[26]

Ives's Albany rooms provided a meeting place for London homosexuals and a base for their literary and political operations. The Order of the Chaeronaea, a secret, quasi-Masonic homosexual order Ives founded, probably convened there. Wilde may have been one of its two hundred and fifty members, as he provided some of the lines for the vow sworn by new recruits to the group. Ives hoped that Wilde would be influential within the movement for homosexual rights and he certainly attended many 'purple' gatherings in Ives's rooms, and often helped out, with money and advice, homosexuals who had fallen foul of the law.[27]

Wilde was also involved in a literary enterprise dedicated to what became known as the 'new culture'. In the autumn of 1894, in Ives's rooms, Wilde and Douglas assisted at the birth of the homosexual magazine the *Chameleon*, another Oxford undergraduate organ for Uranian writers. They offered suggestions concerning its title and contents, and contributed to the first issue. That issue would also prove to be the last: the publishers refused to print any further numbers of what they probably regarded as an obscene magazine. The unique issue of the *Chameleon* boasted a series of Wildean epigrams, such as 'Wickedness is a myth invented by good people to account for the curious attractiveness of others.'[28] It included 'Two Loves', Douglas's most famous poem, at the conclusion of which a figure who represents homosexual passion laments: 'I am the Love that dare not speak its name.' There was also a story by the editor, the Oxonian John Bloxam, entitled 'The Priest and the Acolyte', which vividly describes the love between the eponymous pair and their tragic end in a suicide pact.*

Ives seems to have loaned out his volumes to his homosexual friends. He sent Wilde a copy of Carpenter's *Civilisation*,[30] and, somewhat recklessly, entrusted Douglas with an unidentified tome which the latter absent-mindedly left at the Cadogan Hotel.[31] Ives's book collection may even have been a 'purple' equivalent of Mudie's circulating library. As a 'subscriber', Wilde had access to all the important homosexual literature of the day. His membership of the Ives circle, along with his long-standing interest in Uranian verse, places him at the centre of a group of late Victorian homosexual readers.

This coterie of 'purple' Londoners was by no means homogeneous, as it encompassed temperaments as diverse as those of Ives and Wilde. Although they were united by their interest in the 'new culture' the two men could not have been more dissimilar. The intensely earnest Ives, who thought of himself, in quasi-religious terms, as an

---

* Bloxam, whom Wilde described as 'an undergraduate of strange beauty', makes a comic cameo appearance as an old lady in the first act of *Earnest*. Jack Worthing tells Lady Bracknell that his house in Belgrave Square is 'let by the year to Lady Bloxham . . . a lady considerably advanced in years' who 'goes about very little'. 'Ah,' comments Lady Bracknell, 'nowadays that is no guarantee of respectability of character'.[29]

'instrument' for 'the cause', was at a loss to understand Wilde's mercurial personality; nor could he fathom the characteristically paradoxical, and ironic, form in which it found expression. 'He seems to have no purpose,' Ives complained in his diary, whereas 'I am all purpose . . . He [has] not the gift of responsibility . . . he [is] all Art, and all Emotion.'[32] This voluminous diary consists of the deadly serious whisperings of its author's 'authentic' inner self, at the centre of which lay his homosexuality. It is impossible to imagine Wilde adopting either Ives's tone or his attitude: he rejected outright the notion of an 'essential' self and was keenly aware that his identity had many other sources, such as his race, class, culture and profession. Indeed, the man who often appeared to his friends to have no 'interior life' whatsoever would never have kept a diary in the first place.[33] One day Wilde leafed through the pages of Ives's diary; 'How systematic!'[34] was his only comment.

The fundamental discrepancy between the two men is revealed in their contrasting approach to literature. Ives sent Wilde *Eros' Throne*, his third volume of Uranian verse, which, like its predecessors, was essentially propaganda for 'the cause'. While he found it 'powerful', Wilde complained that the book lacked style. 'Between Truth and Style,' he tried to explain to its author, 'there is always a *désaccord*, unless one is a poet. The ideas in the book are excellent, but the mode of presentation lacks charm. The book stimulates but does not win one.'[35]

For all his sympathy with the volume's message, Wilde was too much of an artist to overlook the inadequacy with which Ives had handled his medium, and his failure to bring content and style into harmony. While Wilde simultaneously adopted a number of readerly personae when he encountered a book — in this case, those of the 'homosexual' and the 'aesthetic' reader — his aesthetic persona was always paramount.

27. "'Arry!'

WILDE'S COPY OF Harry Quilter's volume of art criticism, *Sententiæ Artis*, is in extremely poor condition.[1] Its corners are bumped and its pages have been carelessly cut. Its spine is so cracked that Wilde may have kept it open on his desk with a paperweight. He doubtless handled it in such a rough manner because it was a book he had to review. Reading it was a professional chore rather than a personal pleasure. Indeed, the only satisfaction Wilde derived from the book was pouring scorn over it in one of the most caustic reviews he ever penned, which appeared anonymously, in accordance with *Pall Mall Gazette* protocol, on 18 November 1886.[2]

Wilde's stint as a reviewer in 'Grub Street' began in March 1885 and ended in 1890. Between those years he reviewed around two hundred and fifty books, as well as a number of lectures and plays. Journalism seems to have genuinely interested him, at least at first, but Wilde was primarily motivated by the need to support his family and his own extravagant lifestyle. He laid down his hack's pen as soon as he could maintain them by other means.

Reviewers were offered decent fees but, as the diaries of George Bernard Shaw reveal, they were certainly made to earn them. Shaw would toil away on a *Pall Mall* article for two or three days, while working concurrently on a piece for the *Dramatic Review*.[3] Wilde's schedule would have been equally gruelling. Sometimes two of his reviews were published by the *Pall Mall* in the same week — no mean feat when he was often asked to cover up to eight volumes per article. Wilde doubtless drew on his legendary gift for speed-reading when he perused a book for review, mastering its plot or argument in a matter of minutes and rapidly selecting salient quotations for inclusion in his piece. As he threw one book aside he would have thought of a witty epigram, or epitaph, with which to sum it up before reaching for another volume from the pile beside his desk or divan.

Having failed to establish himself as an artist, Harry Quilter had set himself up, in publications such as the *Spectator*, as, in Wilde's phrase, the 'apostle of the middle-classes'. It was because of Quilter's allegiance to the bourgeoisie that the London-based American artist Whistler famously dubbed him 'Arry, after a lower-middle-class character of that name in *Punch* who dropped his 'aitches'.

Quilter championed the cause of propriety and 'health' in art and literature, condemning the productions of the Impressionists and the Pre-Raphaelite school, and the works of 'fleshly' writers such as Swinburne, as 'morbid' and 'indecent'. Whistler and Wilde were also the objects of Quilter's censorious art sermons on account of their espousal of the Aesthetic creed. 'Arry dismissed Aestheticism as an 'absurd' and 'pernicious' fad, corrosive to 'manly purpose', 'womanly feeling' and the 'moral fibre' of Victorian society.[4]

The animosity was mutual – Wilde loathed Quilter with a passion. When an acquaintance happened to mention the critic, in passing, in the preface to his translations from the poetry of Omar Khayyám, Wilde was less than amused. 'Only one thing I regret,' he told the translator: '– the mention of Quilter in the preface – it seems wrong: Omar would not have liked it.' 'But,' Wilde added, 'they say there is grit in every pearl oyster.'[5]

Wilde's review of Quilter's book was an extremely personal affair. He was writing about a critic who had attacked him as Aestheticism's most famous exponent. To compound matters, Quilter happened to live only a few doors down from Wilde in Tite Street, and probably passed in front of his library window every other day. On reflection, this may explain why Wilde regularly placed a screen in front of it.

Wilde's review is vitriol from start to finish, only slightly diluted by his characteristic humour, which here becomes exceptionally sardonic. One of its opening phrases is 'To many, no doubt, [Quilter] will seem to be somewhat blatant and bumptious, but we prefer to regard him as being simply British'. In summing up, he declares: 'The book will not do . . . the extraordinary vulgarity of the style alone will always be sufficient to prevent these *Sententiæ Artis* from being anything more than curiosities of literature.' In the article, he accompanies quotations illustrating Quilter's obtuseness and slipshod prose style with a mordant running commentary.[6]

Wilde's primary aim in reading *Sententiæ Artis* was to garner examples of Quilter's inadequacy for inclusion in his review. In his copy he highlights errors of judgement, taste, grammar or style, his markings taking the form of schoolmasterly crosses and multiple exclamation marks (sometimes as many as six together), which vividly express his contempt, amusement and incredulity. These, along with heavy underlinings and vertical strokes in both margins, constitute the language of annotation and marking that Wilde used fairly consistently throughout his life. It is a conventional rather than a private idiom, not dissimilar to that exhibited in the volumes Wilde read as an undergraduate.

Wilde doubtless derived a wicked pleasure from spotting the book's spelling mistakes. He marked Quilter's use of 'Steven's' for 'Stevens' with a tick and scrawled the words 'mis-spells name as usual' at the top of the page on which it appears.[7] Wilde may have been amused too by Quilter's feeble criticisms of Aestheticism. The phrase 'A little ugliness, despite William Morris, is a desirable thing' is marked, as is a plea for the revival of a 'sense of propriety' in art.[8] It is, according to Quilter, this quality that distinguishes British from 'foreign' art and makes it so resoundingly superior. Wilde has underlined the most brazen examples of the book's 'Little Englandism', such as its praise of the paintings of the nineteenth-century English artist George Mason as 'fresh as the air on the Sussex Downs, and as national as a Jingo poem'.[9]

The English bourgeoisie was Wilde's *bête noire*. In contrast to George and Weedon Grossmith, who, in *The Diary of a Nobody*, affectionately satirised the middle classes in their portrayal of the city clerk Charles Pooter, Wilde's comments on the class were generally vehement and vicious. He openly despised their obsession with work, domesticity and the accumulation of wealth; and he loathed their common-sensical and anti-intellectual vision of the world. Wilde was equally appalled by their hypocrisy: 'The typical Briton is Tartuffe,' he said, making reference to Molière's famous hypocrite, 'seated in his shop behind the counter.'[10]

In his life no less than in his art, Wilde took immense pleasure challenging the 'seven deadly virtues' so dear to middle-class hearts. Rather than being diligent, he publicly claimed to fritter his time away in restaurants. Where the bourgeoisie were thrifty, he boasted of spending £50 a week at the Savoy. While their outlook was pre-dominantly moral and sentimental, his was entirely intellectual and artistic. And, instead of leading a noble life guided by notions of duty and responsibility, he declared that pleasure was the only thing one should live for, and self-realisation the primary aim of existence.*

---

* Wilde's most extravagant performance as the 'other' of the Victorian bourgeoisie was at the Queensberry trial, where the Pooterish men who comprised the jury – there was a stockbroker, a bank manager and several 'gentlemen' from Clapton – must have thought that the seven deadly sins were being paraded before them.

The amusement with which Wilde read the many passages in *Sententiæ Artis* that espoused middle-class values is almost palpable. He put a bold vertical line beside the critic's astonishing claim that 'the greatest artists have been men who lived simple, kindly lives, generally as middle-class citizens'.[11] He also underlined a passage in which the author describes the no-nonsense (i.e. the no aesthetic nonsense) furnishings that ought, in his view, to adorn the happy home of the 'matter-of-fact business man', his intended reader.[12]

Quilter encouraged his ideal reader to visit the National Gallery in the company of his lady wife, having first enticed the poor silly creature out of the house with the promise of paying for her haircut. Once there, the couple should 'look a little' at Titian and Raphael. 'Yes,' Quilter goes on, 'and also [at] our own Mulready, and Wilkie, and Turner' – artists who will convey an excellent 'notion of what art really is – a help, not a hindrance, to life'. Right after this sentence, in his copy, Wilde has scribbled the word ''Arry!'[13]

When he read the review, 'Arry was so incensed that he dashed off a letter to the *Pall Mall* in which he charged their anonymous reviewer with a whole host of journalistic crimes, from deliberate misquotation to maliciously quoting out of context. The epistle was printed in the paper a week after Wilde's cutting appraisal had appeared.

Wilde was compelled to return to his copy of *Sententiæ Artis* in order to construct a defence. His justification took the form of a letter to the *Pall Mall*'s editorial assistant E.T. Cook, in which he dealt, point by point, with all of Quilter's specific complaints. Cook used the letter as the basis of a lengthy vindication of his reviewer, which appeared alongside Quilter's indictment.[14] The justification proved to be unanswerable and the rest was silence from 'Arry. And so, finally, Wilde put *Sententiæ Artis* back on his bookshelves, where it joined many of his other review copies.[15]

28. 'Ribald titles'

IN THE LATE 1880s and early 1890s Wilde often visited the Librairie Parisienne in Coventry Street, Leicester Square, a bookshop which specialised in French literature. The owner of the shop, Charles Hirsch, said that Wilde was invariably accompanied by a retinue of young men who 'accorded him familiar deference'. The nineteenth-century Socrates browsed the shelves and chatted to the proprietor in French, the language Wilde insisted on using in the store. He purchased several contemporary French novels, sometimes asking Hirsch to deliver them to his Chelsea home. The pair struck up a bookish acquaintance and, when Wilde felt confident of the book dealer's discretion, he enquired if Hirsch also sold 'certain licentious works of a special . . . "Socratic" (i.e. homoerotic) . . . genre'.[1]

Given Wilde's familiarity with the erotic works of the ancient world his interest in modern examples of the genre is hardly surprising. Nor was his curiosity exceptional among writers and gentleman of the period. Wilde knew of Swinburne's mania for titillating titles, which he satisfied by extensive forays into the library of erotica assembled by his friend Lord Houghton.[2] Wilde himself is likely to have explored Houghton's celebrated collection. Having been introduced to the patrician poet and politician by Mahaffy, he visited, on several occasions, Houghton's country house, which became known as 'Aphrodisiopolis' on account of its library.

Wilde was drawn to works of nineteenth-century French literature that had a piquant erotic element. One of his 'bedside books' was Charles Baudelaire's verse collection *Les Fleurs du Mal* which he described as full of 'poisonous honey'.[3] The 'poisonous and perfect' poet had famously defended the volume in court against a charge of offending public morals, partly on account of the graphic obscenity of some of its contents. There is a grisly eroticism about 'Une Charogne', one of Wilde's favourite Baudelaire poems. In it the poet imagines his beloved's corpse rotting beneath the earth, her beautiful body explored by worms and devoured by their kisses.[4]

Théophile Gautier's racy *Mademoiselle de Maupin* was another of Wilde's golden books: during his 1882 tour of America, he could not bear to travel without it.[5] D'Albert, the novel's hero, searches for his ideal of feminine beauty. He finds it incarnate in an unexpected body — that of the pageboy Théodore. At the denouement, D'Albert's master-mistress is unmasked as a girl called Madeline, but not before D'Albert admits to himself the possibility that he loves a young man. The novel ends happily ever after with an orgasm, and the pair slip into a delicious slumber in each other's arms. As soon as D'Albert is asleep, however, Madeline stirs and tiptoes off to the bed of another woman.

During his Parisian honeymoon with Constance in the summer of 1884 Wilde read J-K. Huysmans's *À Rebours*. The novel recounts the long and occasionally lovely aesthetic suicide of Duc Jean Des Esseintes, who renounces human society and the natural world. The jaded epicurean locks himself up in his country home and devotes himself exclusively to artistic pleasures. He luxuriates in the memory of his ancient love affairs, which include relationships with society women, whores, a boy he picks up in the street, and a female ventriloquist who recites, with motionless lips, passages from Flaubert's *Temptation of St Anthony* as they lie in bed together. *À Rebours* provided Wilde with a model for the 'poisonous' book which overwhelms and corrupts Dorian Gray. Its effect on Wilde was profound: he described it as 'one of the best' novels he had ever read.[6] Over the course of his career he would return to drink from it, as from a brandy bottle, when he needed inspiration in his writings.*

At around the same time Wilde devoured Rachilde's novel *Monsieur Vénus*. Wilde narrated its plot to his 'purple' friends with visible excitement, and it is not difficult to see why.[8] Raoule, the novel's heroine, engages in a bitter struggle with an older man known as Le Baron for the love of the young androgynous transvestite Jacques Silvert. In a scene that turns on its head the conventional world of marriage Wilde had recently entered, Raoule, dressed as a man, takes the beautiful young cross-dresser as his wife. When Le Baron hears about the wedding, he shoots Jacques out of jealousy; at the sight of the dying boy, however, he is filled with remorse and bends down to kiss him. 'Leave me alone,' Jacques implores him with his final breath, 'your moustache is tickling me.'[9]

All of these Gallic authors were associated with the Decadent movement in art and literature; *À Rebours* became known as the 'breviary of decadence'. The movement was a reaction against the artlessness and optimism of French Romanticism, and against the belief in unlimited and inevitable progress engendered by the scientific and technological advances of the early nineteenth century. It was also unequivocally anti-bourgeois. Decadent works celebrated art over nature, decay over progress, corruption over innocence, and sickness

---

* Wilde's bedside book during the spring of 1895 was a collection of medieval antiphons (verses from the Psalms) entitled *Le Latin Mystique. Les poètes de l'antiphonaire et la symbolique au moyen âge*. [Mystic Latin. The Poets of the Antiphonary and the Symbolism of the Middle Ages]. The anthology contained pieces from the Bangor Antiphonary, a copy of which stood on the shelves of Des Esseintes. It is possible that Wilde bought the volume after coming across Huysmans's reference to it, so perhaps *À Rebours* influenced his reading as well as his writing.[7]

over health. One of its propagandists hailed the movement as a 'new and beautiful and interesting disease'.[10]

Towards the end of the nineteenth century decadence crossed the English Channel. Pater's *Renaissance* is, in the author's words, a paean to 'that subtle and delicate sweetness which belongs to a refined and comely decadence'; Wilde described it as the 'very flower of decadence'.[11] In the melodious music of Swinburne's passion-tormented poems, the decadent note could also be resoundingly heard.[12]

In *fin-de-siècle* England Wilde became the movement's visible symbol: he seemed indeed to 'exhale Paris'.[13] *Dorian Gray*, with its exploration of artificial worlds and exotic sins, is the English equivalent of *À Rebours*: one reviewer said it was 'spawned from the leprous literature of the French *Décadents*'.[14] *Salomé*, denounced by its first critics as 'morbid, *bizarre*, repulsive, and very offensive', takes as its themes incest and necrophilia.[15]

Wilde's biblical play was originally written in French, a language he ranked, for beauty, with ancient Greek, and far above English. It was penned in 1891 during one of his many sojourns in Paris. 'I wanted,' Wilde said, apropos of his decision to write in French, 'once to touch this . . . instrument . . . which I had listened to all my life . . . to see whether I could make any beautiful thing out of it.'[16] Wilde made the acquaintance of many Decadent authors during his stay in the French capital, and it was in the hothouse of their company that the monstrous flower of *Salomé* grew. In life, as well as in literature, he attempted to imitate the Decadents. To stimulate his 'visions and desires', he knocked back absinthe after absinthe on the boulevards, and chain-smoked 'opium-tainted' cigarettes.[17]

The distinction between works of erotica and outright pornography is largely one of style. The former aim at refinement of treatment and aspire to the status of literary art; in the latter, words are regarded simply as a means of arousing the reader. Unsurprisingly, this stylistic difference weighed heavily with Wilde, who famously declared that style was everything, and subject nothing. While it is impossible to imagine him objecting to pornography on moral grounds, it is easy to see how stylistically crude pornographic productions might offend his fastidious aesthetic sensibility.

Wilde showed little enthusiasm for John Bloxam's tale 'The Priest and the Acolyte', which was published in the *Chameleon* – the Uranian magazine to which Wilde and Douglas also contributed. Wilde criticised the story's crude and slipshod style. It was, besides, 'too direct: there is no nuance: it profanes a little by revelation: God and other artists are always a little obscure'.[18]*

Some of the erotic publications of Leonard Smithers, whom Wilde probably came to know in the first half of the 1890s,[20] were elegant enough for his taste. Brash, flamboyant and spectacularly hedonistic, the publisher and book dealer from Sheffield was, Wilde claimed, 'the most learned erotomaniac in Europe'.[21] Smithers boasted that he would 'publish anything the others are afraid of', and justified the claim on numerous occasions. Under the imprint of the Erotika Biblion Society, he issued translations of masterpieces of erotic literature by authors such as Casanova and Ovid in small and clandestine editions; Wilde would tease him about his fondness for 'bringing out books limited to an edition of three copies, one for the author, one for yourself, and one for the

---

* During Wilde's cross-examination at the Queensberry trial in 1895, he repeated his criticism of the tale. 'I suppose,' Queensberry's barrister asked him, 'I may take it that in your opinion the piece was immoral?' 'Worse,' Wilde replied, 'it was badly written.' Trying to pin Wilde down, the barrister persisted: 'Did you think the story blasphemous?' 'I thought the end,' Wilde responded, 'violated every canon of beauty . . . blasphemous is not my word.'[19]

Police'.[22] Wilde was familiar with Smithers's edition of Catullus, which he may have picked up on a visit to the publisher's shop at 3 Soho Square, outside which the dealer would sometimes display the sign 'SMUT IS CHEAP TODAY'.[23]

Wilde also seems to have enjoyed some of the contemporary erotica Smithers published. The appropriately named *White Stains*, a volume of verse by Aleister Crowley, who would later become famous as a master of the black arts, is representative of Smithers's modern productions.[24] The titles of the poems alone give a taste of its quality: they include 'Necrophilia', 'Ballade de la Jolie Marion' and 'A Ballad of Passive Paederasty'. The volume is obscene, but by no means devoid of humour, intellectual interest or literary merit. Wilde was eager to obtain a copy, after hearing it described by a friend of Smithers – it sounded, he said, like a 'wonderful book'.[25]

The distinction Wilde made between erotica and pornography is illustrated by his dealings with Charles Hirsch at the Librairie Parisienne. His enquiry as to whether the dealer sold homoerotic works under the counter elicited an affirmative response. Over the ensuing months Hirsch supplied him with titles such as *Alcibiade, enfant à l'école* [Alcibiades the Schoolboy], the *Lettres d'un frère à son élève* [Letters of a Monk to his Pupil] and *The Sins of the Cities of the Plain, Or The Recollections of a Mary-Ann* by Jack Saul. Hirsch also furnished Wilde with some 'more recent pamphlets, with ribald titles, printed in Amsterdam', but their 'vulgarity' 'displeased' him and he returned them to the shop.[26] 'Vulgarity' – the cardinal sin in Wilde's personal catechism – doubtless refers to the style as well as to the content of these pornographic books.

The 1881 volume *The Sins of the Cities of the Plain* is the most famous of the titles Wilde purchased. 'Jack Saul', a Mary Ann, or male prostitute, offers a colourful and kaleidoscopic tour of the homosexual underworld of late Victorian London, thinly veiled as fiction. The reader is shown houses where gentlemen pay vast sums of money to be introduced to soldiers; they are also taken inside private rooms where aristocrats dance the night away with men in drag. Saul's description of one such party features the two most notorious transvestites of the period, Frederick Park and Ernest Boulton, (a.k.a. 'Fanny' and 'Stella'). 'Boulton was superbly got up as a beautiful lady, and I observed Lord Arthur [Clifton] was very spooney about her. Park was there as a lady, dancing with a gentleman from the City, a very handsome Greek merchant'.[27]

Along with such carnivalesque scenes Saul describes darker episodes in which rent boys blackmail their aristocratic customers, who knew that exposure meant certain social ruin and possible imprisonment. Between 1892 and 1895 Wilde and Douglas would explore the

---

* Given the distinction Wilde made between erotic literature and pornography it is hard to believe Charles Hirsch's claim that he either edited, or penned, parts of *Teleny: Or the Reverse of the Medal*, the most famous work of homoerotic literature of the 1890s.

According to Hirsch, towards the end of 1890 Wilde brought a thin notebook into his shop, which was tied up with ribbons and stamped with a wax seal. Wilde told Hirsch that one of his friends would soon drop into the shop to pick it up, identifying himself with one of Wilde's cards. A few days afterwards, a young man came and collected the manuscript. A little while later, he returned it with the instruction to pass it on to yet another young man who would also come bearing Wilde's card. The process was repeated several times until, one day, curiosity got the better of the dealer. Hirsch opened the notebook to discover inside a homoerotic story entitled *Teleny: Or the Reverse of the Medal*, written and revised by several hands. In 1893, a slightly amended version of the novel's text was published, in a limited edition of two hundred copies with pink salmon wrappers, by Leonard Smithers.[28]

Could Wilde have had a hand in the novel's production? The most cursory examination of its style makes it appear highly unlikely. Just as Wilde said that the chief argument against Christianity was the leaden prose style of St Paul, so the strongest objection to his authorship of *Teleny* is its cliché ridden and ultra-realistic prose. The graphic sex scenes in *Teleny* aspire to naturalistic 'truth' rather than beauty, and they certainly achieve it. The problem with attributing them to Wilde is that he utterly abhorred realism and disliked 'vulgar' pornography.

underworld evoked in Saul's book, with fervent and reckless enthusiasm. Their experience there was the reverse of the medal of their spiritual Platonic love.

Wilde relished the excitement of his perilous encounters with rent boys. He loved the sex, and the 'camp' banter and masquerade that accompanied it in what, to his eyes, must have seemed like a real-life version of 'fairy-land'. It is hardly surprising then that he read *The Sins of the Cities of the Plain*. He may even have used Jack Saul as his guide to the labyrinth of London's homosexual underworld. While the author is certainly explicit, his style is by no means uncouth or shoddy. He has an eye for evocative detail and a fine ear for the rich and witty argot of London homosexuals, which he serves up with considerable energy and panache.*

29. 'Queensberry rules'

ETWEEN 1891 AND 1895, Wilde penned the four social comedies that established him as one of the most famous playwrights of his day, and earned him the large bags of 'red and yellow gold' he had always coveted. The plays were largely written away from his Tite Street library, in various country holiday homes Wilde rented. He began *Lady Windermere's Fan* in the Lake District in the summer of 1891; *A Woman of No Importance* was composed in Norfolk the following year. In 1893, the greater part of *An Ideal Husband* was completed at Goring-on-Thames; the following summer, sunny Worthing provided the backdrop for the composition of Wilde's masterpiece *The Importance of Being Earnest*.

Perhaps Wilde chose this itinerant lifestyle because it reminded him of his nomadic bachelor years. It certainly offered him relief from the domestic hearth. Family life had become increasingly irksome to him since the centre of his emotional and social life had shifted towards Alfred Douglas. At his country residences, and in the rooms he periodically took at a number of high-class hotels such as the Savoy, Douglas was installed as his semi-permanent guest. The couple invited numerous young men of their acquaintance to come and stay with them. Yet again, given a choice between two alternatives, Wilde contrived to select both[1] – he now had two homes, his family household in Tite Street, and the hotels and holiday residences where he entertained his homosexual friends.

Wilde took books with him everywhere on his travels, carrying them in small suitcases which had a strap on the outside especially designed to hold books.[2] He seems to have enjoyed reading on trains, which was just as well, because he spent a great deal of time aboard them. In the 1880s he used the railways to travel the length and breadth of the country on his English lecture tour. On those journeys he grappled with the complexities of German grammar with the aid of dictionaries and literary works; he may also have passed the time reading Trollope, whose works he mischievously described as 'admirable' only for 'rainy afternoons and tedious train journeys'.[3] Wilde alleviated the boredom of his American odyssey of 1882 by a far more efficacious means: he devoured the writings of the art critic John Ruskin and countless 'paper-bound, yellow-covered' French novels, perhaps relishing the sharp contrast between those old world productions and his new world surroundings.[4]

On one of his English train trips Wilde read another sort of yellow book – *The Yellow Book*, in fact. Wilde bought the famous 1890s Decadent literary and artistic magazine before boarding a train, but on the journey it failed to engage his interest. 'Before I had cut all the pages,' he said, weaving a witty anecdote out of the episode, 'I threw it out of my carriage window. Suddenly the train stopped and the guard, opening the door, said "Mr. Wilde, you have dropped 'The Yellow Book.'"' What was to be done?[5] Wilde was compelled to read on; the only pleasure the experience afforded him was that of pronouncing the magazine 'horrid and not yellow at all'; it is, he declared, 'a great failure. I am so glad.'[6]

Wilde made himself at home in his hotel rooms and country residences by lining them with volumes from his Tite Street library. There was a whole batch of his books in his and Douglas's rooms at the Cadogan Hotel, Knightsbridge.[7] These volumes often served professional purposes. A friend who visited Wilde at Goring-on-

Thames, where he wrote *An Ideal Husband*, said that he surrounded himself with copies of the plays of the contemporary comic dramatists Arthur Jones and Sir Arthur Pinero. Wilde's comedy bears distinct traces of their influence, and he may have used their works as models.[8] Perhaps he also wrote in the presence of their plays as a way of motivating himself to surpass them. When he first turned his hand to the social comedy Wilde boasted that he could pen one in less than three weeks: 'It ought not to take long,' he remarked, 'to beat the Pineros and the Joneses.'[9]

From the autumn of 1892, Wilde rented rooms at 10 St James's Place, Piccadilly, ostensibly in order to work undisturbed.[10] Yet it was also a convenient place to which he and Douglas could invite their countless lovers, as well as the numerous rent boys they were introduced to by their friend, the pimp and ex-Marlborough School boy, Alfred Taylor. They often visited Taylor's rooms in Westminster, where booze and boys were always in plentiful supply. Occasionally the prostitutes and their clients dressed in drag and conducted mock marriage ceremonies. Wilde and Douglas also entertained Taylor's boys in fashionable West End restaurants.

Perhaps it was Douglas's exalted social status that encouraged Wilde to be so reckless. Though not untouchable in Victorian society, lords were excused much. They could certainly get away with more than an Irish lord of language who caricatured the English aristocracy in his plays and ridiculed the vulgarity of its middle class. Yet it would be wrong to blame Douglas entirely for Wilde's rash behaviour, which was of a piece with the public and political nature of his life and art. He may have felt impelled to challenge, through his actions, Victorian protocol and the false and hypocritical values that underpinned it. Having said that, Wilde's sexual excesses were also a compulsive habit. 'I deliberately went to the depths in search for new sensations,' he said, 'Desire, at the end, was a malady, or a madness, or both.'[11]

The rent boy and former valet Charlie Parker described Wilde's *pied-à-terre* at St James's Place. 'The sitting room was a sort of library,' he said. 'There were a good many books about.'[12] Wilde probably transferred some of his working library there from his Tite Street study, which was no longer the nucleus of his writing life.

Wilde's truancy from home distressed his family. On one occasion, when he had been away from Tite Street for a more than usually prolonged period, Constance turned up unannounced at the Savoy where he was staying with Alfred Douglas, ostensibly to deliver his post, but really to implore him to return home. Wilde tried to make light of the matter by saying that he had been absent from their house for so long that he had forgotten the address; Constance, not knowing whether to laugh or cry, did both.[13]

Although Wilde's library was no longer his special writer's den, it continued to feature prominently in the drama of his life. On one portentous occasion in 1893, Wilde's manservant Arthur entered the room to inform his master that a young man called William Allen was at the door, craving an audience. Having been shown in, Allen, a rent boy of Wilde's acquaintance, explained that he had come to return one of Wilde's letters in which he had extravagantly professed his love for Alfred Douglas. 'A very curious construction,' Allen commented menacingly, 'can be put on that letter.' He had, he said, been offered £60 for it from a party hostile to Wilde, but being a decent sort of fellow, he preferred to first offer Wilde the opportunity of buying the letter back for the same sum.

'If you take my advice,' Wilde responded, 'you will . . . sell my letter. I myself have never received so large a sum for any prose work of that length; but I am glad to find that there is someone in England who considers a letter of mine worth £60.' Allen was bewildered by Wilde's reply and left the house in a state of some embarrassment.

Five minutes later Wilde was disturbed again, this time by a different rent boy, Robert Clibborn, who offered the incriminating letter to Wilde for free. 'There is no use,' Clibborn complained, as he handed over the soiled epistle, 'trying to "rent" [i.e. blackmail] you as you only laugh at us.' Noticing how grubby the letter was, Wilde reprimanded the boy: 'I think it quite unpardonable,' he said, 'that better care was not taken of this original manuscript of mine.' Clibborn apologised, and Wilde gave him a sovereign. Escorting the boy to the front door, Wilde told him that he was leading a 'wonderfully wicked life'. 'There is good and bad,' Clibborn said, 'in every one of us' — a remark that impressed Wilde so much that he called the young man 'a born philosopher'.[14]*

The incident conveys something of the delight Wilde derived from the danger the boys brought into his life, and the bravado with which he confronted that danger. After the encounter Wilde continued to play with fire, no doubt because he was supremely confident that he would never get burnt. And there is no reason to suppose that he ever would have been, had 'class' not entered the play in the form of Douglas's father, the Marquess of Queensberry, or 'Q' as Wilde called

---

* The episode captures something of the pleasure Wilde took in the unpretentious company of working-class youths. They were, in his eyes, refreshingly unfettered by Victorian convention, both morally and intellectually. Wilde's fondness for the motley fellowship of former music-hall comedians, grooms and bookmakers' assistants-turned-whores which congregated at Alfred Taylor's rooms, doubtless appalled the Pooterish jury at his trials in 1895. The barristers who cross-examined him expressed their stern disapproval in words that might have been borrowed from *Earnest*'s Lady Bracknell. 'The valet and the groom,' one suggested, were hardly the right sort of people for a gentleman to consort with. Wilde replied that he 'didn't care twopence what they were. I liked them.'[15] The transcripts of Wilde's trials indeed suggest that he was condemned for his social solecisms as well as for his 'offences' against sexual 'morality'.

him. Wilde's downfall and imprisonment did not come about on account of his 'homosexual' relations with rent boys: they were a consequence of his foolish attempt to take on a marquess in court.

Q was a very dangerous man to challenge. Hot-tempered, belligerent and fond of histrionic public outbursts, he was the inheritor of an ancient name, and a peer of the realm, who could pull rank whenever the occasion required it. His relations with his son had never been amicable; after Bosie's spectacular failure at Oxford and his refusal to pursue a career, they became openly hostile. Bosie's intimacy with Wilde, which Q interpreted in a less than Platonic light, pushed the relationship between father and son to breaking point.

In April 1894 Q wrote a letter to Bosie, in which he characterised the friendship as 'loathsome and disgusting'. He threatened to cut his son off without a penny if it did not cease immediately. Bosie, who had inherited his father's cantankerous temper, replied with the telegram: 'WHAT A FUNNY LITTLE MAN YOU ARE'.[16] Over the ensuing weeks, the quarrel raged on and Wilde found himself caught up in a virulent family feud. Later he described himself as the 'catspaw' in Bosie and Q's 'ancient hatred' of each other.

The danger of Wilde's position was made painfully clear to him when, on the afternoon of 30 June 1894 at around four o'clock, Q visited Tite Street unannounced, in the company of a burly body-guard. Arthur showed them into the library, then went upstairs to inform Wilde, who was (as usual) dressing. On entering the room Wilde found Q standing by the window. Wilde moved over to the fireplace but Q ordered him to sit down. 'I do not allow anyone to talk like that to me,' Wilde replied, 'in my house or anywhere else.'

Q accused him of 'disgusting conduct', a charge which Wilde flatly denied. He then walked over to Wilde and began gesticulating uncontrollably and cursing violently. The bodyguard had to intervene to ensure that his master stopped short of assault. 'If I catch you and my son together again in any public restaurant,' Q shouted, 'I will thrash you.' Wilde displayed remarkable fortitude throughout, and even had the equanimity to make a joke about the famous rules for boxing which Q had established. 'I do not know,' he said, 'what the Queensberry rules are, but the Oscar Wilde rule is to shoot at sight.' With that he ushered Q and his sidekick out of the room, and told Arthur never to admit them again.[17]

Wilde was shaken by the confrontation, and not only, perhaps, because of its aggressive character. Q's visit had brought violence and vulgarity into Wilde's palace of art: brutal reality had knocked down the door of his 'Holy of Holies' and marched straight in. When Wilde later compared Q's campaign of aggression against him to a 'foul thing' assailing a 'tower of ivory', it is not impossible that he had this encounter, and his library, in mind.[18]

Q's campaign intensified and became public. It culminated with the infamous card he left at Wilde's club in February 1895 with the words 'To Oscar Wilde posing Somdomite [*sic*]' written on it in his barely legible hand. It was Q's 'booby trap', and Wilde walked right into it by prosecuting him for libel.

Wilde's foolhardy decision was certainly influenced by Douglas, who urged him on out of a desire to see his father humiliated. Wilde may have felt, too, that Q's card placed him in an intolerable social position. It is also possible that, as a magus of the word, convinced of his power to effortlessly alter 'the minds of men and the colours of things' through language, Wilde genuinely believed that he could captivate a jury. Whatever 'vulgar' facts Q's defence might adduce to justify the charge that Wilde 'posed' as a sodomite, he would weave, out of his magical words, a far more compelling reality.

But alas, when the Queensberry trial opened on 3 April 1895, the paradoxical and philosophical language Wilde employed in his defence was thoroughly worsted by the mundane language of the law. Q and his team of private detectives had the facts on their side, having bribed several rent boys to testify against Wilde. The testimonies of the boys (or rather the mere knowledge that they existed) proved far more persuasive than Wilde's witty and winged words. He withdrew from the case two days into the trial, partly to prevent this evidence coming to light and also because it was obvious that he was fighting a losing battle. Where he had hoped to be the author and hero of a clever comedy, Wilde found himself the protagonist of a tragedy that was thoroughly Greek but far from gracious. Hubris had provoked the wrath of the Gods, and Doom entered the stage with running feet.

The suspicion remains, however, that Wilde did not perform his role unwillingly. All of his life he had felt a strong premonition of impending disaster. That sensation had been nurtured by encounters with palm readers, one of whom had informed him that he had 'the left hand . . . of a king, but the right . . . of a king who will send himself into exile'.[19] This presentiment seems to have been strong on the eve of the trial. When a friend advised him to withdraw from the proceedings he demurred. 'That would be going backwards,' he said. 'I must go as far as possible . . . Something must happen . . . something else.'[20]

Did Wilde purposely fulfil his 'destiny'? Certainly, the way his life conforms to the contours of a Greek tragedy cannot be entirely coincidental. Replete with portents, hubris, a wailing chorus of devoted friends and the bloody intervention of destiny, Wilde's biography might have been written by Aeschylus; or, rather, penned by Wilde himself, using the great dramatist as his model. In this way he achieved his ambition of turning his life into a work of art.

In Wilde's tragedy, the Home Secretary, his erstwhile friend Herbert Henry Asquith, played the part of Doom. On the very afternoon that the libel case against Queensberry collapsed, he decided to issue a warrant for Wilde's arrest. Asquith was not legally bound to do so and his haste was extraordinary – Wilde's friend, Lord Henry Somerset, had tactfully been given ample time to leave the country in similar circumstances. It seems likely that Q made a deal with the Liberal government of the day. In exchange for Wilde's head, or so the theory goes, Q offered the cabinet his silence on a potentially embarrassing matter – the Prime Minister Lord Rosebery's love affair with another of his sons, Drumlanrig, Bosie's elder brother. Other aspects of the trial seem to support this hypothesis: the names of 'exalted persons' were deliberately kept out of the proceedings, and it was not thought necessary to call Alfred Douglas into the witness box.[21]

At around 6.30 p.m. on 5 April, Inspector Richards of Scotland Yard tracked Wilde down to room 53 of the Cadogan Hotel. 'We have a warrant here, Mr Wilde, for your arrest for a charge of committing indecent acts,' Richards announced as he entered the room, in which there were several half-packed suitcases which bore witness to Wilde's vacillating resolve to flee the country. 'Where shall I be taken?' Wilde enquired. 'To Bow Street,' came the reply.

Wilde, who had been drinking heavily, rose unsteadily to his feet, perhaps with the aid of Robbie Ross who was there with him.[22] He asked Richards if he might bring along with him a yellow book that was lying on the hotel bed. The inspector assented and, when Wilde emerged on to Sloane Street from the hotel's portico, he was observed carrying the tome. 'Arrest of Oscar Wilde,' read one newspaper headline the following day, 'Yellow Book under his arm.'

The volume was erroneously reported in the press to have been the Decadent magazine *The Yellow Book*. Later scholars have claimed that it was actually *Aphrodite*, an erotic novel by Pierre Louÿs,[23] but that book was not published until 1896. The volume's yellow cover strongly suggests that it was a French novel – and how fitting if it had been either Balzac's *A Harlot High and Low* or Stendhal's *Scarlet and Black*. The heroes of those golden books of Wilde's youth are both condemned to prison on account of their inordinate pride, and for want of powerful allies.

The yellow book kept Wilde company that night in the cells at Bow Street police station, where he slept badly. He would spend a few nights there before being transferred to Holloway prison to await his trial, fixed for 26 April, on charges of 'gross indecency' and 'sodomy'. The latter indictment was particularly serious: until 1861 sodomy had been a capital offence; after that date, men were still sentenced to life imprisonment for it. Fear of the draconian law is rumoured to have prompted an exodus of around six hundred homosexual gentlemen, who fled England for France on the evening of Wilde's arrest.[24] A couple of days later Robbie Ross absconded to the continent on the insistence of his mother; Douglas courageously chose to remain.

Soon afterwards, Constance left Tite Street to seek refuge in the country, taking Cyril and Vyvyan with her. A few weeks later mother and sons left England for the continent, where they lived under the name Holland, a family name of Constance's. Meanwhile, Wilde's two comedies, *An Ideal Husband* and *The Importance of Being Earnest*, continued to play to packed houses in the West End. In the interests of propriety, however, the author's name was removed from the playbills.

PART III

A Library
of Lamentations

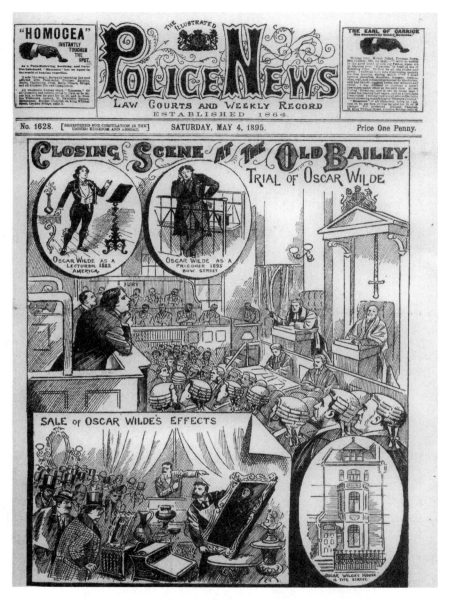

The Illustrated Police News *depicts Wilde's first trial and the sale of his possessions at Tite Street.*

30. 'May I say nothing?'

HOLLOWAY PRISON HAD the forbidding exterior of a medieval castle, with its Gothic turrets and tall central tower, but life inside was not excessively grim. It was principally a jail for men and women who, like Wilde, were awaiting trial. Inmates were allowed to pay for extra food, which was delivered to them from restaurants on the nearby Holloway Road; they were also at liberty to wear their own clothes, to see visitors every day and to furnish their cells.

Only a year previously, Wilde had referred to Holloway in an early manuscript draft version of *Earnest*. In the scene, later dropped from the play, Algernon is arrested for having failed to settle an enormous bill at the Savoy Hotel (one of the creditors that later pressed a claim for payment at Wilde's own bankruptcy proceedings). When Grigsby, the Savoy's solicitor, informs the profligate aristocrat that he will be incarcerated in Holloway if he refuses to pay up, Algy declares that it is 'perfectly ridiculous' to be 'imprisoned in the suburbs for having dined in the West End'. Grigsby assures Algy that the prison is actually rather 'fashionable and well-aired'. There are also, he says, 'ample opportunities of taking exercise'. 'Exercise!' exclaims Algy. 'Good God! No gentleman ever takes exercise.'[1]

Wilde suffered as he counted down the days to his trial, but that interim was relatively bearable. Not only was the regime at Holloway fairly relaxed, but it conformed to the idea of prison life he had derived from books. Balzac's Lucien de Rubempré compares his cell to a cheap room in Paris's Latin Quarter; Stendhal's Julien Sorel conducts lengthy interviews in jail with his lovers. These scenes evidently dominated Wilde's imagination, as his pre-1895 writings contain several glib and romanticised references to prison life.

In Holloway Wilde could assume the role of one of his fictional heroes. He drew, in particular, on his own youthful tragedy *The Duchess of Padua*. In the play, the star-crossed lover Guido Ferranti professes his undying devotion to the Duchess of Padua in the darkness of his prison cell. Now Wilde poured out his love for Alfred Douglas in a series of letters. 'Every great love has its tragedy,' he told his 'dearest boy', 'now ours has too . . . What wisdom is to the philosopher, what God is to his saint, you are to me.'[2]

Unconvicted prisoners at Holloway enjoyed the privilege of reading as much, and more or less whatever, they liked. In his first letters from the prison, Wilde complained bitterly about the lack of books. To alleviate his boredom, the friends who visited him brought along numerous volumes. Douglas supplied Wilde with several titles, so did his friend, the author, newspaper editor and occasionally charming rogue, Frank Harris. Harris may have given him a copy of Plato's *Apology*, in which Socrates eloquently defends himself in court from the charge of corrupting youth. He probably hoped that Wilde would draw courage and inspiration from the book — a rather bizarre notion, given that Socrates eventually lost his case and was condemned to death.[3]

Wilde asked Ada Leverson to send 'some Stevensons — *The Master of Ballantrae* and *Kidnapped*', probably because he craved comfort reading. Wilde had always regarded Stevenson as a 'delightful master of delicate and fanciful prose', though he was critical of some of his realistic excesses: 'there is,' he commented apropos of *The Black Arrow*, 'such a thing as robbing a story of its reality by trying to make it too true.'[4] The Sphinx sent Wilde the Stevensons, along with a copy of Shakespeare's plays.[5] Perhaps the prisoner turned to the Bard's dramatic trials and tragic prison scenes for strength and for some rhetorical tips.

However agreeable these volumes may have been, they could not even begin to console Wilde for the loss of his own books. On 24 April, just before his trial, his beloved collection was auctioned off, along with all the other effects from his 'House Beautiful', at the demand of his creditors. The principal creditor was the Marquess of Queensberry, who, at his trial, had been awarded £600 costs which Wilde was liable to pay; Q doubtless realised that a request for immediate payment would bring about a public sale of Wilde's goods. 'I hope you have copies of all my books,' Wilde wrote to Alfred Douglas, referring to the first editions of his own published writings. 'All mine have been sold.'[6] Even before the sale, Wilde's 'Holy of Holies' had been despoiled. Robbie Ross visited the library straight after Wilde's arrest, in order to secure some of the choicest items. When Ross arrived at Tite Street he was horrified to discover that someone had been there before him. The lock on the library door was broken and some of Wilde's letters and manuscripts had been stolen.[7] The identity of those papers, and of the culprit, remains a mystery to this day.

Wilde's trial at the Old Bailey began on 26 April and lasted five days. During the proceedings the wealth of highly damning, and extremely graphic, evidence that Queensberry had accumulated from Wilde's rent boys was heard in open court. Wilde's counsel managed to undermine the reliability of many of the boys' statements, and in the dock Wilde excelled himself in eloquence when he was asked to elucidate the meaning of Douglas's poetic phrase the 'Love that dare not speak its name'. 'It is,' Wilde declared, '[a] deep and spiritual affection that is as pure as it is perfect . . . It is in this century misunderstood, so much misunderstood that it may be described as the "Love that dare not speak its name" . . . The world mocks at it and sometimes puts one in the pillory for it.' The public galley burst into spontaneous and prolonged applause at the conclusion of the speech. One of Wilde's friends claimed that it influenced the jury, who were unable to arrive at a unanimous verdict.[8] The judge fixed a retrial for 20 May, and, after a week's delay, Wilde was released on bail.

Wilde took a cab from Holloway to the Midland Hotel at St Pancras, but was immediately asked to leave. He travelled to another hotel, where he met with a similarly hostile reception: some of the other clients threatened to tear the establishment apart if he was permitted to stay.[9] Their antagonism was fairly representative. Wilde had become the most hated man in England – his 'diabolic sins' provided the theme for countless sermons and the subject of sanctimonious articles in the national press.

Wilde had no alternative but to head for his mother's house at 146 Oakley Street, Chelsea. He had been reluctant to seek refuge at Speranza's in part because his brother Willie, from whom he had been estranged for some time, also resided there. Willie was an alcoholic wastrel, who sponged off his increasingly impecunious mother and his younger brother, whose success he envied but affected to despise. When Wilde knocked on the door of the house it was opened by Willie. 'Give me shelter or I shall die in the streets,' Wilde said, before falling 'down on [the] threshold like a wounded stag'.[10]

For about ten days, during which he was violently ill, Wilde was a guest at Oakley Street, sleeping on a camp bed in the corner of a small room. He derived some comfort from his mother's hoard of books. Speranza's collection had dwindled since her Dublin days, as she had been forced to sell some of it to keep the wolfish bailiffs from the door. Nevertheless, the library at No. 146 was still 'crowded with books from floor to ceiling, and in many places along the floor'.[11] Some of the volumes that had accompanied Wilde through his Merrion Square childhood would almost certainly have been there – among them, no doubt, Speranza's *Poems*, her anthologies of Irish folk tales, and her copies of Macpherson and Keats.

During his stay Wilde revisited the works of Wordsworth, who had always been one of Speranza's idols. He read the Lake poet's sonnets aloud in the company of the journalist Robert Sherard (an old friend from his bachelor days) perhaps from the very copy he had first perused in Dublin as a boy. Wilde's forthcoming retrial, and the sober character of most of Wordsworth's lines, made the occasion a solemn one, but humour suddenly broke through. When Wilde came across a sonnet in which the poet rhymed 'love' with 'shove' he burst out laughing, and exclaimed, 'Robert, Robert, what does this mean?'[12]

In his account of those dark days, Sherard mentioned Speranza's copy of the witty and rambling *Essays* of Montaigne. He and Wilde may have read them together.[13] Sherard certainly quoted to Wilde the philosopher's famous line: 'Were I accused of stealing the towers of Notre Dame the first thing I should do would be to put the frontier between myself and the *gens de la justice*.' This was precisely what Sherard, and many of Wilde's other intimates, urged him to do in the interim between his trials; Frank Harris even hired a steam yacht and stocked it with food and books, so that Wilde could sail in comfort to France.

Wilde's brother and mother condemned these schemes as craven and dishonourable. Willie implored Wilde to stay to 'face the music' like 'an Irish gentleman'; Speranza's exhortation was even more forceful. 'If you stay,' she told him, 'even if you go prison, you will always be my son . . . But if you go, I will never speak to you again.'[14]

These words are redolent of the speeches that Fingal and Ossian made to their warrior heir Oscar.

Wilde spent the latter half of his interval of freedom at Ada Leverson's house at 2 Courtfield Gardens, Kensington, where he lodged in the nursery on the top floor. Like Sherard and Harris, the Sphinx courageously stood by Wilde in his adversity, though she courted opprobrium by doing so. Wilde passed his time there, among the toys, receiving visitors such as W.B. Yeats, and a tearful Constance.

In Leverson's company Wilde made a point of being light-hearted, inventing marvellous parables for her pleasure and chatting pleasantly to her about books in an effort to keep his imminent trial from his mind.[15] It was during his stay at Courtfield Gardens that he uttered his immortal epigram about the heroine of Dickens's *The Old Curiosity Shop*. 'One must have a heart of stone,' Wilde quipped to the Sphinx, 'to read the death of Little Nell without laughing.'[16]

Sir Alfred Wills, the judge at Wilde's second trial, considered him culpable from the outset, and gave a damning summing-up. The charge of 'sodomy' was dropped, but the jury returned a verdict of guilty on several indictments of 'gross indecency'. Wills gave Wilde the maximum sentence of two years' hard labour — a punishment he described as 'totally inadequate' for the crime. As the judgment was delivered, Wilde almost swooned in the dock. With a face contorted with anguish, he mumbled, 'And I? May I say nothing, my lord?'; the judge waved him away.

Despite the famous English shibboleth about a man being innocent until he is proven guilty, the press had almost universally condemned Wilde on his arrest. 'Open the windows!' the *Daily Telegraph* now declared triumphantly. 'Let in the fresh air!'

Harry Quilter was equally exultant — he claimed that Wilde's 'vices' were the inevitable consequence of his 'immoral' Aesthetic credo, and reminded his readers of his own tireless attempts to 'knock' the 'high priest' of Aestheticism 'on the head'. Wilde's downfall was, he announced, a blow for decency and morality, which would now become, once again, the touchstones of literature and art. 'There will,' Quilter declared, 'come back into the world some substitute for the old faith in God, and reverence for those things which are fair, lovely, and of good report'.*[17]

---

* Quilter's prophecy was not fulfilled. The Modernist literary movement that grew out of the 1890s, and Edwardian art critics such as Bernard Berenson, ignored the values Quilter espoused and drew heavily upon the Aestheticism of Pater, Swinburne and Wilde.

Quilter lived on into the twentieth century, but in intellectual terms he was never at home in it. History has completely forgotten his work and his name only survives today because of the minuscule part he played in the lives of great aesthetes such as Wilde and Whistler.

31. 'Humanity's machine'

A FTER THE SENTENCING, Wilde was taken in a windowless
Black Maria from the Old Bailey back to Holloway. On his
arrival, he was left in no doubt as to his changed status: he was
now a convicted felon and was permitted none of the privileges he had
enjoyed while awaiting trial.

Wilde surrendered all his personal property, then stripped naked
for a detailed medical inspection, after which the prison doctor
pronounced him fit enough to perform hard labour. Next, he bathed
in grimy water, and had his hair cut short. Then he put on his convict
costume – a cap and an ill-fitting grey suit with arrows printed all over
it. Finally, the long litany of prison regulations was barked out to him:
'Prisoners shall preserve silence by day and by night . . . They shall not
be idle, nor feign sickness to evade their work.'[1] There were so many
rules that the recitation could take up to forty-five minutes; afterwards
Wilde was led off to his cell.

About two weeks later, Wilde made the short journey down the
Caledonian Road from Holloway to Pentonville, a prison for convicted
felons. His cell there was around thirteen feet long, seven feet wide
and nine feet high. Its walls were whitewashed and spotlessly clean, as
was its shiny asphalt floor. A copy of the prison regulations was
pinned to the wall, and a bible, a prayer-book and hymn-book stood
on a small shelf. A plank of wood placed across two trestles would
serve Wilde as a bed.

At Pentonville Wilde was introduced to the gruelling and monotonous daily routine of the Victorian prisoner. He was woken up in the morning at 5.30 by the tolling of the prison bell, which gave out a shrill and strident peal.[2] On hearing it, Wilde rose, washed himself quickly with freezing water, then cleaned his cell and its contents. Everything had to be spick and span for inspection by the warders. After their rigorous examination, Wilde was allowed out to empty his slops from the bucket he used, during the night, as a lavatory.[3] Having breakfasted on thin cocoa and stale bread at 7.30, he left his cell for around forty-five minutes' exercise with the other prisoners. They paced around the 'slippery asphalt yard' in single file and in silence. Being exceptionally tall, Wilde's long strides brought him quickly to the heels of the convict ahead of him; whenever this happened a warder would separate them immediately to prevent any communication.[4]

At around 9.30, the prisoners were marched off to chapel where wooden panels had been placed between the individual pews to prevent the prisoners seeing each other. The inmates had to endure the chaplain's long and often virulent sermons, in which their 'dishonesty, over-indulgence' and 'wickedness' were castigated. The author of 'The Soul of Man under Socialism' found these tirades exasperating. Wilde longed to 'rise in my place and . . . tell the poor, disinherited wretches around me that . . . they are society's victims, and that society has nothing to offer them but starvation in the streets, or starvation and cruelty in prison'.[5]

Wilde's dinner at noon, eaten in his cell, typically consisted of bacon and beans or suet pudding. He was also given weak tea there at around 5.30. During the day, he performed at least six hours' hard labour, mostly in his cell. He 'picked oakum', which involved separating the fibres in a tarry rope, or turned the 'crank' handle to pump water or grind corn. The gas jets that lit his cell were turned off at eight, when the prisoner had to retire to his hard plank bed.

The regime under which Wilde would struggle to survive had been instituted by the Prison Act of 1865. The Act established the 'Separate System' throughout England, which was designed to isolate inmates from the outside world and from each other. Conversation between convicts was strictly forbidden at all times; even eye contact was severely punished. Inmates were locked in their solitary cells for up to sixteen hours a day. Advocates of the system claimed that it would 'deprive the prisoner of the contaminating influence' of their fellows.[6] They also argued that in 'the solitude of the cell, alone with a wounded conscience' and his bible, the inmate would inevitably turn to God.[7] Isolation was a potent means of control: it encouraged prisoners to focus exclusively inwards, rendering them docile and weak, and destroying their will to resist authority.

Wilde abhorred the puritanical character of the system, with its emphasis on solitary bible reading and its insistence that the prisoner learn to respect the seven deadly Victorian 'virtues' of industry, thrift, obedience, abstemiousness, duty, piety and chastity. He also loathed the scientific rationality that informed the regime. With meticulous precision, space and time were ordered and controlled in the prison. Each cell, landing and wing was identical in dimension; every action of every day was measured to the second, and each day replicated its predecessor. The Separate System was, in Wilde's vivid phrase, 'humanity's machine'.

The diet was so inadequate that Wilde lost a considerable amount of weight – perhaps as much as twenty pounds in his first month. One newspaper reported that the prisoner was so ill that the governor contemplated transferring him to the infirmary.[8] Alarmed by these reports, Wilde's well-connected aristocratic friend Lady Brooke persuaded Richard Haldane, a Liberal MP of her acquaintance, to visit the prison. Haldane, a kind-hearted and cultivated man, was a member of a Home Office committee investigating the prison system, and had right of access to jails throughout England. The MP visited Wilde on 12 June 1895. At first, the prisoner refused to speak to him. Haldane managed to draw Wilde out, however, by putting a friendly hand on his shoulder, and by broaching the subject of his future literary plans. He urged Wilde to compose a great work based on his terrible experiences and, with that end in mind, promised to procure for him books and writing materials. These were the first sympathetic words Wilde had heard since his sentencing, and he burst into tears.

Haldane's proposal constituted an extraordinary relaxation of the prison rules. For the first three months of his sentence, a Victorian convict was only allowed to read the Bible, and the prayer-book and hymn-book that remained permanently in his cell. Additional works of pious literature could be supplied at the chaplain's discretion.[9] Wilde was given a copy of John Bunyan's famous seventeenth-century Protestant allegory *The Pilgrim's Progress*, but derived from it neither pleasure nor consolation.[10] When the first three months of a prisoner's sentence were up, he was permitted to borrow one book a week from the prison library.

When Haldane asked Wilde which titles he wanted, he nominated 'Flaubert's works'. Haldane explained that, as Flaubert had been charged with indecency over his novel *Madame Bovary*, it was unlikely that the request would be acceded to. Wilde laughed at this comment, which he doubtless regarded as typical of the stupidity of the prison authorities.[11] Their literary chat, and the promise of books, raised his spirits and, with Haldane's help, he enthusiastically drew up a list of requests. This included Pater's *Renaissance*, and a number of volumes by Cardinal Newman. (The full list is reproduced in Appendix II a., See p. 319).

Haldane purchased all of the selected volumes, perhaps with the financial help of Lady Brooke, and sent them to Pentonville.[12] Although Wilde had yet to serve three months of his sentence, the books were issued to him at the rate of one title per week. The governor meanwhile informed the Commission that 'several books' had been sent to the prison by Wilde's friends.[13] As convicts were forbidden to receive anything from the outside world,[14] these volumes were immediately returned to their donors. One of the benefactors was anonymous so the gift could not be sent back: instead the book would be handed to the prisoner on the day of his release.

It is a pity Wilde was not allowed to see the volume (which has not been identified) or the touching note that accompanied it. 'Please give Mr Wilde the book,' it read. 'I have never ever seen him but it must indeed be a hard heart utterly unacquainted with <u>God's love</u> that does not bleed for such a shipwrecked life . . . I feel this book which I send, may be helpful. Faithfully yours, an Irishwoman.'[15]

32. 'Silence'

ILDE'S CONDITION WORRIED Haldane. Less than a month after his visit the MP had the prisoner transferred from Pentonville prison to Wandsworth, in south London. He probably thought Wilde would benefit from the more salubrious environment outside the city; he also knew William Morrison, Wandsworth's chaplain, and could closely monitor the prisoner's condition through him.

Haldane asked Pentonville's governor to send on to Wandsworth the ten books that had been purchased for Wilde. They arrived a month and a half after the prisoner's transfer.[1] While Wilde waited, no doubt with great impatience, for the delivery of his little library of books, he turned to the King James Bible. Like so many Victorian prisoners, he must have read it from cover to cover, perhaps more than once. Wilde had always been enchanted by the 'beautifully artistic' stories of the Old Testament, as well as by the personality of Jesus. Back in the 1860s, at the Protestant Portora school, he had learned many of its verses by heart. The ease and frequency with which Wilde quotes the King James version in some of his prison letters suggests that he once again committed much of it to memory. It is highly likely, however, that Wilde was also permitted, in his first days at Wandsworth, to peruse books from the prison library, which was overseen by Haldane's friend, the chaplain.

*

The libraries of Victorian prisons were largely comprised of three types of books: educational volumes, religious books and popular fiction. In one of the prisons in which Wilde was confined these categories were represented fairly equally, with roughly three hundred volumes of each.[2]

The educational books were extremely rudimentary. Arnold's *Phonic Reader Primer* and that publisher's 'Albion Readers' were typical titles; both were aimed at the semi-literate working class who made up the vast majority of the prison population. There were also practical handbooks on various trades.[3] Obviously, none of them was of the slightest interest to Wilde. The same is doubtless true of the pious titles on offer. Typical of these books was Joseph Kingsmill's *The Prisoner's Manual of Prayer* which includes the prayer: 'Take me, O gracious God, under thy protection this night; I am a vile, unworthy sinner . . .'[4]

Popular literature was heavily censored by the chaplain. Novels that referred to sex, prisons or politics found no place on the prison library's shelves.[5] It is something of a surprise, then, that *any* title managed to pass the censor, but there was a wealth of 'goody-goody' Victorian novels to choose from. In these works virtuous characters are awarded happiness and evildoers come to a bad end which, as *Earnest's* Miss Prism remarked, is 'what fiction means'.

The prison authorities added a new terror to Wilde's punishment by effectively force-feeding him the sentimental, didactic and realistic fiction he despised. Out of excruciating boredom, Wilde was compelled to read 'everything' that was on offer at the various prisons in which he was confined, 'several times' over.[6] Some members of the prison hierarchy evidently believed that Wilde would benefit from a steady diet of 'wholesome' reading. During a conversation with one official, Wilde was asked which book he most coveted. When he named Flaubert's luxuriant and sensual historical novel *Salammbô*, he was rebuked: 'It is that sort of nonsense which has brought you here.'[7]

One 'goody-goody' novel available to Wilde was Sir Walter Besant's three-volume work *The Ivory Gate*.[8] The hero, Mr Edward Dering, is a city solicitor who, after a life dedicated to hard work and the accumulation of wealth, suddenly recognises the 'visionary dreamer' within himself and the infinite spiritual and social possibilities available to humanity at large. After his awakening he preaches a gospel of altruism: if man, he says, 'lays down his garb of selfishness and puts on the white robes of charity', Utopia can be established on earth. The novel ends with a beatific vision in which the hero suddenly sees a 'long procession of those who work and sing at their work and are happy, work they ever so hard, because they work for all and all for each.'[9] This is, of course, precisely the sort of badly written moralistic fiction that Wilde excoriated, with such devastating eloquence, in his writings. Besant was indeed one of Wilde's *bêtes noires* – a sort of novelistic equivalent of Harry Quilter, who exemplified for him all that was anti-intellectual, sentimental and inartistic about middle-class English fiction. He found Besant's 'universal benevolence' positively nauseating and was equally appalled by the author's didacticism, and his disdain for what he referred to as '*mere* style' – a phrase that greatly amused Wilde. Worse still, Besant was an arch-realist, whose voluminous *oeuvre* constituted, in Wilde's view, a tedious attempt to 'exhaust the obvious'.

Novels like Besant's espoused some of the guiding principles of the Separate System, such as diligence and duty. As works of realism, they also resembled the world of the prison in their cold objectivity. Both worlds, real and fictional, denied their inhabitants the freedom of interpretation or discussion, and neither offered them an outlet for their inner world of feelings, dreams and fantasies. Such parallels may explain why Wilde's criticism of the prison system was often reminiscent of his strictures against the realistic novel: it was 'stupid', he complained, because it lacked 'imagination'.

Prison libraries also contained thrillers and murder yarns such as Fergus Hume's *The Lone Inn*. The immensely popular productions of this New Zealand crime writer were regarded as innocuous because they generally attributed crime to the personal 'wickedness' or psychological deficiency of the felon, rather than to social circumstances. Wilde probably found such popular 'trash' more congenial than Besant: at least the story had a clearly defined structure, and the author did not consciously set out to preach.

Not that Wilde had anything complimentary to say about the choices available to him. 'The books,' he remarked in a letter to the press written after his release, 'that compose an ordinary prison library are perfectly useless. They consist chiefly of third-rate, badly-written, religious books, so-called, written apparently for children, and utterly unsuitable for children or for anyone else.'[10] One of Wilde's proposals for prison reform was that prisoners have free access to an adequate selection of good literature.

Like the titles on offer, the conditions in the prison were far from conducive to a pleasant, or rewarding, reading experience. The perpetual state of exhaustion, hunger, illness and depression 'paralysed', in the words of one inmate, 'the reading faculties'.[11] Victorian prison cells were, moreover, hardly designed for reading. The murky light that filtered through the tiny barred and begrimed windows and the meagre light emitted by the gas jets barely allowed the prisoner to make out the printed words.

Reading in these circumstances inevitably caused eyestrain and sight loss, and Wilde's vision became impaired, particularly during the winter months of his incarceration, when he read by gaslight after sundown.[12] He would stand up in his cell next to the artificial light, holding his book right up against the flame and peering closely at the pages, which he turned very slowly.[13] This image of uncomfortable, unhurried and isolated reading contrasts sharply with all our previous pictures of Wilde the reader.

Relief from conventional literary prison fare arrived on 17 August in the form of the ten books that had been bought for Wilde by Haldane. At the end of that month, the Liberal MP also sent to Wandsworth's library, through his own bookseller, some 'volumes of Pater which Oscar Wilde was anxious to have'.[14] The new additions to Wilde's store were *Greek Studies*, in which Pater discusses various aspects of Greek literature and culture, *Appreciations*, his anthology of essays on English literature, and *Imaginary Portraits*, a collection of four historical stories.

Wilde's copy of the latter has survived. On its inside cover there is a little table of rows and columns, in which the date '1–10–95' is written.[15] This was probably the day on which Wilde returned it to the library. In the margin on page 141, the date appears again, next to a tiny rip. It must have been written by the chaplain, or his assistant, the schoolmaster's orderly, who inspected books for damage on their restitution to the library. Next to the volume's half-title are two numbers, '541' and '1189', doubtless its library shelf-mark.

The book is in very poor condition. Its edges and corners are knocked; its cover and many of its pages heavily soiled with smudges and dust marks. These blemishes vividly conjure up the unwholesome circumstances in which the volume was read, and the filthiness of the hands that held the book after performing hard labour. The volume contains markings that are probably Wilde's. Few other inmates are likely to have requested Pater, and no one else would have been allowed to mark the book. Of the stories in the volume, Wilde seems to have been particularly drawn to 'Duke Carl of Rosenmold', a fictional sketch of an early precursor of the German Enlightenment of the eighteenth century. Wilde had described the tale, on first reading *Imaginary Portraits* a decade earlier, as an allegory of 'the passion for the imaginative world of art'.[16] Vertical lines mark passages referring to Bach and Goethe. Wilde's curiosity was also excited by some musings on the Enlightenment's conception of the imagination and by a number of abstruse paragraphs on metaphysics.[17]

These markings suggest that Wilde's enquiring intellect was still very much alive. He evidently retained the requisite mental power to engage the book in a readerly dialogue; he was also robust enough to query some of its claims. On page 104 there is a question mark next to Pater's dubious statement that the lives of Dutch artists were generally 'exemplary in matters of domestic relationship.'

Yet Wilde's markings also convey despair. Page 111 contains what must be the most poignant example of all Wildean marginalia – a single exclamation mark next to the word 'silence'. Did he draw attention to the word because it was charged with terror for him? Under the Separate System the prison was pervaded by a deafening silence; 'condemned' to that silence, 'the wretched man,' Wilde commented, 'confined in an English prison, can hardly escape becoming insane.'[18]

Wilde drew comfort from the books Haldane sent him. When Robert Sherard visited him at the end of August, reading was the only subject he could discuss with equanimity; all other topics caused him to break down. Similarly, in October, when he was granted special permission to see his solicitor friend Arthur Clifton, Wilde mentioned the pleasure his copies of Pater and Newman afforded him.

Both visitors were horrified by Wilde's appearance and by his account of life inside. During his talk with Clifton, Wilde spoke of the 'savage' treatment meted out to him.[19] Wilde 'cried a great deal', Clifton recalled, and said repeatedly that 'he did not think he would be able to last the punishment out'.[20]

Wilde was displaying signs of partial deafness — a consequence of a fall in chapel, which permanently damaged his ear. Because of that fall, and chronic diarrhoea, Wilde was allowed to spend some time in the infirmary. He did not enjoy much respite there, however, as the doctors treated him cruelly. Wilde's condition became so serious that the Home Secretary sent two medical experts to examine him for mental and physical illness. Wilde's health evidently concerned them as they strongly recommended that he be transferred from London to the country, where he might profit from the fresher air, and Reading Gaol was eventually settled upon. Once again, Wilde's guardian angel, Haldane, was probably at work behind the scenes.[21]

33. 'Books in his hand'

A T TWO O'CLOCK on the rainy afternoon of 21 November 1895, Wilde stood on the centre platform at Clapham Junction station awaiting his train for Reading 'in convict dress and handcuffed, for the world to look at'. The worthy burghers of London going to, and coming from, the City, saw the prisoner and laughed. 'That was,' Wilde recalled, 'before they knew who I was. As soon as they had been informed, they laughed still more.' One of their number spat in Wilde's face. He had to endure their abuse until his train arrived at 2.30. 'For a year after that was done to me,' he wrote, 'I wept every day at the same hour and for the same space of time.'[1]

After alighting at Reading station Wilde completed the short trip to the prison which, like Holloway, Pentonville and Wandsworth, had the neo-Gothic appearance of a medieval castle. After the customary medical inspection, Wilde was taken up two shiny iron staircases and along a narrow walkway to cell C.3.3. – the third cell on the third floor of Block C. It was no bigger than his previous dwellings, but it had two large south-facing windows which let in a fair amount of light (see plate 12). This would be his home for the next eighteen months.

The report on Wilde's condition at Wandsworth recommended a 'variation of employment' such as 'bookbinding' or 'garden work'. Instead of hard labour, Wilde would now 'be employed with the schoolmaster in sorting, repairing and distributing books'; he was also given three hours of garden work a day.[2]

As 'schoolmaster's orderly' Wilde's main task was to issue and collect library books. This afforded him a rare and welcome opportunity of talking with his fellow convicts, and about a subject dear to his heart. Once a week Wilde brought the prison library's catalogue round to each inmate's cell. He must have given the prisoners excellent advice about which books to choose, striking up, in the process, many friendships which would endure beyond his release. After the convicts had chosen their titles, Wilde went back to the library, where he took the selected books down from the shelves and put them on a trolley. He then made his rounds of the cells to deliver the books. When issuing each prisoner with a volume, he wrote its catalogue number on a blue library card that was kept in the convict's cell. After a week, the prisoner could exchange the book for another title, provided that it was returned undamaged. Another of Wilde's duties was to cover the library books with brown paper and rebind them. He told one of his first visitors at Reading how much he enjoyed this chore. If he could not read all the volumes he wanted, he could at least 'hold books in his hand'.[3]

The visitor in question was Constance. Though seriously ill and utterly broken psychologically, she had travelled, in February 1896, to see Wilde, all the way from Genoa in Italy, where she now lived with Cyril and Vyvyan. She made the trip to break to Wilde the terrible news that his mother had died as she could not bear the idea of him hearing the report from the lips of a stranger.

Wilde was overwhelmed with anguish and remorse. He believed that his mother had died 'broken-hearted because the son of whose genius and art she had been so proud . . . had been condemned to the treadmill for two years'.[4] His distress was undiminished by the fact that the tidings did not surprise him. Wilde claimed that, on the eve of Constance's visit, Speranza's spirit had appeared in his cell dressed in her outdoor cloak. He had asked her to take it off and sit down, but she shook her head sadly and vanished.[5]

It was a fittingly theatrical and bookish denouement to the relationship between mother and son, pregnant as it was with so many literary associations. Speranza's spirit played the role of the banshee — the phantom woman of Irish folklore whose appearance portends the death of a family member. She was also performing the part of Odysseus' mother, who features in Book XI of Homer's *Odyssey*. Odysseus descends into Hades, the underworld of the Greeks, and there, among the shadows of the dead, he encounters the ghost of his mother. They engage in conversation, at the conclusion of which Odysseus tries to embrace his mother, but, phantom-like, she eludes his grasp. Curiously, the episode had made a great impression on Wilde at Oxford, where he recounted the 'wonderful' and 'affecting' scene in an essay.[6]

Speranza's wraith seems, too, to have been mimicking Everallin, the mother of Oscar in Macpherson's Ossianic poems. In one episode, Everallin's ghost appears to Oscar's father Ossian, 'in all the light of her beauty; her blue eyes rolling in tears'. She exhorts him to 'Rise, and save my son; save Oscar prince of men', who is in mortal danger. It is possible that Speranza recited this marvellous scene to Wilde as a boy, and he may have recalled it now as he lay in jail. Certainly he interpreted her ghostly visitation as an attempt to warn him of some imminent danger. Speranza's spirit reappeared to him on many occasions later in his life and always, he believed, to that end.[7]

On her deathbed Speranza had asked if her 'dear Oscar' might be permitted to visit her, but she must have known that he would not be allowed. Now that she was dead, Wilde was not even granted permission to attend her funeral.[8] A month after it took place he asked a friend to retrieve, from Oakley Street, all of 'the books of *my own writing* I gave my dear mother'.[9]

The Wandsworth medical report had proposed that Wilde continue to enjoy special reading privileges. He was to have access to his little collection of personal classics, which had been transferred from Wandsworth to Reading. On their arrival, their Wandsworth shelf-marks were replaced with new ones, and the words 'Reading Prison' were written on the half-title pages.[10] As an additional concession, Wilde was now permitted to read two volumes rather than one per week.

In February 1896, seven titles were added to his store. These were: Dante's *Divina commedia*, accompanied by an Italian grammar and dictionary to help Wilde with the poem's medieval Italian; two massive folio volumes containing the entire surviving corpus of Greek and Latin poetry and drama; the equally weighty Liddell and Scott's *Greek Lexicon*, and Lewis and Short's *Latin Dictionary*. More Adey, the translator of Henrik Ibsen and another of Wilde's 'chivalrous' and supportive friends,[11] procured the volumes and dispatched them to Reading. He was one of several people who sent the prisoner books during his confinement; others included the Sphinx and Robbie Ross.

The seven volumes were most welcome to Wilde. The works of classical literature proved to be of little use, however, as reading them brought on terrible migraines.[12] Along with the headaches, Wilde complained that his attention span, which had been ground down by ill health and depression, was often no longer equal to the effort of reading such literature.[13] He bemoaned, too, the fact that Reading's governor – the despotic drunkard H. B. Isaacson – deliberately obstructed his reading. He 'loves to punish', Wilde told a friend, 'and he punishes by taking my books away from me'.[14]

Fortunately for the prisoner, Isaacson's days at Reading were numbered. He was replaced in July 1896 by Major James Nelson, whom Wilde would later describe as the most 'Christ-like' man he ever met.[15] Around the time of Nelson's arrival, Wilde composed a harrowing petition to the Home Secretary in which he expressed the fear that he was slowly becoming insane. In interviews with friends too, he seemed haunted by the spectre of madness: he asked Robbie Ross if he thought *'his brain seemed all right?'* and predicted that his confinement would slowly 'deprive him of his mind'.[16] In his petition to the Home Secretary, Wilde attributes his dire mental condition to 'the fearful system of cellular confinement', and to the absence of 'writing materials whose use might help to distract the mind'. He also laments the lack of 'suitable or sufficient books' that are 'so essential to any literary man' and 'so vital for the preservation of mental balance'.

Wilde then makes an impassioned plea for wider access to literature. 'By special permission,' he writes, in the third person, in accordance with prison protocol, 'the petitioner is allowed two books a week to read: but the prison library is extremely small: it hardly contains a score of books suitable for an educated man.' As for those books that had been ordered specifically for him, 'he has read and re-read them till they have become almost meaningless'. Consequently, 'the world of ideas, as the actual world, is closed to him: he is deprived of everything that could soothe, distract, or heal a wounded and shaken mind.' Wilde concludes with the most pathetic paean he ever penned to books: 'Horrible,' he says, 'as all the physical privations of modern prison life are, they are as nothing compared to the entire privation of literature to one to whom Literature was once the first thing of life, the mode by which perfection could be realised, by which, and by which alone, the intellect could feel itself alive.'[17]

The Prison Commission responded by instructing the new governor to provide Wilde with 'foolscap paper, ink and pen, for use in his leisure moments in his cell' (in the event, he was given a notebook). It told Nelson to ascertain whether Wilde had indeed read all the books available to him; if that was the case, then he could ask the prisoner to request further titles. In addition, the Commission instructed the governor to 'use his discretion' with regard to the number of books Wilde was issued per week.[18] In his reply Nelson said that while Wilde had not actually read '*all* the books in the prison library', he had perused all those titles 'he considered worth reading'. He also enclosed a list of books for which the prisoner 'would be extremely grateful'.[19]

This list contains over twenty titles, written out in Wilde's neatest hand (see plate 13). Some of his requests, such as a novel by the French Decadent author Huysmans, have been crossed out by Nelson, perhaps because of their controversial nature. Ernest Renan's heterodox *Life of Jesus* and his *Apostles* were allowed to remain, but only if they were purchased in original French-language editions, presumably to ensure that none of the other prisoners could read them. Some of Nelson's excisions may be due to the fact that he was limited to a budget of £10, the annual amount allocated to prison book purchases. It is, however, highly likely that Wilde's friends paid for at least some of the books. (The full list of titles appears in Appendix II b., pp. 319–20).

When the new books began to arrive Nelson took one of them round to cell C.3.3. Entering the room, he cheerfully announced, 'the Home Secretary says you are to have books.' Holding out the volume he had brought with him, he said, 'here is one you may like, I have just been reading it myself.' Wilde was so overwhelmed by the governor's kindness that he broke down and wept. 'Those,' he told him, 'are the first kind words that have been spoken to me since I have been in [Reading] gaol.'[20]

This was just one of the many ways in which Nelson 'used his discretion' when applying the regulations in Wilde's case. The prisoner was allowed to retain up to perhaps a score of volumes permanently in his cell, which assumed the appearance of a small library.[21] He was also granted the extraordinary privilege of keeping his gas jet lights on all night so that he might read for as long as he wished.[22]

Yet despite these blessings, Wilde's suicidal depression is still palpable in the piteous appeal for an early release he wrote to the Home Secretary on 10 November 1896. He thanked the Prison Commission for having added his book requests to the prison library, but said that even 'these alleviations, for which the prisoner is naturally very grateful, count for but little in relieving the terrible mental stress and anguish that the silence and solitude of prison-life intensify daily'.[23]

Wilde's plea for an early discharge was not granted, but he was permitted to order more books, provided they were paid for by his friends. The Commission's decision was probably prompted by Nelson, who informed them that Wilde had 'read and re-read all the books' that 'were specially supplied for him'.[24] Once again, Wilde drew up a list of titles, which More Adey then purchased and dispatched to Reading. (The catalogue is reproduced in Appendix II c., p. 320.)

One final consignment of books was sent to Wilde before his release. He appears to have broached the idea of compiling a further list of requests during an interview with Adey in January 1897.[25] A little while later Adey wrote out the catalogue, which he submitted for Haldane's approval at the end of the month. This was duly granted, along with Major Nelson's consent, once again with the proviso that Wilde's friends supply the books.[26] Wilde probably made numerous revisions to Adey's list, because it had to be sent a second time to the

Home Office and to Nelson for their authorisation. (The amended list can be seen in Appendix II d., pp. 320–1.) The only item Nelson objected to was an issue of the periodical the *Nineteenth Century* that contained an article on the prison system 'with which,' he said, 'it is not desirable the prisoner should be acquainted'.[27]

34. 'The greatest consolation'

PRISONERS TYPICALLY RETURN, in their imagination, to the past: 'we have', Wilde commented, 'nothing else to think of'.[1] Some seek in it relief from the tyranny of the motionless present, which Wilde compared to 'one long moment of suffering', drawing comfort from their store of recollections. Others turn to it in an attempt to understand what has brought them to the prison gates.

It was probably for these reasons – and also because new readerly challenges may have seemed too daunting – that Wilde travelled back in time through his prison reading. Many of the titles on his request lists had been familiar to him from his youth, their pages redolent with memories. When he took up his Liddell and Scott's *Greek Lexicon* and his Greek Testament, they may have reminded him of the copies of the same titles that had once stood in his father's library. The volumes of Tennyson, Keats, Chaucer, Spenser, Wordsworth, Arnold, John Dryden, Malory and Robert Burns that Wilde read in prison would likewise have taken him back to Merrion Square, where his mother's poetry collection had doubtless contained them all.

Wilde could also return to the past with the help of the vast library he carried around with him in his head. During exercise in the prison yard he paced around 'with bended head . . . usually muttering snatches of prose or verse from his favourite authors'.[2] In 'his lonely cell', too, 'night after night', he would pass the wakeful hours continually talking to himself, as though 'laughing to imaginary visitors'.[3] Perhaps he was acting out scenes from plays, or passages of dramatic verse.

And, when Wilde intoned poetry, did he hear an echo of the voice that had first recited verse to him? Many of the phrases Speranza had quoted to her boy certainly came back to him in prison. He recalled, in particular, four lines from Goethe, translated by Carlyle, which his deceased mother had loved to chant:

> Who never ate his bread in sorrow,
>   Who never spent his midnight hours
> Weeping and wailing for the morrow,
>   He knows you not, ye Heavenly powers.

As a youth Wilde declined to 'admit the enormous truth hidden' in the quatrain. Now, however, he drew consolation from it.[4]

The works of classical literature and the commentaries on ancient culture Wilde read in prison would have reminded him of Trinity and Oxford. His requests suggest that, along with his Dublin childhood, it was to his 'flower-like' time as an Oxonian that he most devoutly wished to return (he ordered the works of a number of authors, such as Newman and Pater, whom he had read there). It is possible that he trod the backward path to Oxford in order to return to his intellectual point of departure. Having reached it, he hoped to set forth again on a new adventure.

As well as evoking memories of the past, the books Wilde requested helped him make sense of it. When he opened *Poetae Scenici Graeci*, the gargantuan folio volume containing the surviving body of Greek poetry and drama, he re-read a passage in the *Agamemnon* and discovered in it a key to his personal history. It appears in a speech of the Chorus concerning Helen of Troy. The beautiful Helen was the cause of the war described in Homer's *Iliad*, fought by the Greeks in order to recover her from the Trojans.

In the passage Aeschylus compares Helen to a charming lion's whelp who is welcomed into the house of a generous lord and nurtured there with loving indulgence. In its infancy, the whelp returns the lord's love, but when it grows into a lion it reveals the fierce nature of its race, turning on its master and devouring his children. So too would Helen, now pampered at Troy, where Prince Paris had sequestered her after stealing her away from the Greek noble Menelaus, one day prove to be the agent of the city's destruction. As an undergraduate, Wilde had been irresistibly drawn to these lines. In an Oxford essay he paraphrases and then praises them as 'the highest triumph of Greek genius'.[5] Now, as he sat in his prison cell at Reading, he realised that they had a striking autobiographical resonance.

In the early 1890s, Wilde had metaphorically, and literally, invited into his house and spoilt Alfred Douglas. Bosie had been the god of Wilde's romantic idolatry; he had also, or so Wilde now came to believe, been one of the instruments of his downfall. 'In the most wonderful of all his plays,' Wilde wrote to Douglas from prison, 'Aeschylus tells us of the great Lord who brings up in his house the lion-cub . . . And the thing grows up . . . and destroys the lord and his house . . . I feel that I was such a one as he.'[6]*

Such reflections prompted Wilde, during the first year of his sentence, to turn violently against his former 'dearest of all boys'. He never regretted the homosexual nature of his relationship with

---

* This is yet another case of Wilde's life imitating art. It is also an example of the way in which time seems to bend in his biography. In his youth, he was fascinated by a passage in a play; later he came to realise that it had been an omen – not unlike the ones that appear throughout Aeschylus' works. Could it be that he was unconsciously drawn to the lines as an undergraduate, precisely because they were premonitory?

Douglas, but during his imprisonment he came to the conclusion that the life of 'studied materialism' and 'sensual excess' he had shared with Bosie had been 'unworthy' of him both as a man and as an artist. He also attributed much of the blame for his incarceration to Douglas, who had urged him to take legal action against his father.

Wilde also turned to literature to make sense of the present. Dante's *Divina commedia*, above all other books, helped him understand the hideous world of the prison. Wilde read the famous account of the poet's visionary journey through Hell, Purgatory and Heaven in the original medieval Italian, with the aid of a prose translation and various commentaries, and an Italian grammar and dictionary.

On his odyssey, the Florentine poet, guided first by the Latin author Virgil and then by his Platonic love Beatrice, travels up through the circles of the different dimensions of the afterlife, interviewing, on his way, the souls who dwell there. In the *Inferno*, the spirits he encounters are plagued by terrible tortures: the carnal are caught up in ceaseless winds, the gluttons are lashed by the rain, and the heretics rend their own flesh. The souls that live forever in Paradise bask in the glory of God.

Wilde's sufferings in prison were heightened by the monotonous simplicity of his surroundings. It was this, together with its ultra-rational uniformity, that made life in jail so inhuman and so impossible to describe. Describing a prison was, Wilde said, 'as difficult as describing a water-closet . . . one could merely say that it was well, or badly, papered: or clean or the reverse: the horror of prison is that everything is so simple.'[7] Words could get no purchase on the spartan world of the prison; nor could emotions or ideas. This opened up a chasm between the inmates' tragic feelings and the banal character of the environment around them: 'everything is so commonplace', as Wilde put it, yet 'so degrading, and hideous' and so 'revolting in its effect'.[8] In consequence, realistic descriptions were completely inadequate to the task of evoking prison life – how could an objective account convey the horror and anguish that ate away at the convict's soul?

Yet where realism failed, fantastic and visionary literature could succeed, as Wilde discovered when he opened one of the books in the *Divina commedia*. 'Dante!' he remarked after his release, 'I read Dante every day in the Italian, every page of him; neither the *Purgatory* nor the *Paradise* was intended for me . . . But the *Inferno*! What else was I to do but adore it? Hell – were we not dwelling in it? Hell: that was the prison.'[9]

Wilde was familiar with the author he hailed as 'the supreme modern poet' long before his incarceration.[10] With characteristic disdain for historical facts, his mother had actually claimed descent from Dante. Wilde had referred frequently to the Florentine poet in his youthful verse and his Tite Street library contained an English translation of the *Divina commedia* with John Flaxman's sinuous black and white illustrations.

During his 1882 lecture tour of America Wilde had visited a jail in Nebraska. There he found a prisoner engrossed in the pages of Dante's masterpiece. 'Strange and beautiful,' he commented afterwards, 'that the sorrow of a single Florentine should, hundreds of years afterwards, lighten the sorrow of some common prisoner in a modern gaol.'[11] Now that he himself languished in prison, he recalled the portentous incident. He told More Adey that he finally understood how Dante could have charmed the American convict because the Italian poet 'was the greatest consolation that he had.'[12]

The *Inferno* articulated for Wilde the full horror of his experience, conferring significant form on the hell that was prison life. It was one of those great works that used imaginative and poetic 'lies', and visionary fantasies, to tell a truth that realistic literature could not even begin to hint at. As a man who always came to life through books, Wilde had to place his sufferings in a literary context — to fashion and to fix them with burning poetic words. The *Divina commedia* offered Wilde the script that he required in order to understand and to survive his sentence.

When Wilde came to describe prison life, and his own experience, he frequently alluded to Dante's poem. He compared the suicidal despair he had felt at Wandsworth to that of certain characters in the *Inferno* who succumbed to the sin of wilful sadness.[13] Yet, in some respects, the prison world was so appalling that not even Dante's words could adequately express it. Next to a Victorian jail, indeed, some aspects of the Florentine's hell seemed positively congenial. In the *Inferno*, as Wilde remarked, 'people could [at least] move about, could see each other, and hear each other groan. There was *some* human companionship.'[14]

After his release Wilde often acknowledged his enormous debt to Dante. He told one acquaintance that the Florentine had 'saved' his 'reason';[15] to another he vividly evoked the pleasure that he had derived from the *Divina commedia*. 'You can imagine,' he said, 'how I tasted every word.'[16] Of all the figurative comparisons Wilde made between food and literature this is the most poignant, for what else was there to taste in prison but words?

35. 'Words of grace'

AFTER SERVING THE first year of his sentence, Wilde's thoughts increasingly turned from the past to the present, and to the world beyond the prison gates. While the list of requests he drew up in June 1895 is comprised exclusively of old favourites and literary classics, the lists written after July 1896 contain many recently published titles such as Stevenson's and Rossetti's letters, and new novels by Huysmans, Meredith and Thomas Hardy. From the summer of 1896, Wilde clearly wished to catch up on all the latest literary gossip and to keep abreast of fresh artistic developments.

The return of Wilde's curiosity concerning his contemporaries probably indicates an improvement in his spirits. Their works, in turn, further lightened his mood and inspired letters composed in his old witty vein. 'Stevenson['s] letters most disappointing . . .' he wrote to Robbie Ross. 'I see that romantic surroundings are the worst surroundings possible for a romantic writer. In Gower Street Stevenson could have written a new [*Three Musketeers*]. In Samoa he wrote letters to *The Times* about Germans.'[1]

Wilde's reawakened interest suggests that he was gradually starting to think of himself again as part of the outside world and slowly preparing for his return to it. He made himself ready by reading the numerous contraband newspapers and periodicals that his warder friends smuggled into his cell. Previously, Wilde had devoured newspapers, throwing them down after a couple of minutes with a sigh of dissatisfaction and mild disgust. Now, in his cell, he pored over their pages, hungrily eating up every crumb of information.

Towards the end of his sentence, Wilde looked towards the future. From around December 1896, he evidently began to believe that some sort of future awaited him on the continent, because he embarked on the study of a number of European languages. This represents a significant sea change in his mood: previously he had doubted whether he would live to see the day of his release.

His list of requests for December 1896 includes a number of German and Italian language study books. Wilde had always been sardonic about German: in *Earnest* Lady Bracknell describes it as a 'thoroughly respectable language', while Cecily Cardew calls it 'horrid'. Wilde had visited Germany in 1889 partly, or so he joked, because he 'thought it would be a superb opportunity for forgetting the language'.[2] Even during his imprisonment Wilde managed to make jokes about German, remarking that jail was the 'proper place' to study it.[3]

Wilde seems to have been fonder of Italian. He probably learned as much from Dante as he did from the grammar books he consulted as he later described his Italian conversation as an 'astonishing . . . mixture of Dante [and] the worst modern slang'.[4] One of the didactic manuals he studied was Biaggi's *Practical Guide to the Italian Language*, which contains a translation exercise that might have amused him. The student is asked to render Dickens's account of the death of Little Nell into simple Italian – presumably without laughing. Wilde also ordered a French–Italian conversation book and, in the list of requests compiled at the end of his sentence, he asked for a Spanish grammar.[5] He probably envisaged a semi-nomadic existence for himself on the continent after his liberation. There was, he would have realised, no place for a pariah such as himself in what he later referred to as the 'God-forsaken' and 'sea-lashed' isle of England.[6]

Wilde also began to see a future for himself as a writer. On the eve of his release he requested a number religious titles, in part because he contemplated writing an essay on Christ. Wilde outlined his vision of Jesus in the religious and philosophical passages of the long auto-biographical letter he wrote to Alfred Douglas at Reading, which has become known as *De Profundis* (1905).*

Wilde composed the epistle, on twenty folio sheets of blue ruled prison paper, between December 1896 and March 1897, at night, by gaslight in his cell. He used his plank bed as a table – 'it was,' he remarked, 'a very good table, too.'[8] Wilde was extremely grateful for the opportunity to write at all, a privilege forbidden to Victorian convicts. Under Nelson's benign regime he was permitted to keep writing materials permanently in his cell.

The composition of *De Profundis* grew directly out of Wilde's prison reading. If his copy of Pater's *Imaginary Portraits* is anything to go by, its genesis can be traced back to the marginalia he began, perhaps with Nelson's permission, to write in books. From the passages he marked, he doubtless selected significant excerpts to transcribe into the notebook he had been given in the summer of 1896. 'The brain,' Wilde said, 'loses its life . . . becomes fettered to the monotony of suffering [so] I take notes of the books I read, and copy lines and phrases in poets . . . I cling to my notebook: it helps me: before I had it my brain was moving in very evil circles.'[9]

* Around two-thirds of the letter is comprised of Wilde's account of his relationship with his lover, and constitutes a fierce diatribe against Douglas. The remainder consists of Wilde's reflections on moral and literary matters. Although ostensibly a private communication addressed to Bosie, Wilde wanted his other friends to have access to the letter, and particularly to those passages dealing with general philosophical matters. It is also clear that Wilde wrote it with posthumous publication in mind, though he apparently failed to specify exactly which parts of the letter he intended to be published.[7]

As well as being therapeutic, note-taking inspired in Wilde those literary stirrings that would eventually find expression in *De Profundis*. The mere handling of pen and ink, the immersion in ideas, the opportunity to luxuriate once again in language, awoke his creative powers. A number of the quotations Wilde garnered in his notebook were probably used in his long letter, which is striated with echoes, allusions and citations from his prison reading. Old writerly habits die hard, and the author of the heartfelt autobiographical epistle was still a beast who fed off books.

'Every morning,' Wilde wrote in *De Profundis*, 'after I have cleaned my cell and polished my tins, I read a little of the Gospels, a dozen verses taken by chance anywhere. It is a delightful way of opening the day.'[10] Wilde's reading of the 'four prose poems about Christ', in his Greek Testament, inspired the reflections on Jesus' personality that appear in his long prison letter.

Wilde's interpretation of Christ is predictably heterodox: Jesus wanders across the pages of *De Profundis* uttering sublime paradoxes and parables, like some latter-day Socrates, and preaches a humane and utterly human message of tolerance, sympathy and self-realisation. Yet, like many more orthodox Christians, Wilde also turned to Jesus' life when he tried to invest his own appalling sufferings with significance. Towards the end of his prison letter he reached the conclusion that 'Nothing in the whole world is meaningless, and suffering least of all', and it was Jesus, the 'eternal mouthpiece' of 'the inarticulate, the voiceless world of pain', who led him to it.[11]

Books offered Wilde spiritual guidance. They were also full of 'words of grace', to use his vivid phrase, in another sense.[12] The convict was confined within a present time that was monolithic and two-dimensional, and which stultified the mind. 'Thought', in Wilde's words, 'to those that sit alone and silent and in bonds', is 'no "winged

living thing" as Plato feigned it, but a thing dead'.[13] Yet over the
course of his prison sentence, books loosened the bonds that shackled
Wilde's mind.

A little while before his release he triumphantly declared that
'Time and space . . . are merely accidental conditions of Thought.
The Imagination can transcend them, and move in a free sphere of
ideal existences.'[14] This represents the hard-fought victory of a
spirit and an artistic temperament so indomitable that even the
torture of the Separate System could not break them. It was a
battle that the prisoner played out and won in the margins of his
books. The markings in Wilde's copy of Pater's *Imaginary Portraits*
convey something of the wildly oscillating moods of despondency
and hope he experienced during his struggle. Although on page 111 he
annotated the terrible word 'silence'– a word redolent of the hideous
world of the prison – by the end of the book he was soaring away
from the prison on the wings of Pater's words, marking, on page 170,
the following marvellous sentence: 'Surely, past ages, could one get at
the historic soul of them, were not dead, but living, rich in company
for the entertainment, the expansion of the present.'[15] How apt the
phrase 'the expansion of the present' seems – it was exactly the effect
Pater's book must have had for Wilde.

'When I read Walter Pater,' Wilde remarked of one of the volumes
that had been sent to him, 'I shall have two friends to think of' – the
author, and the person who donated it. In that instance, the generous
benefactor was Arthur Humphreys, to whom Wilde wrote after his
release: 'The knowledge that many . . . books were a gift from a good
fellow such as yourself, made me touch and handle them with as much
pleasure as though they had been, each of them, the hand of a friend:
indeed each of them *was* to me the hand of a friend, and lifted me

from the mire of despair and pain where I had, for a whole year, been lying.'[16]

Always an eminently gregarious reader, Wilde contrived to enjoy the social aspect of books even during his confinement. In letters to acquaintances he wrote wittily about literature; he talked books whenever he could with the friendlier warders. When one asked him if Marie Corelli, the late nineteenth-century queen of popular sentimental trash, 'could be considered a great writer?' it was more than Wilde could stand. 'Now don't think I've got anything against her *moral* character,' he remarked, 'but from the way she writes *she ought to be here*'; 'You say so, Sir,' was the warder's bewildered response, 'you say so.'[17]

Wilde discussed literature whenever he could with his fellow inmates. As schoolmaster's orderly, he recommended titles to them from the prison library; he also sent them clandestine notes that touched on literary matters. 'Have had a very good Sunday,' he writes in one of these, 'reading Goethe's *Faust*, a very great work of art.'[18] Wilde evidently believed that great writing was accessible to the uneducated working-class prisoners who were now his peers, and that, in Ruskin's words, the society of books is, or ought to be, classless.

When Wilde compiled his lists of book requests, he bore the other inmates in mind. All the titles sent to him (at least before Nelson's arrival at Reading) were deposited in the prison library and became immediately accessible to the other prisoners. Wilde was aware of this. On one list he wrote 'The library here contains no example of any of . . . Dickens's novels. I feel sure that a complete set of [his] works would be as great a boon to many amongst the other prisoners, as it certainly would be to myself.'[19]

A similar motivation prompted Wilde to ask for Stevenson's *Treasure Island*. Six weeks after his friends sent it to the library, he was gratified to learn that it was 'in great request and much appreciated' by the other prisoners.[20] Encouraged by the enthusiasm of the inmates, Wilde asked for more Stevenson, along with volumes by Walter Scott and H.G. Wells.[21] He intended, on regaining his liberty, to present the prison library with a further 'dozen good novels' by the likes of Jane Austen and Thackeray.[22] As Wilde sent money after his release to all of his 'great friends in Reading' ('*my* pals', he called them, 'hearts of gold')[23] it is possible that he carried out this charitable plan.

Wilde was forbidden to take his books with him on his discharge: they were, as he put it, 'sentenced to perpetual imprisonment' in the library. Not that he complained about this. On the contrary, it cheered him to think that the books might 'soothe and heal other troubled minds and breaking hearts'.[24] Wilde knew, of course, from personal experience what an 'anodyne from pain' books could provide.[25] 'Passionately,' he later reflected, 'as I loved literature from boyhood. I had no idea that some day that one supreme art would save both mental and physical life for me.'[26]

36. 'Dazed with the wonder'

ON THE AFTERNOON of 18 May 1897, Wilde left Reading gaol for Pentonville, the prison from which he would be released at dawn on the following morning. In the company of two warders he took a cab from Reading to Twyford station where he waited on the platform for the London train. He was overwhelmed there by the sight of a blossoming laburnum tree – the first he had seen in two years. Opening his arms to its yellow petals, he exclaimed, 'Oh beautiful world! Oh beautiful world!' The warders, anxious that the prisoner should remain incognito, begged him to be quiet. 'Now, Mr Wilde,' one of them admonished, 'you mustn't give yourself away. You're the only man in England who would talk like that in a railway station.'[1]

In *De Profundis*, Wilde had eagerly anticipated the prospect of reading and owning 'beautiful books' on regaining his liberty: 'what joy,' he asked, 'could be greater?'[2] For that reason, along with his horror of 'going out into the world without a single book', he once more turned, on the eve of his release, to his faithful friends, asking them to purchase for him a library of choice volumes. He sent Robbie Ross, now installed as his literary executor as well as his all-round Sancho Panza, a list of specific requests (reproduced in Appendix II e., pp. 320–1) and invited him to add to it other titles by 'Flaubert, Stevenson, Baudelaire, Maeterlinck, Dumas *père*, Keats, Marlowe, Chatterton, Coleridge, Anatole France, Gautier, Dante (and all Dante literature); Goethe (and ditto) . . . you know the sort of books I want'.[3]

Wilde told Robbie that he would regard it as 'a great compliment' if his friends clubbed together to buy him the volumes. The little library would be a symbol of their solidarity as well as a collection of golden books.[4] Once again friends such as Ross, Humphreys, Adey, Beerbohm, and the journalist and wit Reginald Turner (whom Wilde described as 'wonderful . . . purple and perfect'), responded to his appeal with generosity. Adela Schuster, a society hostess who had assisted Wilde financially during his trials, and whom he described as 'one of the most beautiful personalities I have ever known', sent him over ten volumes.[5]

At dawn on the morning of 19 May the gate of Pentonville prison opened and Wilde stepped out into the Caledonian Road. Before he was discharged, his personal possessions were returned, and among them he would have found the volume that had been sent to him by the anonymous Irish well-wisher.[6] And so Wilde's imprisonment ended, just as it had begun on the night of his arrest, with a book.

Outside the prison, Adey and Stewart Headlam, the socialist author and defrocked vicar who had stumped up part of Wilde's bail in 1895, awaited him in a cab. As soon as they sped off down the hill towards King's Cross Wilde started talking books. 'He was eager to talk about Dante,' Headlam said, 'and insisted on writing down for me the best way to study him and the best books to read.'[7] The cab carried them to Headlam's house in Upper Bedford Place, Bloomsbury, where a number of Wilde's intimates awaited him, the Sphinx among them. After washing and changing, Wilde talked and laughed the morning away in their company. 'The dear Governor . . . and his wife,' he told them, 'asked me to spend the summer with them . . . Unusual, I think? But I don't feel I can. I feel I want a change of scene.'[8]

Wilde planned to take a cab to Croydon and then go on, by train, to Newhaven. There he would board the steamer for Dieppe, which he had settled on as a suitable place for his residence. He could not, however, resist the temptation of stopping off at Hatchard's bookshop on his way. He wanted to make a few quick purchases, his very last on English soil; he may also have wished to see the shop's manager, Arthur Humphreys. The visit turned out to be a poignant epilogue to Wilde's English career as a reader and book collector. To his distress, someone in the shop recognised him and pointed him out to a number of the other customers.[9]

Wilde crossed the Channel by the overnight boat. At 4.30 on the following morning he arrived at Dieppe harbour where Robbie Ross and Reginald Turner awaited him. They had engaged a room for Wilde at the Hôtel Sandwich, under his new pseudonym, Sebastian Melmoth, which combined the first name of the Christian martyr whose iconography he adored with the surname of the hero of *Melmoth the Wanderer*. 'In his room,' Turner informed his friend Max Beerbohm, 'we have put a lot of flowers. All the books we have collected are on the mantelpiece, and your own two works are in the centre to catch his eye.'[10]

When he greeted his friends at the port, Wilde was in childish high spirits; it was only on entering the hotel room, full of beautiful books and flowers, that he broke down and wept.[11] His distress was short-lived, however. Throughout the following day he regaled his two friends with witty anecdotes about life in Reading Gaol, which had already become, in his imagination, 'a sort of enchanted castle of which Major Nelson was the presiding fairy'.[12]

A few days later Wilde and his friends visited Berneval-sur-Mer, a little coastal village west of Dieppe, and decided that it would be the ideal place for him to live. Wilde would pass the summer of 1897 there swimming, sunbathing and enjoying the company of the locals. Gradually he reacclimatised himself to freedom and to the natural world, which, at first, overwhelmed him with its splendour. 'I cannot write much,' he confessed, 'for I am nervous – dazed with the wonder of the wonderful world: I feel as if I had been raised from the dead. The sun and the sea seem strange to me.'[13]

During his first few weeks at Berneval Wilde took rooms in the Hôtel de la Plage, after which he rented the two-storey Chalet Bourgeat.[14] He set out his little library in his new home, and visitors remarked on the profusion of books throughout the rooms.[15] Much of his summer was spent reading in the chalet or in the long grass on Berneval's chalk cliffs, or on its brilliant white stony beach.

Wilde greatly enjoyed the volumes Max Beerbohm had donated to his store. Among these were the 'inimitable' Max's novel *The Happy Hypocrite* and *Works*, a collection of witty essays, both of which displayed Wilde's marked influence on Beerbohm's prose. 'I cannot tell you,' Wilde thanked him, 'what a real pleasure it was . . . to find your delightful present for me.'[16]

Reginald Turner sent Wilde a number of volumes including a guidebook to Berkshire, which doubtless included references to Reading Gaol, widely regarded as the architectural jewel of the town. Turner must have bought it as a joke – the joke being that Wilde could consult it whenever he pined for jail. 'Thank you so much for the charming books,' the recipient wrote with heavy irony: 'the guidebook to Berkshire is very lax in style, and it is difficult to realise that it is constructed on any metrical system. The matter, however, is interesting, and the whole book no doubt symbolic.'[17]

An old friend of Wilde's parents, the Irish poet Aubrey de Vere, showed his support by giving Wilde a copy of Volume V of his *Poetical Works*.[18] Expressions of solidarity came from other Irish quarters – Shaw sent the books he had written since Wilde's imprisonment.[19]

The Hôtel de la Plage, Berneval.

A host of French men of letters presented Wilde with books. André Gide's novel *Les Nourritures terrestres* [The Fruits of the Earth],[20] which contains many passages that were directly inspired by Wilde's conversation, found its way to Berneval via an acquaintance. Wilde found the book self-indulgent; he did not think Gide's personality sufficiently interesting to justify his navel-gazing. '*To be an Egoist,*' he remarked dryly to a friend apropos of the book, '*one must have an Ego*'.[21] To the author himself Wilde offered the following advice: 'dear, promise me . . . never to write *I* anymore. In art, don't you see, there is no first person.'[22]

Wilde's library of French literature was augmented by Henry Davray, 'a charming fellow' and a 'good English [Literature] scholar', who would later translate some of Wilde's writings into French.[23] Davray collected a number of volumes of contemporary literature for Wilde, all of which had been inscribed to him by their authors. Wilde was overjoyed at receiving the books: 'I am greatly touched,' he said, 'by the sympathy and attention shown to me by you and other French writers. I hope to thank each of the authors individually.'[24] These gifts demonstrated to Wilde that the French continued to regard him as an artist, and not simply as a notorious ex-convict. That was his reputation in England, where many libraries and shops boycotted his books.

Some English authors were, however, extremely sympathetic. Along with Beerbohm's offerings, Wilde received the *Verses* of Ernest Dowson, perhaps the greatest volume of English lyric poetry of the 1890s.[25] Wilde was impressed by the work of the 'sweet singer', a resident of the nearby village, Arques, who, he said, wrote 'words with wings'. He was equally drawn to Dowson's 'persistently and perversely wonderful' (if occasionally morose) personality.[26] They drank and talked away several mornings and evenings together and, after one session, legend has it that the poet took Wilde to a Dieppe brothel, where he had sex with a woman for the first time in years. 'Tell it in England,' Wilde is reported to have said of the incident, 'where it will entirely restore my reputation.'[27]

The most momentous English book Wilde received over the summer was Alfred Douglas's *Poems*, which the author sent along with numerous volumes by other authors.[28] Bosie had spectacularly fallen out of Wilde's favour during his imprisonment. Yet, typically, although their rift was dramatic, it also proved to be short-lived. A week after his release Wilde was again addressing Douglas as 'My dearest Boy'; by the end of the month 'dearest' had blossomed into 'darling'.

Wilde's darling boy, who was desperate to get back into his lover's good books, dispatched a copy of his verse collection as a peace offering at the start of June. It was one of an edition of only thirty copies, printed on Dutch hand-made paper.[29] Wilde's copy of *Poems* is in a far from immaculate condition, so it was probably well thumbed by him, even though he was already familiar with the bulk of its contents, which had been composed before his trials.

As a poetry reader, Wilde typically focused on the stylistic and technical qualities of verse, but he found it difficult to ignore the biographical resonances in *Poems*. The verses are littered with sobriquets such as Narcissus, Jonquil and Fleur-de-Lys, which Wilde had, in happier days, conferred on his lover. The volume includes Bosie's famous poem 'Two Loves' and verses such as 'Amoris Vincula', which alludes to Wilde's incarceration. And then there is the blank dedication page. Just before the volume's publication in 1896, Wilde had discovered, via a friend who visited him in Reading, that Bosie intended to dedicate *Poems* to him. At the time, full of venom towards his former lover, Wilde thought the idea revolting, and vetoed it.

These intimate biographical associations diminished *Poems* as a work of art in Wilde's eyes. He also objected to its occasionally forthright tone. 'Of course,' Wilde commented, alluding to the social ostracism Bosie had suffered because of his association with his imprisoned lover, 'your . . . personality has had . . . to express itself *directly* . . . but I hope you will go on to forms more remote from actual events and passions. One can really, as I say in *Intentions*, be far more subjective in an *objective* form than in any other way.'[30]

Over the course of the summer, Wilde's friends continued to supply him with books. They were, he said, especially welcome to him because 'Dieppe, like all provincial towns in France, not merely has no books, but does not know in what garden those yellow flowers grow'.[31] Wilde was not the only one who bemoaned the dearth of books in the town: the customs officials at the harbour were also bored for want of decent literature. Wilde remedied the situation by passing on to them his copies of the elder Dumas's novels after he had read them.[32]

Wilde was particularly touched by the munificence of Leonard Smithers, who sent him a 'prize-packet' of books.[33] The redoubtable publisher became a regular drinking partner of Wilde's in August, and the pair could often be seen wandering around Dieppe with 'monsters to the sound of music', as Wilde put it, and wearing 'vine-leaves' in their hair (Wilde's phrase, borrowed from Ibsen's play *Hedda Gabler*, for intoxication). Wilde described Smithers as 'quite wonderful and depraved' and as a 'delightful companion, and a dear fellow, very kind to me'.[34]

As well as becoming friends, the pair formed a literary alliance which would bear fruit in the publication of Wilde's last three books – *The Ballad of Reading Gaol, Earnest* and *An Ideal Husband* – all of which Smithers courageously brought out, between 1898 and 1899, when no other publisher would touch them. The publisher's gift to Wilde probably included a number of titles that he himself had recently issued, such as Beerbohm's *Caricatures of Twenty-Five Gentlemen* and Dowson's playlet *The Pierrot of the Minute*[35] which had been beautifully illustrated by Aubrey Beardsley.

37. 'Infamous Saint Oscar'

FTER HIS RELEASE Wilde picked up a volume of Baudelaire's letters only to abandon it half-way through. He found the poet's correspondence 'unpleasant': it was, he complained, 'all about publishers and money'.[1] Wilde had probably experienced more than his fill of the tedious and the mundane in prison. His Berneval reading, with its emphasis on poetry and fantasy, suggests a desire to escape from the commonplace and the realistic to the shores of old Romance.

Wilde had a particular craving for that fantastic masterpiece, *The Temptation of St Anthony*. Flaubert's youthful production vividly evokes the psychedelic visions of the hermit saint, and his bizarre conversations with a number of historical and mythical figures. It is closer to a prose poem, or indeed to a film script, than it is to a conventional novel. The book was an integral part of Wilde's post-prison plans. He placed it at the top of the list of requests he drew up a month before his release; around the same time, he told a friend that he hoped to rent a little apartment, for the coming summer, in 'some French or Belgian town, with some books about him, of course Flaubert's *Temptation of Saint Anthony* among them'.[2] At Berneval Wilde also renewed his acquaintance with many other old literary friends.[3] Baudelaire's *Fleurs du Mal* had been a golden book of his youth, as had Maeterlinck's *Plays*.

Some of the titles Wilde read suggest that he wanted to prepare himself, through his reading, for the role of the saint or outcast. His pseudonym, Sebastian Melmoth, captures the dual elements of this new persona and testifies once more to his desire to turn his life into an imitation of literature. W.B. Yeats's short story collection *The Secret Rose*[4] contains 'The Crucifixion of the Outcast', a tale in which a Bard of the olden times is martyred. Wilde also perused various mystical books, and a number of biographies of St Francis. Wilde had always revered the saint of Assisi: 'With the soul of a poet,' he commented, 'and the body of a beggar he found the way to perfection.' The life of St Francis was for him 'the true [*Imitation of Christ*]: a poem compared to which the book that bears that name is merely prose'.[5] On his release, Wilde identified the saint as his role model: 'My path is now that of Saint Francis,'[6] he told a friend, with all the sincerity of an actor entirely, albeit only momentarily, absorbed in his role. With greater irony and considerably more accuracy, he referred to himself as the 'Infamous Saint Oscar of Oxford, Poet and Martyr'.[7]

Wilde hoped his books would reawaken an imaginative faculty that the prison system had tried to paralyse, and inspire in him 'literary (i.e. creative) longings'.[8] He had in mind a play about Pharaoh and Moses, and he would dazzle friends by outlining its plot and evoking its scenes. 'The King is marvellous,' he would say, 'when he cries to Moses, "Praise be to thy God, O prophet, for He has slain my only enemy, my son!"'[9] In order to put it down in black on white, he required, he said, 'books about Egypt, full of the names of beautiful things, rare and curious meat for the feast'.[10] This is why, on the eve of his release, he had asked his friends to purchase Flinders Petrie's *Egyptian Decorative Art*[11] for him and any 'good book on Ancient Egypt'.

Wilde probably requested *Thaïs*,[12] the novel of his acquaintance Anatole France, for similar reasons. He intended to return to his 'beautiful, coloured, musical' drama 'La Sainte Courtesane', which he had left unfinished in 1893. Wilde's play is set in the African desert soon after Christ's death, and features a hermit and a courtesan. It draws heavily on *Thäis* and on Flaubert's *Temptation*, for both its subject and style. In prison the courtesan had, Wilde said, occasionally whispered 'wonderful things' in his ear; now he was determined to write her words down. France's novel would serve him as a model and help him re-enter the imaginative world of his play.

In Reading Wilde had eagerly looked forward to taking up his writing career again. After a period of reading 'beautiful books' he would, he believed, be able to rediscover his 'creative faculty'.[13] Yet he was acutely aware of what a challenge this would be: 'the two long years of silence,' he said, 'kept my soul in bonds. [But] it will all come back, I feel sure, and then all will be well.'[14]

And come back it certainly did. At Berneval Wilde began his last original work, *The Ballad of Reading Gaol*, which recounts the execution of the murderer Charles Thomas Wooldridge, hanged in Reading during Wilde's incarceration there. The rousing 650-line composition is part poetry and part propaganda against the Separate System. It fulfilled a promise he had made to a warder friend at Reading: 'if I write any more books,' he had said, 'it will be to form a library of lamentations . . . for those who have suffered . . . I shall be a mouthpiece for the world of Pain.'[15]

The *Ballad* was written under the influence of the creative mood induced by Wilde's reading. It was also directly inspired by two poems that he had with him in his Berneval library: A.E. Housman's *A Shropshire Lad*, and Coleridge's 'The Rime of the Ancient Mariner', both of which he quarried for stylistic effects. As ever, Wilde's own distinctive ideas, images and lines, crystallised around phrases that he read.

And so Wilde spent the summer of 1897 with his head in books. They amused him, healed him, revived his desire to write, and gave him a new, and dramatically appropriate, sense of himself. The elation he had felt on his release remained with him for much of the summer, during which he was filled 'with wonder at all the beautiful things that are left to me: loyal and loving friends: good health' and 'books' – 'one of the greatest of the many worlds God has given to each man'.[16]

Yet Wilde had countless hardships to endure. At Dieppe he was frequently insulted by English tourists, and cut by some of his former friends. 'I staggered as though I had been shot,' he said of one such encounter, 'and went reeling out into the street like a drunken man.'[17] Around three months into his stay, the remoteness of Berneval began to depress him. After two years in prison, Wilde wanted more than the intermittent companionship offered him by those English friends of his who occasionally came on what he called 'pilgrimages to the sinner'. Finally, there was the weather, which became 'too British for anything' as summer turned to autumn.[18]

So it was that in September, when Alfred Douglas held out to him the offer of a home in Naples, Wilde found the temptation impossible to resist. In returning to Bosie he knew that he would alienate many of his friends, who thought a reunion would be damaging to Wilde from a legal and a social point of view. He was equally aware that he would infuriate Constance. After his release Wilde's wife had written him several cordial letters, which suggested that she had not entirely ruled out the possibility of a reconciliation. However, seeing in Douglas's company the 'only hope of again doing beautiful work', and the possibility of constant, loving, companionship, Wilde left for Naples, arranging for his books to be sent on after him by ship.[19]

38. 'There they lie'

A FTER AN INTERVAL of two and a half years, the second act of Wilde and Douglas's 'tragic romance' was played out at the Villa Giudice, in the exclusive Neapolitan quarter of Posillippo.[1] Their new home overlooked the Bay of Naples and offered superb views of Vesuvius and the islands of Ischia and Capri. It was, in every respect, the opposite of Reading Gaol: salubrious, beautiful and a paradise for the body.

Wilde's books finally arrived in November, two months after he had dispatched them from Dieppe by 'long sea'. Over the autumn and winter his collection was supplemented by an old acquaintance, Stanley Makower, who sent his novel, *The Mirror of Music*, which Wilde praised as a 'most subtle analysis of the relations between music and a soul'.[2] The book was issued by John Lane, Wilde's former publisher, who advertised his company's back catalogue at the end of the volume. Wilde, who often browsed book advertisements, would have been saddened, though hardly surprised, to find none of his own books on Lane's list.*

* With his recently acquired proficiency in Italian, it is also likely that Wilde purchased several works of Italian literature at Naples. He certainly acquired *La citta morta* [The Dead City] a play by Gabriele D'Annunzio.[3] In this rather portentous drama two modern day Italian couples visit the ruins of Argos where, according to Aeschylus's play, King Agamemnon met his bloody fate at the hands of Clytemnestra (Wilde himself had visited the site during his 1877 tour of Greece). The characters are vouchsafed terrible visions of the events that took place at Agamemnon's court, as the ancient past intermittently breaks through the fabric of the present.

Wilde struggled to put black upon white at Naples. He completed his *Ballad* there, but left his other manifold projects unfinished. Perhaps they were not even begun. The warm climate and the pagan atmosphere of the city seduced the ex-convict into a life of sensual ease. After two long years of suffering, during which the puritanical prison system had coerced him into concentrating exclusively on his mind and soul, it was perfectly natural that Wilde should now live entirely for his body. His Neapolitan days and nights were monopolised by brandy and boys.

There were other reasons for Wilde's artistic sterility. He was wearied by the continual want of money, and depressed by the impossibility of ever again winning artistic or social renown. He was often recognised and reviled at Naples, chiefly by English residents and tourists. Prison had, in any case, kicked out of Wilde the joy and the energy requisite for writing. He was now unequal to the sustained intellectual concentration, and to the sheer physical force and willpower demanded by artistic creation. 'Something is killed in me,' he admitted, 'I feel no desire to write. I am unconscious of power. Of course my first year in prison destroyed me body and soul. It could not have been otherwise.'[4]

Not that Wilde laid down his pen forever beside the Bay of Naples. He picked it up again later to revise *Earnest* and *An Ideal Husband* which had been performed, but not published, before his trials. These were issued in 1899, not under his name, for fear that no shop would stock them, but semi-anonymously, as the work of 'the author of *Lady Windermere's Fan*'. Wilde probably also returned to 'La Sainte Courtesane', only to abandon his manuscript – quite literally, by leaving a portion of it in a cab. He is reported to have laughed off the loss; a cab, he commented, was the proper place for the play.[5]

Wilde's original inventions were now reserved exclusively for his conversation, and written only on the air. His talk was as extraordinary as ever. During one wonderful flight of fancy outside a café, Wilde's listener, a journalist of his acquaintance, swore that he saw a resplendent golden angel walking towards Wilde. On closer inspection the figure seemed to be a cross between a Christian messenger and the Greek god Apollo, because in his hand he carried an enormous lyre. Having reached their table, the cherub stood for a while beside the great *seanchaí* as the marvellous words gushed out of him.[6]*

Wilde's listeners urged him to commit his tales to paper, but he demurred. 'It is enough,' he said, 'that they actually exist; that I have been able, in my own mind, to give them the form which they demand . . . if I could hope to interest others as I seem to have interested you, I would; but the world will not listen to me now.'[7]

Writing was not the only thing that presented Wilde with difficulties. Two years' hard labour had so enervated him that he now found sustained and intense periods of reading a trial. 'If I . . . read,' he said, 'a book that makes, as all fine books do, a direct claim on me, a direct appeal, an intellectual challenge of any kind, I am utterly exhausted in the evening, and often sleep badly.'[8] Wilde had always read with his body as well as his soul and now his body was no longer up to the task.

At the beginning of 1898 Wilde was forced to part from Douglas by Constance, who threatened to stop the allowance she paid him if they continued to live together. Bosie's mother assailed her son with similar financial threats. In any case, there had been the usual

---

* After a few moments the journalist realised that the figure was a hallucination: the image of a golden statue of Apollo on a nearby building had somehow been projected into the air and then refracted by the rays of the afternoon sun. Yet this did not dispel the magic of the moment and, ever after, whenever the journalist met Wilde, he always 'saw' the golden angel in his mind's eye.

theatrical ructions between the pair, and their Naples reunion probably failed to live up to their expectations. Douglas departed first, leaving Wilde alone with his library in the Villa Giudice. When the time came for Wilde to go, he left his books there. 'My friends,' he later remarked, apropos of the volumes he had been given on his release from prison, 'presented me with a box full of beautiful books – Keats, and so on. They are at Naples. There they lie'.[9]

When Wilde closed the front door of the Villa Giudice on his golden books, he was shutting tight the portal to his past and the doorway to what was, and had always been, his true home. In his youth, he had frequently moved between cities and residences, but he had always carried his books with him. Wilde was also closing the door on his future as a writer. Without the inspiration and the physical proximity of books, there was no way that an author such as he was would ever write again.

Lines from *The Tempest* come to mind. At the end of the play the half-man, half-beast, Caliban, urges his fellow conspirators to steal the books of Prospero, his tyrannical master:

> . . . Remember,
> First to posses his books; for without them
> He's but a sot, as I am, nor hath not
> One spirit to command.

39. 'Interested in others'

T HE REMAINDER OF Wilde's life would demonstrate the literal truth of Caliban's claim that a magician without a library is nothing but a 'sot'. An inveterate drinker, Wilde spent his twilight years in the cafés of Paris (where he eventually settled after leaving Naples) knocking back absinthe after absinthe as he talked of marvellous things or turned the pages of a book.

Wilde had always enjoyed combining the pleasures of the written word with wine, as the wine-splashed pages of one of his under-graduate books attest. Accounts of his final years often depict him with a glass in one hand and a volume in the other. 'He would sit for hours' in Parisian cafés, remembered one friend, 'sipping his *apéritif* and reading.'[1] Another acquaintance portrays him at a roadside café in Cannes with a copy of Virgil for company.[2] Wilde himself said, 'whenever I enter a strange town I always order [*The Temptation of Saint Anthony*] and a packet of cigarettes, and I am happy.'[3] He was even happier when there was a little drop of poison on the table next to his book.

This leisurely course of café reading, fortified by alcohol, was a new experience for Wilde. Previously he had devoured books, meta-phorically and literally, scouring the pages that moved so rapidly in front of his eyes for delicious morsels for quotation, or for phrases and images that he could use in his own writings. Speed, intensity, concentration, impatience — these are the defining qualities of his pre-prison reading. Yet now, having put aside his pen, he no longer gobbled up books, but tasted them. Rather than gulping them down in one go, he sipped them along with his *apéritif*.

Wilde's style of reading reflects a more general alteration in his attitude to the world, which he summed up during one of the many symposia he enjoyed in the company of his old friends. At a café near the Opéra in Paris, Wilde told a group of acolytes that he liked a particular work of fiction by the English writer Laurence Housman, precisely because 'a few years ago it would have interested me so much less'. 'At that time,' he said, 'I represented the symbol of my age [and] was only interested in myself. Now, in an age to which I do not belong, I find myself interested in others.'[4]

Interested in others, interested in others' books, interested, also, in other sorts of books. Wilde made many new literary discoveries at this time. He delighted in the popular novels of 'that new strange writer of things impossible in life, who writes under the name of Benjamin Swift'[5] – the pseudonym of the Scotch writer W.R. Paterson. He also read the Norwegian novelist Knut Hamsun and the English fiction writer A.W. Clarke, neither of whom he is likely to have encountered before. Wilde struck up other new bookish acquaintances during his frequent visits to Galignani's and Brentano's bookshops, where he would dawdle around the shelves. On one visit to Galignani's he was gratified to see, inside the front window, his own name blazoned on a placard advertising one of his plays.[6] He would also have glimpsed the reflection of his now rather portly frame, superimposed on the display.

At Brentano's Wilde picked up the following titles, which are itemised on a book bill that has survived.[7]

The Ambassador by John Oliver Hobbes
Beatrice Harraden and the Remittance Man by Hilda Stratford
A Child of the Jago by Arthur Morrison
March Hares by Harold Frederic

The last book bill ever made out to Wilde, from Brentano's.

The Amateur Cracksman by E.W. Hornung
Poetical Works (four volumes) by Alfred Lord Tennyson
Colonel Starbottle's Client by Bret Harte
A Protégé of Jack Hamblin by Bret Harte

Apart from Tennyson's poems and Hobbes's play, these were all recently published works of popular fiction. *The Amateur Cracksman* is a thriller that features Wilde's old haunt, the Albany in Piccadilly; *March Hares* is a historical novel that also uses London as a backdrop, and *A Child of the Jago* is a classic account of poverty in the East End. The Hilda Stratford volume, meanwhile, contains two novels with a Californian setting. The bill supports the idea that Wilde was an intrepid literary adventurer in his final years. This may have been the first time he had ever read the novelists Hilda Stratford and E.W. Hornung. Only Tennyson and Bret Harte could be described as old literary flames.*

Popular fiction no doubt offered Wilde comfort reading, and a distraction from the sorrowful mysteries of his present, in which he was perpetually pestered by pecuniary worries, and cut by erstwhile friends. It may also have diverted his attention from the joyful and glorious mysteries of his distant past, memories of which would only have highlighted the depressing circumstances in which he now lived.

Not that Wilde was averse to literary trips down memory lane: Gautier, Flaubert and Balzac were his constant companions, just as they had been in his youth. Youthful reading was indeed very much on Wilde's mind at this time: with one friend he discussed Lucien de Rubempré and Julien Sorel, his favourite boyhood characters. Wilde concluded his comments with a melancholy reflection: 'Lucien hanged himself, Julien died on the scaffold, and I died in prison.'[10]

Wilde also accepted as gifts some evocative book relics of his former days. After the 1895 auction of Wilde's goods, the dealers who snapped up his books put them on the open market, and some were secured by his friends. Wilfrid Chesson, a Tite Street neighbour, purchased from a Chelsea bookshop Wilde's bible, a copy of Shakespeare's *Sonnets* replete with his annotations, and his working copies of *Vera* and *The Duchess of Padua*, his early dramatic efforts.[11]

---

* Another author Wilde reacquainted himself with at this time was Henry James. A decade previously, Wilde had gently mocked the American novelist's efforts, remarking that he seemed to write 'fiction as if it were a painful duty'.[8] While he continued to regard James as one of those authors 'one ought to read' but was 'not bound to like', Wilde was greatly impressed by the ghost story 'The Turn of the Screw' (published in 1898). He described it as a 'most wonderful, lurid, poisonous little tale, like an Elizabethan tragedy . . . James is developing,' he added, 'but he will never arrive at passion, I fear.'[9]

In the summer of 1898 Chesson travelled to France to restore the books to their former owner. Wilde welcomed all of the titles with the exception of *Vera*, in which he would not 'profess the slightest interest'.[12] Over coffee and cigarettes in the courtyard of a café, he rewarded Chesson for his kindness by regaling him with tales, and witty snippets of literary criticism, that may have reflected his recent reading. Wilde seems to have called a truce with his old enemy, Dickens: 'There have been no such grotesques,' he said enthusiastically of the novelist's characters, 'since the Gothic gargoyles.' He also lavished praise on Kipling, supporting his candidacy for the office of Poet Laureate. It would, he commented, be 'such a change, so artistic. There was Tennyson, with his idylls, . . . his dainty muse, and here is Kipling, who makes his muse say, "Go to Hell".' Wilde was caustic, however, about the level of detail contained in Kipling's novel *Captain Courageous*, which is set partly on a schooner: 'I object,' he said, 'to know all about cod fishing.'[13]

Wilde was equally grateful when his friend, the Irish-American poet Vincent O'Sullivan, returned to him another batch of his books. Yet the sight of his old copy of G.L. Craik's two-volume *History of English Literature* among them, which had been awarded to him as a prize at Portora school, provoked only scorn. 'However could you imagine?' he said. 'Do take those dreadful things away. Don't keep them yourself. Give them to a cab-driver.'[14]

Wilde was 'charmed' with a similar gift from the journalist and publisher George Bedborough, who sent him a copy of one of his 'dear father's' books and a *Salome* with 'dainty' pencil drawings in it by Max Beerbohm.[15] How strange it must have been to leaf through these volumes on the Paris boulevards – they would have seemed like archaeological remains from a lost world.

Paris was the base to which Wilde always returned after his periodic trips away: in a bid to prove that he was worthy of his Melmothian pseudonym, he wandered around Geneva, Rome, Genoa and Sicily in his final years. In the various Parisian hotel rooms he rented, Wilde amassed a sizeable collection of books, which were impounded whenever he defaulted on his rent.* His library was comprised of personal classics, presentation copies and new gifts from old friends.

A steady stream of presentation copies continued to flow to Wilde from England, courtesy of writers such as George Ives and Bernard Shaw. A substantial number of French authors too, such as André Gide and Pierre Louÿs, continued to pay homage to the 'Lord of Language' and former 'King of Life'.[17] Leonard Smithers regularly sent Wilde parcels of the books he published, such as the beautiful edition of Ben Jonson's play *Volpone* which contained illustrations by the recently deceased Aubrey Beardsley and a eulogy of Beardsley by Robbie Ross.[18] Wilde was curious to see Ross's essay because he knew that his devoted Horatio would be writing his own eulogy one day.

Wilde continued his custom of showering books on his lovers, past, present and future. They were either mementoes of passion, or talismans that would, if he was lucky, help to incite it. When he presented Douglas with *An Ideal Husband* he touchingly inscribed it 'To Bosie: the beautiful poet'.[19] He sent copies of the *Ballad* to the other great loves of his life: Robbie Ross and Constance. Wilde's wife, who was 'frightfully upset' by the 'wonderful poem',[20] died a few weeks after receiving it, in consequence of an unsuccessful operation on her spine. With her died Wilde's last hope of seeing 'his poor dear boys' again; Cyril and Vyvyan were now under the guardianship of

---

* There was another connection between Wilde's debts and his books during this period. When he was more than usually hard up, Wilde would give his books to friends as security for loans. He handed his copy of John Webster's Jacobean tragedy *The Duchess of Malfi* over to Henry Davray for this purpose.[16]

Wilde in Rome in 1900.

Constance's family and attended school in England. When he visited Constance's grave in Genoa's Staglieno Cemetery in 1899, Wilde was overwhelmed by regret and 'with a sense, also, of the uselessness of all regrets'.[21]

So far as new loves were concerned, Wilde had frequent recourse to his old strategy of seduction by books. During one of his trips to Italy he displayed wicked ingenuity by tempting a Sicilian seminarist with a prettily illustrated book of devotion.[22] He also sent a number of his own works to a young man called Louis Wilkinson, along with a collection of short stories by the French author Paul Adam, one of which featured a homosexual prisoner.[23] Wilkinson had contacted Wilde to ask his permission to put on, at his public school, a dramatised version of *Dorian Gray*. Wilde accompanied his gifts with some delightful letters in which he charms the young man with book chat.

Wilkinson's replies reveal that Wilde had lost none of his old magic. With every fresh book he received, the young man felt 'more and more' in love with 'the genius who wrote' them.[24] He was also very appreciative of Wilde's suggestions regarding his reading. 'I shall always,' he wrote, 'be grateful to you if you trouble to recommend me particular poetry to read: I am thankful to say that I play neither football nor cricket, so I am really comparatively at leisure.'[25] It is a shame that the pair were destined never to meet, because Wilkinson sounds exactly Wilde's type.

40. 'Rest peaceably'

WILDE'S FINAL RESIDENCE was the Hôtel d'Alsace at 13 rue des Beaux-Arts, on Paris's left bank, a stone's throw away from the Seine. His room contained a desk, a narrow bed, curtains that had turned the colour of purple wine with age, and a mantelpiece on which there was a hideously ornate marble clock (see plate 15). Although it was clean, the room could hardly be described as luxurious.

At the foot of the bed, against the wall, there were a few shelves on which Wilde set out his books. They were not capacious enough to accommodate all of the three hundred or so volumes he had amassed over the previous two years and most of the books were strewn across the floor or piled up in the corners of the room.[1] The bohemian setting recalls Wilde's rooms on the Kitchen Staircase at Magdalen; indeed, some of his friends compared his Parisian abode and lifestyle to that of a student.[2]

Robert Sherard remembered some of the titles from Wilde's last library. There was Gautier's *Émaux et Camées*, and countless French novels by authors such as Huysmans and Balzac. Wilde had also assembled a considerable body of prison literature. This included numerous pamphlets and magazine articles on prison reform, as well as several novels concerning prison life, such as Hornung's *The Rogue March* and Tolstoy's *Resurrection*, which Wilde read in a French translation.[3]

The hotel's kindly patron, Monsieur Dupoirier, remembered Wilde as a great reader: 'one rarely saw him,' he said, 'without a volume in his hand.' He would sit for hours in the quiet hotel courtyard with a book and a glass of wine, or a fine brandy when he was in funds. Wilde passed many of his afternoons in this fashion, turning the pages of his book, as the shadows lengthened across the yard. After sundown, he left the hotel to enter what he called 'the circle of the boulevards', meeting up with faithful old friends such as the Sphinx and Robbie Ross, and forging new friendships in the cafés. He wearied many a moon with his talk there, enjoying nights that were, in his phrase, lit up with 'beauty and wine'. When he woke up,

The Hôtel d'Alsace in the early twentieth century.

a little worse for wear in the mornings, he would nurse his hangover by reading in bed.

During the autumn of 1900 bed was the only place where Wilde could read. He was more or less confined there with an illness, now believed to have been 'middle ear disease', which he had contracted in prison. But, of course, all of the physical and psychological sufferings he had endured in jail contributed to his premature death. Major Nelson reckoned that men of Wilde's class usually died within two years of completing a sentence of hard labour; it is a testimony to the robustness of his constitution, and to the benevolence of men such as Nelson and Haldane, that Wilde survived for three and a half.

Wilde's end would come on 30 November 1900. Before death entered the hotel room, he played out what has become one of the most famous final scenes since the demise of Socrates. This featured a spectacular last-minute 'conversion' to Roman Catholicism, the creed Wilde had dallied with throughout his life. As we have seen, Wilde had been baptised both as a Catholic and as a Protestant, but he had been raised in the latter faith. For aesthetic, as well as theological reasons, he evidently believed that the Roman faith was the 'only [one] to die in'; the conversion was also consistent with his role as the 'Infamous Saint Oscar'. 'The Catholic Church,' he declared, 'is for saints and sinners alone. For respectable people the Anglican Church will do.'[4] Wilde's last scene was illuminated by some characteristically funny and flamboyant verbal flashes that have passed into history. 'I will never outlive the century,' he remarked at one point. 'The English people would not stand for it.'[5]

Reginald Turner, the friend who nursed Wilde during his final illness, doubtless read to him as he lay in bed. As he approached his end Wilde became inarticulate and babbled of books in French and English.[6] In one of his last lucid intervals he mentioned *Senator North,* a popular novel by the American author Gertrude Atherton: 'This is a fine study of the American politician,' he commented, 'and possesses the quality of truth in characterisation. What else has the lady written?'[7] The remark suggests that Wilde indulged in a diet of light reading just before he 'crossed the bar'. During his 1882 tour of Nebraska prison he had visited the cell of a 'murderer with melancholy eyes' who had been condemned to death by hanging. The prisoner chose to while away the three weeks left to him on earth by reading novels. Wilde had taken a rather dim view of this at the time: it was, he thought, 'a bad preparation for facing either God or nothing'.[8] Yet the same could be said of Wilde's own reading during his final days – it hardly points to a serious state of mind at the last.

As his life slowly ebbed away from him, Wilde uttered the apparently nonsensical remark, 'Could you get a Munster to cook for me?' and then added, 'one steamboat is very like another.'[9] He was delirious when he said this, on account of his illness and the numerous cocktails of champagne and morphine he downed to dull his pain. Yet his words were not complete gibberish: 'The Munster' was a steamboat that ferried passengers across the sea from Wales to Ireland. As he approached his end, Wilde was going back, in his mind, to his native home and point of origin. Perhaps he was also expressing a wish to return in body as well as in imagination. His remark brings to mind a number of stories in his mother's collections of folklore, which describe the terrible longing experienced by Irish corpses interred abroad. 'The souls of the Irish,' as Speranza says in her commentary to these tales, 'will not rest peaceably unless laid with their forefathers and their own people.'[10]

Just before the end, Wilde was suddenly deprived of the power of speech. Yet if he was no longer able to talk books, he could at least gaze at them on the shelves at the end of his bed. Their spines would have been among the last things he ever saw. Wilde believed that, as people become older, the colours of the world become progressively less vivid and vibrant to their eyes, and that, as they approach death, the world loses all of its hues and turns grey.[11] If that is indeed the case then he would have seen, from his bed, the myriad bright colours of his books slowly drain away, in the moments before his eyes finally closed at 1.50 p.m.

It would have been apt if Balzac's *A Harlot High and Low* had been among the volumes that Wilde fixed his eyes on just before he gave up his ghost. The novel ends with Lucien de Rubempré's funeral, which takes place at the church of St Germain-des-Prés, after which the young poet's body is interred at Père Lachaise cemetery. Wilde's own funeral mass would be said at the same church on 2 December, and Père Lachaise would also be his final resting place. In his posthumous existence Wilde continued to imitate art.

During his glorious days of 'purple and gold' Wilde had, on various occasions, outlined his fittingly bookish vision of what heaven would be like. On arrival he wanted to be handed 'a number of volumes in vellum' and then 'be told' that they 'were his'.[12] There would also be a copy of Pater's *Renaissance* waiting for him to savour.[13] Inside the 'Elysian fields' he hoped to find his literary heroes, lounging around reading 'shadowy copies' of *Dorian Gray* with approval (the cover of Gautier's copy ought, he thought, to be 'powdered with gilt asphodels').[14] All of these books would be produced by magical means, for there would be no place in paradise for publishers.[15]

In the 1920s the medium Mrs Travers Smith claimed to have contacted Wilde's spirit. The messages she received suggest that his bookish vision of heaven turned out to be accurate. His ghost, it seems, now dwells in a sort of Elysian library, where he reads the publications of posterity and passes terrible judgement upon them.

'Flaubert's secret,' he commented during one seance, is 'quite unknown' to Arnold Bennett; at another he dismissed James Joyce's *Ulysses* as 'vomit continued through countless pages'.[16] That last criticism sounds far too crude for Wilde and, of course, Mrs Smith was probably a charlatan. Yet it is pleasant, nonetheless, to think that Wilde is still reading and discussing other people's books beyond the grave, just as we continue to read and talk about his.

'Tutti gli angeli'

TWENTY YEARS AGO, when I was sixteen, I was browsing the shelves of a second-hand bookshop in Cambridge. The black and white spine of the Oxford Authors edition of Oscar Wilde's writings caught my eye and I took it down. It was cheap, I liked the sweet smell of its pages, and I knew that Wilde was a 'Lord of Language' from the beautiful fairy tales that had been read to me as a child. I bought the book and, later the same day, I started to read *Dorian Gray*.

By the end of the first chapter I was overwhelmed. Wilde's elegant prose and his agile intellect dazzled me; I was thrilled, too, by his effervescent, Mozartian wit. I became intoxicated on the novel – as though Wilde's writing really was, to borrow the phrase of one of his friends, the 'champagne of literature'. *Dorian Gray* offered me a portal into intellectual, literary, social and moral universes that I was ready, and eager, to enter. I had received a strict Catholic upbringing, and my state-school education had left me almost entirely ignorant of literature and philosophy. Wilde's musical words charmed me out of myself, and I followed his pipe laughing into a brave new world.

Like many of its first readers back in the 1890s, I was so enchanted by the novel that I read it fifteen, or perhaps even twenty times, sometimes finishing it and beginning it again on the same day. To break the spell, or perhaps to prolong it, I turned to the other works in the Oxford Authors volume. Nearly all of them met Wilde's criteria of the perfect form of pleasure – they were exquisite but they left me hungry for more. So I scoured the shelves of the public library for editions of his obscurer writings, and I plundered the second-hand bookshops of Cambridgeshire and Bedfordshire of their Wilde biographies. *Dorian Gray* had turned me into a confirmed Wildean; reading it was the beginning of a lifelong romance.

It was also the beginning of my great literary mission. In a moment of quixotic madness, I resolved to read all the books my hero had read. I had been denied a half-decent education in the humanities by the state-school system; now, in the first year of my A-level course, I decided to stop attending school on a regular basis and resolved to educate myself instead in the public library. Over the next two years I only went to school one or two days a week; my more enlightened teachers approved of my truancy, the others failed to notice it. Wilde would be my Virgilian guide to the circles of world literature; his life and art the thread with which I would navigate the labyrinth of the history of ideas. I hoped, too, that he would be a sort of Socratic mentor, who would help me give birth to a new self.

I began by devouring the authors that had meant most to him: Plato, Keats, Shakespeare, Flaubert, the Greek tragedians, Dante, Baudelaire. Then I moved on to less familiar fare, gobbling up Chatterton, Pater, Rossetti, Ruskin, Dowson and Huysmans. It was a long and exhilarating voyage of discovery – I read, in Dickens's phrase, 'as if for life'.

My odyssey took me a fair distance in a worldly sense too – as far as Magdalen College, Oxford, to which I applied, in the winter of 1990, because it had been Wilde's alma mater. I spent the day before my interview wandering around Magdalen's snow-covered grounds, absorbing the ancient spirit of the place. The past seemed to haunt the present there; every staircase, every arch, was alive for me with some Wildean association. I re-read *Dorian Gray* that evening, more excitedly than ever, in a room not far from Wilde's former quarters at the college. The novel's magical words and the beautiful surroundings inspired me: at the interview I spoke with uncharacteristic assurance, and even a certain Wildean panache. My interviewers were either impressed or amused by my performance. Two weeks later I was told that, if I achieved the requisite grades in my A levels, a place at the college would be mine.

After attaining the grades I left Cambridge for Oxford. For two of my years at Magdalen I occupied a room on the kitchen staircase that contained the beautiful russet oak fireplace from Wilde's Tite Street library. It gave me a thrill to rest my arm, and my wine glass, on the mantelpiece; I also loved reading, next to the fireplace, the very works that Wilde had penned in its presence a century earlier.

As a member of Magdalen, I had access to its marvellous collection of Wildeana, which includes the manuscripts of a score of his witty undergraduate letters, and a heavily annotated typescript of the first two acts of *Lady Windermere's Fan*. I passed many happy hours in the college's archives, which overlook its cloisters, poring over these relics.

At Oxford my Wildean literary mission continued. With every book I read, I seemed to draw closer to my hero. I began to realise just how important Wilde's golden books had been to him. I felt, too, that his biographers had placed undue emphasis on the dramatic external episodes of his life, and not enough on the inner world of his intellect and imagination. It seemed to me that the great events of Wilde's biography, to adapt his own phrase, had taken place in his brain.

Influenced, no doubt, by the transformation his writings had wrought in my own existence, I became convinced that Wilde's life had been profoundly altered by his reading. I traced his sexuality back to the pages of Plato; in Greek tragedy I identified the model he had copied when he composed the tragicomic play that was his own life. Could Wilde, I wondered, have made his whole life up with the aid of his favourite authors?

At times, on my quest, I felt like Jorge Luis Borges's fictional hero Pierre Menard. An author of the early twentieth century, Menard attempts to enter into the mind of his hero, Cervantes, by saturating himself in the literary and historical culture of sixteenth-century Spain. He achieves such a perfect state of identification with Cervantes that he spontaneously produces several verbatim passages from *Don Quixote*.

As my literary adventure progressed, in the back of my mind the idea of writing a book about Wilde the reader slowly took shape. It would be an entirely new kind of literary biography – an attempt to tell the story of an author's life, and to illuminate it, exclusively through the books that he had read.

After leaving Magdalen I continued to retrace Wilde's steps around the shelves of the library of world literature, but it was not until I began my research for this book three years ago, that I actually drew up a list of his reading. In compiling it, I realised, to my horror, just how unfeasible my mission was. The principal source of information regarding the contents of Wilde's library is the Tite Street Catalogue, which includes an inventory of some of the books sold at the action of his household goods on 24 April 1895. On examining the list, I soon became aware that it was woefully incomplete, identifying, as it does, only a fraction the volumes sold that day and often with incorrect or incomplete information. Some of its gaps could, I knew, be filled by the numerous references Wilde made to his reading in his letters and published writings. Yet, even with the help of such allusions, I would only be able to identify the titles of around half of the books in his library.

Having produced a list of volumes that I was certain Wilde had read (or at least owned), I was forced to confront the even more depressing truth that, intellectually, I was simply not up to the task of comprehending them all. In my heart I had, of course, always known this, but it was only when I embarked on my research for *Oscar's Books* that the full force of the realisation hit me.

Wilde was deeply versed in the writings of the ancients, and he travelled extensively in the realms of French, German and Italian literature (he probably read a bit of Gaelic and Spanish, too). I had Italian, and a smattering of French, but, so far as all the other foreign-language titles were concerned, I had to rely on translations, where they were available. Nor was language the only obstacle. I found many of the books on the list hard going – I became lost in the labyrinthine commentaries on Hegel, and the opaque pages of Herbert Spencer and Mallarmé induced in me a sort of vertigo.

There was also the overwhelming question of *how* Wilde had read these volumes – would I really be able to empathise with this most subtle, sophisticated and imaginative of readers? Wilde's intellect had, after all, been forged by two preposterously gifted parents, and by the finest Liberal Arts education available in late nineteenth-century Dublin and Oxford.

The education system that moulded Wilde's mind, unfortunately, no longer exists. In the Victorian period, writers such as Matthew Arnold and Cardinal Newman argued that the aim of education, at every level of the system, should not be to prepare students for a specific profession. Instead, it ought to endow them with a broad knowledge of the humanities, and an intimate familiarity with those classic works of literature that contained the best that had been known and thought throughout history. This, they believed, would sharpen the student's mind, enrich his experience of the world, and encourage him to think independently. Much of the teaching Wilde received, and the education he gave himself through private reading, was directed towards these ends.

Wilde reckoned that 'any fairly educated reader' of his day ought to have read, in their original languages, the *Satyricon* of Petronious Arbiter and Gautier's verse collection, *Émaux et Camées*. He was, of course, speaking as a member of an Oxford-educated intellectual elite, yet how many of today's Oxford graduates, not to mention 'any fairly educated reader', have even heard of titles such as these, let alone read them in translation?

For that matter, how many of us in the twenty-first century are familiar with even a quarter of the cheaply published modern and ancient classics that, according to Jonathan Rose's brilliant book *The Intellectual Life of the English Working Class* (2001), Victorian autodidacts gorged themselves on? The aim of our education system – and this is especially true of English State-schools – is to prepare students for their niche within the world of work. And in that world a catholic knowledge of literature has practically no market value; an ability to regurgitate law or engineering textbooks is rewarded twenty times better. It is ironic that Wilde characterised his own period as an 'age of the over-worked and the under-educated'; an age in which people were 'so industrious that they become absolutely stupid' and where thought was 'degraded by its constant association with practice'. What would he say if he came back to visit the philistine, workaholic, mortgage-enslaved England of our day?

Curiously, I was not disheartened by these reflections; rather, they spurred me on. The intellectual gulf that separates us from Wilde made, I felt, a survey of his reading all the more important. By acknowledging the cultural divide, my work would also stand as a warning against our rather facile identification with him. We like to think of Wilde as one of ourselves – as a man whose sexual rebellion made him way ahead of his benighted times. Yet, in intellectual and existential terms, Wilde is utterly alien to us, and we are far closer to that emblem of the Victorian middle class, Charles Pooter.

I knew that the bulk of Wilde's books had been purchased by dealers at the Tite Street auction and then placed on the open market. Subsequently, they had been dispersed throughout the world. I had always assumed that they had been lost without trace, yet I was wrong: around fifty of the books are now housed in public and private collections of Wildeana in America and England. As soon as I learned this, I made contact with their custodians, and was delighted to find that virtually all of them were willing to put the volumes at my disposal. Only one or two Wilde scholars have ever inspected these books; none have made more than a passing reference to them in their works. I was excited by the thought that I would be the first commentator to go through them all carefully and to discuss them at length.

Prior to consulting one of Wilde's books, I purchased or borrowed a copy of the same edition. I took this along with me and transcribed into it all of Wilde's annotations and markings, to produce a duplicate of his copy. Using the library of replica editions I assembled over the course of my research I would, I hoped, be able to recreate the world of Wilde's reading.

After perusing a few of Wilde's volumes I became familiar with his idiosyncratic markings – the multiple exclamation marks that articulated incredulity or amusement, the heavy underlinings and marginal strokes that identified phrases of particular significance. I would always read the book before examining Wilde's copy, and try to guess which sections of the text would especially interest him. The occasions on which I was able to correctly predict Wilde's response convinced me that my investigation was proceeding along the right lines.

I remember sitting in the living-room of a beautiful house in Boars Hill, Oxford, excitedly turning the pages of Wilde's copy of the *Iliad*. The copious annotations it contained allowed me to follow the lightning-quick movements of his readerly mind. I was particularly delighted to discover that he had underlined, in the introduction, a passage concerning the possible oral origins of the Homer's epic. Given his upbringing in a profoundly oral culture, I had imagined that Wilde would be drawn to the issue, and it was gratifying to have this confirmed.

Other markings I discovered vividly evoke some of Wilde's readerly emotions. The British Library has a copy of Elizabeth Barrett Browning's *Aurora Leigh* which Wilde glossed in an extremely personal way. He thrilled to certain lines in the poem, writing 'very fine' next to the phrase 'Alas my Giotto's background!' Alongside a glorious description of a Tuscan sunset he scribbled, 'I have seen this exactly'. Reading these words it was as though I could overhear the excited tone of Wilde's internal reader's voice.

Other books conjured up Wilde's physical presence. When I leafed through his copy of W.H. Mallock's *The New Republic* in Magdalen's Old Library, I laughed when I came across a jam stain on one of the pages – practically the only mark in the book. I imagined Wilde, a century earlier, in his rooms on the other side of the college's cloisters from where I was sitting, holding the volume in one hand and a slice of bread and jam in the other.

Examining the copy of Pater's *Imaginary Portraits* Wilde had read during his imprisonment was a harrowing experience. Its soiled pages – touched by hands that had performed six hours of hard labour each day – evoked the full horror of his incarceration. As I looked down at the pages, something that Robbie Ross had said after a visit to the prisoner came into my mind: 'how can a civilised country,' he commented, '– the English, being Protestant, are of course not *Christian* – keep any man in such an appalling condition.'

In December 2006 I was awarded a £5,000 prize by the Royal Society of Literature/Jerwood Foundation for my proposal for this book, which was judged to be the second-best proposal for a work of non-fiction for that year. It seemed a generous and timely gift from the gods of literature because it would go some way towards paying the extortionate rent on my London studio flat.

On the very day I picked up the cheque from the RSL a friend telephoned to tell me that Wilde's copy of Swinburne's *Essays and Studies* – a book whose existence I had been hitherto unaware of – would be auctioned at Sotheby's the following week. I felt a rush of excitement, followed by a greedy acquisitiveness: I was determined to get my hands on it. When I told my friend about my windfall she advised me to stake it all on an absentee bid. If it was 'meant to be', she said, then £5,000 would be enough.

Five thousand pounds was a pretty paltry bid – other books from the Tite Street library had, I knew, previously fetched as much as £25,000. Yet my friend's optimism was infectious and, on the morning of the auction, I felt sanguine about my chances. I spent the day going through some of my notes, but was too excited to concentrate on work. In the middle of the afternoon the phone rang. It was an acquaintance of mine who works at Sotheby's calling to let me know that my bid had been successful. I immediately dashed off to Bond Street to pick up the book.

On returning to my flat I washed my hands, then carefully examined my treasure. I smoothed my fingers over its ribbed royal blue cover and savoured the musty smell of its foxed and yellowed pages. The words 'Oscar Wilde Magdalen College July 1877' had been inscribed on the initial blank leaf in Wilde's beautiful charactery. Inside, there were a number of fascinating and distinctive markings. I was excited to see that he had underlined the phrase 'the essence of an artist is that he should be articulate', because I knew that it had appeared, in slightly altered form, in one of his American lectures. I was also amused to find that he had placed a large exclamation mark beside a savage and witty dig at Wordsworth, to express, perhaps, his delight or surprise, or a mixture of both.

Remembering that Wilde had copied some lines from the volume's final paragraph into one of his Oxford notebooks, I looked up the relevant entry in my notes. '*Rien n'est vrai que le beau,*' read Wilde's notebook transcription. 'Beauty may be strange, quaint, terrible, she may play with pain as with pleasure, handle a horror till she leaves it a delight . . . *La beauté est parfaite.*'

I turned to the last page of *Essays and Studies* expecting to find an annotation or at least some markings. To my disappointment, the margins were empty. However, in the blank leaves at the end of the book, I was thrilled to discover something that appeared to connect the volume with Wilde's notebook entry. On one of the end pages there was a faint mirror-image impression of some characteristic Wildean doodles — one was of the profile of a medieval knight, another of a paper kite. In moments when his attention strayed from his reading, Wilde embellished his notebooks with such sketches, and, during my research, I had seen countless examples of them.

The images at the back of *Essays and Studies* must have been imprinted by some half-dried ink doodles that Wilde made in his notebook, the relevant page of which would have rested between the end leaves of the volume while he made his transcription from it. As soon as I realised this, I saw exactly how his Swinburne and the notebook would have been arranged on Wilde's desk. I pictured him bending over them in his room at Magdalen, his eyes darting from the volume to the notebook as he took his notes – his mind and body in rapid and harmonious motion. And so a vivid and an archetypal image of Wilde the reader rose up from the end leaves of the copy of *Essays and Studies*, which had once been his and now was mine.

From the moment I acquired the volume that I now refer to as 'my precious', I regarded it as a sort of imprimatur for *Oscar's Books*, and as a talisman that would help me complete my work. It has rested on my desk throughout the composition of this book, just as it once lay on Wilde's.

After *Essays and Studies* fell from the heavens into my lap, I was convinced that the gods of literature were on my side, and I felt sure that I would make further semi-miraculous discoveries. When I visited many of Wilde's former residences in Ireland, England and France, I half expected to find, mouldering away in a cupboard somewhere, a forgotten pile of his books.

Before my trip to Naples in the spring of 2007, I was almost certain that I would unearth some treasure at the Villa Giudice, which Wilde had rented in 1897. In this case my belief was founded upon something more solid than the conviction that I was blessed: I knew that Wilde had left a small library of books behind him on his departure. According to Wilde's greatest biographer, Richard Ellmann, an Englishwoman who had stayed at the villa twenty-five years later had found Wilde's volumes still there on the bookshelves.

As I walked from the harbour up the Via Posillipo, with the Bay of Naples on my left shimmering in the late morning sun, I was supremely confident that I would talk my way through the villa's gates and into the building. Once inside, I would locate the books and purchase them for a trifling sum from their owner, who would, I hoped, be unaware of their provenance. If he was alert to their Wildean association, then I would simply ask to inspect the volumes.

At the very least, I looked forward to an afternoon buried among Wilde's copies of Keats, Flaubert and Dowson, with occasional breaks for ice-cream and grappa-laced espresso.

A few moments after I pressed the buzzer at the imposing iron gate of No. 37 Via Posillipo – the address, or so Ellmann said, of the Villa Giudice – the concierge, an elegantly attired man in his early sixties, came out and, with a friendly smile, asked my business. After firing off the litany of polite Italian phrases I had learned for the occasion, I explained that I was writing a book about Wilde, and would be extremely grateful for a quick tour of his former residence.

At the mention of Wilde's name the concierge's face twisted into a grimace. *'Porco Belin!'* he bellowed out a conventional Italian expression of annoyance, 'not another Oscar Wilder.' After a deep sigh, he continued. 'Ever since the publication of Ellmann's biography we have been plagued by the pilgrims of dear Oscar (*'Caro Oscuro'*). But *porco Dao, e la Madonna, e tutti gli angeli in colonna* (literally, 'Bloody God, and the Madonna and all of the angels standing on a column') – Ellmann got the address wrong! I am deeply sorry for you – yes, you inspire in me much pity – but this is not, nor has it ever been, the Villa Giudice.'

I am still not sure if he was lying. There was something suspiciously theatrical in his manner (though theatricality is *de rigueur* in Naples) and I half suspect that Wilde's books may still be gathering dust on the shelves of No. 37. His story was, however, fairly plausible; Ellmann had died before putting the finishing touches to his monumental biography and, inevitably, it contains a few factual errors. Indeed, Ellmann had led me on a couple of Wilde-goose chases prior to my Neapolitan misadventure.

I tramped back down the Via Posillipo in melancholy mood. Not even the sight of Ischia – suddenly made visible as the wind scattered the sea mist – could raise my spirits. It was, I supposed, a classic case of hubris: the gods were punishing me for presuming that I would effortlessly walk into the villa and then off with the books; I had taken their assistance for granted. By the time I reached the train station, however, my humour improved. My failure was not, I reflected, a sign that the gods had turned against me, but their clear directive that I end my wanderings and start putting black upon white. And so, about a week later, I began writing *Oscar's Books*.

A biography of Wilde the reader which explores the influence books had on him, and many other readerly issues besides, must necessarily limit itself to certain sections of his bookshelves. My choices have been dictated by my own taste and by my intellectual limitations. Had I had the culture, and the time, I would have written more about Wilde's love of French fiction, and his adventures in the literature of the ancient world. I would also have explored, in detail, his passion for authors such as Arnold, Goethe, Thackeray, Newman, Ruskin, Huysmans, Carlyle, Poe, Shakespeare, Meredith, Ralph Waldo Emerson and Robert Browning – all of them Wildean favourites. Likewise, I would have enjoyed investigating Wilde's possible interest in authors with whom he has rarely been associated, such as Jane Austen, Arthur Rimbaud, Lewis Carroll and Kierkegaard.

In making my selections I have also been guided by a determination to include in my book as much unpublished and unfamiliar material as I possibly could. Over the course of my research, I compiled an archive of previously unconsidered Wildean treasures. This includes copies of his unpublished reviews and lectures, the notes I took when I examined the surviving fifty or so books formerly in Wilde's possession, and also a number of Wilde's book bills.

My archive also contains the notes I made when I inspected every book Wilde is known to have either owned or read. In compiling my inventory of these titles, I drew on three main sources: the Tite Street

Catalogue, the allusions to books contained in Wilde's letters and writings, and all the references to volumes formerly belonging to Wilde that I could find in book dealers' and auctioneers' catalogues. I took my list along to the British Library and spent around six months going through all the items. I cannot claim to have read every word of every book on my inventory – I 'tasted' them, to use Wilde's phrase, and scoured their pages for paragraphs that might have caught his eye. Where possible, I called up the same edition Wilde read in order to get an idea of his taste in the 'apparel of books' and an impression of the physical appearance of his library.

My quest to read every one of Oscar's books, which I embarked on twenty years ago, has not been accomplished. Yet I hope to have realised another dream of mine – to write a biography of Wilde the reader.

I wanted to use some lines from Borges's poem 'Mis Libros' [My Books] as an epigraph for this book. I think that Wilde would have agreed with the idea they express. (They certainly chime with a statement he made during a lecture: 'A man is only half himself,' he said, ' . . . [Chatterton] praises men of genius because they are more himself than he is.') Instead of placing the lines at the beginning of *Oscar's Books*, I have chosen to reproduce them here, for the benefit of those readers who, like Wilde, always begin books at the end.

> My Books (which do not know that I exist)
> are as much part of me as is this face . . .
> . . . I feel now that the quintessential words
> expressing me are in those very pages
> which do not know me, not in those I have written.*

* Jorge Luis Borges 'My Books', *The Book of Sand* (London, 1979), p. 179, trans. Alastair Reid.

Wilde's Letter to the *Pall Mall Gazette* on the Subject of 'The Best Hundred Books'

(Printed in the paper on 8 February 1886)

To the Editor of the Pall Mall Gazette

Books, I fancy, may be conveniently divided into three classes:

1. Books to read, such as Cicero's *Letters*, Suetonius, Vasari's *Lives of the Painters*, the *Autobiography of Benvenuto Cellini*, Sir John Mandeville, Marco Polo, St Simon's *Memoirs*, Mommsen, and (till we get a better one) Grote's *History of Greece*.

2. Books to re-read, such as Plato and Keats: in the sphere of poetry, the masters not the minstrels; in the sphere of philosophy, the seers not the *savants*.

3. Books not to read at all, such as Thomson's *Seasons*, Rogers's *Italy*, Paley's *Evidences*, all the Fathers except St Augustine, all John Stuart Mill except the *Essay on Liberty*, all Voltaire's plays without any exception, Butler's *Analogy*, Grant's *Aristotle*, Hume's *England*, Lewes's *History of Philosophy*, all argumentative books and all books that try to prove anything.

 The third class is by far the most important. To tell people what to read is, as a rule, either useless or harmful; for the appreciation of literature is a question of temperament not of teaching; to Parnassus there is no primer and nothing that one can learn is ever worth learning. But to tell people what not to read is a very different matter, and I venture to recommend it as a mission to the University Extension Scheme.

 Indeed, it is one that is eminently needed in this age of ours, an age that reads so much that it has no time to admire, and writes so much that it has no time to think. Whoever will select out of the chaos of our modern curricula 'The Worst Hundred Books,' and publish a list of them, will confer on the rising generation a real and lasting benefit.

 After expressing these views I suppose I should not offer any suggestions at all with regard to 'The Best Hundred Books,' but I hope that you will allow me the pleasure of being inconsistent, as I am anxious to put in a claim for a book that has been strangely omitted by most of the excellent judges who have contributed to your columns. I mean the *Greek Anthology*. The beautiful poems contained in this collection seem to me to hold the same position with regard to Greek dramatic literature as do the delicate little figurines of Tanagra to the Pheidian marbles, and to be quite as necessary for the complete understanding of the Greek spirit.

I am also amazed to find that Edgar Allan Poe has been passed over. Surely this marvellous lord of rhythmic expression deserves a place? If, in order to make room for him, it be necessary to elbow out someone else, I should elbow out Southey, and I think that Baudelaire might be most advantageously substituted for Keble. No doubt, both in *The Curse of Kehama* and in *The Christian Year* there are poetic qualities of a certain kind, but absolute catholicity of taste is not without its dangers. It is only an auctioneer who should admire all schools of art.

(Source: *Complete Letters*, pp. 276–7)

Lists of Books Requested by Wilde, 1895–97

(I have added translations of foreign titles in square brackets.)

a)
Requested in June 1895

St Augustine: *Confessions*
De civitate dei [The City of God]
Pascal: *Pensées* [Thoughts]
Provincial Letters
W. Pater: *Studies in the History of the Renaissance*
T. Mommsen: *The History of Rome* (5 vols)
Cardinal Newman: *The Grammar of Ascent*
Apologia Pro Vita Sua [Defence of his life]
Two Essays on Miracles
The Idea of a University

(Source: *Complete Letters*, p. 653, n. 2)

b)
Requested in July 1896

This list is written in Wilde's hand and contains his annotations. The titles in square brackets were deleted by Major Nelson.
A Greek Testament
Milman's *History of the Jews* & [*Latin Christianity*]
[Stanley's *Jewish Church*]
Farrar's *St Paul*

Tennyson's Poems (complete in one volume)
Percy's *Reliques* (the collection of old ballads)
Christopher Marlowe's Works
[Buckle's *History of Civilisation*]
Carlyle's *Sartor Resartus* and Life of *Frederick the Great*
[Froude's *Short Studies on Great Subjects*]
A prose translation of Dante's *Divine Comedy*
Keats's Poems
Chaucer's Poems
Spenser's Poems
[Letters of R. Louis Stevenson, edited by Sidney Colvin]
[Walter Pater's posthumous volume of essays]
Renan's *Vie de Jésus* and *Les Apôtres* [The Life of Jesus and The Apostles] (The chaplain sees no objection to these if they are in the original French)
[Taylor's *Primitive Culture*]
Ranke's *History of the Popes*
Critical and Historical Essays by Cardinal Newman
[*En Route* by J-K. Huysmans. Translation of the French by C. Kegan Paul. I would of course prefer it in the French if it would be allowed. If not I would like to read it in the

319

translation. It is a book on modern Christianity.]

[Lecky's *History of Rationalism*]

Emerson's Essays (If possible in one volume)

Cheap edition of Dickens's Works. The Library here contains no example of any of Thackeray's or Dickens's novels. I feel sure that a complete set of their works would be as great a boon to many amongst the other prisoners as it certainly would be to myself.

(Source: *Complete Letters*, p. 660, n. 1)

c)

Requested in December 1896

Gaston de Latour by Walter Pater, MA (Macmillan)

Milman's *History of Latin Christianity*

Wordsworth's Complete Works in one volume with preface by John Morley (Macmillan. 7/6)

Matthew Arnold's Poems. One volume complete. (Macmillan. 7/6)

Dante and Other Essays by Dean Church (Macmillan. 5/-)

Percy's *Reliques*

Hallam's *Middle Ages* (*History of*)

Dryden's Poems (1 vol. Macmillan. 3/6)

Burns's Poems ditto

Morte D'Arthur ditto

Froissart's Chronicles ditto

Buckle's *History of Civilisation*

Marlowe's Plays

Chaucer's *Canterbury Tales* (edited by A. Pollard 2 vols 10/-) Macmillan

Introduction to Dante by John Addington Symonds

Companion to Dante by A. J. Butler

Miscellaneous Essays by Walter Pater

An English translation of Goethe's *Faust*

EDUCATIONAL

Ollendorff's *German Method* 5/6

Key to the same. 3/6

Wilhelm Tell. Hamiltonian System. 5/-

German–English Dictionary

Faust by Goethe (in the original)

Key to Mariotti's *Italian Grammar*. 1/-

Guide to the Italian Language by A. Biaggi. 5/-

Biaggi's *Prosatori Italiani* [Italian Prose Writers] 5/-

Italian–English Dictionary

(Source: *Complete Letters*, p. 673, n. 3)

d)

Requested in March 1897

A French Bible

German Grammar

German Conversation Book

French–Italian Conversation Book

Dante: *Vita Nuova* [The New Life]

Dante: *Vita Nuova*. English Translation

Goldoni: *Commedie* [Comic Plays]

Augustin Filon: *L'Art dramatique en Angleterre* (*Le Théâtre Anglais*, 1896) [English Dramatic Art]

Journal des Goncourt. Latest volume

Pressensé: *Vie du Cardinal Manning* (1896) [Life of Cardinal Manning]

Huysmans: *En Route* (1895)* [On the Road]

Letters of Dante Gabriel Rossetti (1895)

Robert Louis Stevenson: *Valima Letters* (1895)

George Meredith: *Essay on Comedy* (1897)

Ditto: *Amazing Marriage* (1895)
Thomas Hardy: *The Well-Beloved* (1897)
Harold Frederic: *Illumination* (1896)
Nineteenth Century for 1896
Robert Louis Stevenson: *Treasure Island*

* This is the religious novel of which Mr Gladstone wrote in terms of such high commendation. [The request for *Treasure Island* and the note on *En Route* were written by Wilde. The rest of the list was compiled by More Adey.]

(Source: *Complete Letters*, p. 682, n. 2)

e)
Books requested in April 1897
This list was compiled by Wilde at the end of a letter he wrote to Robbie Ross on 6 April 1897.

FRENCH BOOKS
Flaubert: *Tentation* [The Temptation of St Anthony]
Trois Contes [Three Tales]
Salammbô
Mérimée: Novels
Anatole France: *Thaïs* and his latest works
Pierre Louÿs: Novel [*Aphrodite*, 1896]
La Jeunesse: Novel [*L'imitation de Notre-Maître Napoléon*, 1897] [The Imitation of Our Master Napoleon]
Maeterlinck: Complete [i.e. Complete Works]
Baudelaire: *Fleurs du Mal*
Strindberg: Last plays
Ibsen: Translation (*Eyolf. Borkman*) [i.e. Little Eyolf. John Gabriel Borkman]

Montaigne
Gautier: *Émaux et Camées*
French Bible (University Press)
French–English Dictionary
Some mystical books
Murray: *Greek Literature* [Gilbert Murray, History of Ancient Greek Literature]
Quarterly Review for April
Hogarth on Alexander the Great (Murray) [D. G. Hogarth, Philip and Alexander of Macedon]
Quo Vadis? (Dent, translation of novel by Sienkiewicz)

ENGLISH
Epic and Romance [W.P. Ker]
St William of Norwich [*The Life and Miracles of St William of Norwich*]
Ancient Ideals [H.O. Taylor]
Wagner's Letters to Roeckel (Arrowsmith)
[J.A.] Symonds: *Italian By-Ways*
Hettinger on Dante. Translated by Father Bowden
Mrs Mark Pattison: *Renaissance [of Art] in France*
Dom Gasquet: *Historical Essays*
Yeats: *The Secret Rose*
A.E.W. Mason *The Philanderers* (Macmillan). Also his previous novel [*The Courtship of Morrice Buckler*, 1896]
A Bible.
Flinders Petrie on Egypt [*Egyptian Decorative Art*, 1895]. Any good book on Ancient Egypt.
Translation of Hafiz, and of Oriental love-poetry.
Morrison: article in *Nineteenth Century* on Prisons and Sir Edmund Du Cane's reply. Morrison's Criminology Series.

Spanish–French Conversation Book.
Calderon: *Mágico Prodigioso* (translated).
[The Wonder-Working Magician]
Devoción de la Cruz. [The Devotion of the Cross]
Spanish Grammar.

Guide-Book to Morbihan, Finisterre district. Quimper, Vannes.
Guide-Book to Pyrenees.
Salomé.

(Source: *Complete Letters*, pp. 791–3)

Bibliographical Note

My notes contain references to most of the volumes I consulted during the preparation of this book. Here I list only the works that have been indispensable to me, and those which I recommend to anyone wishing to pursue their interest in Wilde.

The following biographical works have been of invaluable assistance: M. Holland and R. Hart-Davis (eds.), *The Complete Letters of Oscar Wilde* (London, 2000); E.H. Mikhail (ed.), *Oscar Wilde: Interviews and Recollections*, 2 vols (London, 1979) and R. Ellmann, *Oscar Wilde* (London, 1987); H. Pearson, *The Life of Oscar Wilde* (revised edition, London, 1954) is also well worth reading, particularly for its matchless reconstruction of the social world in which Wilde moved. The following biographies of Wilde, which were written by his friends, are extremely evocative: R. Sherard's *The Real Oscar Wilde* (London, 1917?), *The Life of Oscar Wilde* (New York, 1906) and *Oscar Wilde: The History of an Unhappy Friendship* (London, 1902); F. Harris, *Oscar Wilde, His Life and Confessions* (New York, 1930). Some of Wilde's friends also left vivid memoirs and recollections: V. O'Sullivan, *Aspects of Wilde* (London: Constable, 1936); [John Paul Raynaud] and Charles Ricketts, *Oscar Wilde: Recollections* (London, 1932); Laurence Housman, *Echo de Paris* (London, 1923) and Ada Leverson, *Letters to the Sphinx* (London, 1930).

The following modern biographical works focus on specific aspects of Wilde's life: Davis Coakley, *Oscar Wilde: The Importance of Being Irish* (Dublin, 1994) discusses Wilde's Irishness and his upbringing in Ireland; Neil McKenna, *The Secret Life of Oscar Wilde* (London, 2003) deals with Wilde's homosexuality, and Thomas Wright (ed.), *Table Talk: Oscar Wilde* (London, 2000) offers a portrait of Wilde the storyteller and anthologises his finest spoken stories. M. Holland (ed.), *Irish Peacock and Scarlet Marquis: The Real Trial of Oscar Wilde* (London, 2003) contains the transcript of the Queensberry trial, and is expertly annotated and introduced. H. Montgomery Hyde, *The Trials of Oscar Wilde* (Edinburgh, 1948) includes valuable accounts of Wilde's two trials. Anthony Stokes, *Pit of Shame* (Winchester, 2007) contains fascinating information on Wilde's time at Reading Gaol.

The best affordable edition of Wilde's writings is *The Collins Complete Works of Oscar Wilde, Fifth Edition* (London, 2003). I. Murray (ed.), *Oscar Wilde: The Oxford Authors* (Oxford, 1989) offers a judicious selection of Wilde's finest works and is brilliantly annotated by the editor. Anyone still hungry for more Wilde should try to acquire second-hand copies of the following lesser-known writings at www.abebooks.co.uk: *Reviews by Oscar Wilde* (London, 1908) a collection of Wilde's book reviews and *Miscellanies by Oscar Wilde*, an anthology of Wilde's other journalistic writings and some of his lectures; R. Ellmann (ed.), *The Artist as Critic* (Chicago, 1968) is an inexpensive collection of Wilde's journalism and criticism.

Those whose interest in Wilde is of a more scholarly nature, and who can afford the £60 or so asked for each tome, may wish to purchase the volumes of *The Complete Works of Oscar Wilde* which the Oxford University Press is currently in the process of publishing. B. Fong and K. Beckson (eds.), *Poems and Poems in Prose: The Complete Works of Oscar Wilde, Volume I* (Oxford, 2000) is especially valuable as it contains a wealth of hitherto unpublished material. The forthcoming volume of Wilde's journalism, edited by Professor John Stokes, also promises to include a number of articles and book reviews that have never previously been attributed to Wilde.

Anyone who would like to explore the wealth of secondary critical literature concerning Wilde should turn to the excellent bibliographies: I. Small, *Oscar Wilde Revalued* (Greensboro, 1993) and I. Small, *Oscar Wilde: Recent Research* (Greensboro, 2000). K. Beckson (ed.), *Oscar Wilde: The Critical Heritage* (London, 1970) provides a fascinating selection of the late Victorian critical reception of Wilde's works and K. Beckson, *The Oscar Wilde Encyclopaedia* (New York, 1998) is a useful reference book. The best bibliography of Wilde's own writings is Stuart Mason, *Bibliography of Oscar Wilde* (London, 1914), an elegant and eccentric mine of Wildean information.

Those who wish to keep up with all the Wildean gossip, of a scholarly and also of a more general nature, should subscribe to the following publications: *The Wildean*, a biannual journal of the Oscar Wilde Society, which is expertly edited by the Society's chairman, Donald Mead. The journal comes free with membership to the OWS (www.oscarwilde society.com); *The Oscholars*, a monthly internet bulletin crammed full of fascinating information on all matters Wildean, which also offers a whole library of scholarly essays. It is superbly edited by the indefatigable David Rose, and is available, free of charge, at www.oscholars.com.

Acknowledgements

It gives me great pleasure to acknowledge the many people who have helped me over the course of my research. I have given full details of specific debts of gratitude in my notes, but I would like to offer more general words of thanks here to the following people: Dr Colin Harris, Head of Modern Papers at the Bodleian Library, Oxford, and his helpful assistants; Mrs Verity Andrews, Archives Assistant of Reading University Library; Dr Robin Darwall-Smith, Archivist of Magdalen College and his predecessor, Dr Janie Cottis; Dr Christine Ferdinand, Magdalen's Head Librarian; John B. Thomas III, Curator of the Pforzheimer Collection at the Harry Ransom Humanities Center in Texas; the staff of the Public Records Office in Kew Gardens; the staff of the London Library; the librarians at the Pierpont Morgan Library, New York; the staff of the Science 2 reading room in the British Library, and the staff of the following public libraries which, at the time of writing, continue to stock books: Muswell Hill Library, Hampton Hill Library, Bedford Library.

My special thanks to Laura Fielder, Dr Elizabeth James and Sally Brown of the British Library, who gave me access to the Eccles Bequest of Wildeana at a time when the material was still being catalogued; and to the William Andrews Clark Junior Memorial Library in Los Angeles, which granted me the Short-Term Fellowship that enabled me to spend a month examining its extensive collection of Wildeana. The Clark librarians skilfully guided me through their vast archive, and Bruce Whiteman, the Head Librarian, gave freely of his expert advice.

I am extremely grateful to two private collectors, Julia Rosenthal and Jeremy Mason, who generously put at my disposal both their Wildean treasures and their profound knowledge of Wilde. The hours I spent in their homes were among the most rewarding and pleasurable of my research. My conversations with Julia Rosenthal, over the last two years, have been a constant source of inspiration. I also thank Nali Dinshaw for furnishing me with information regarding her Wilde collection.

I have benefited enormously from the help of the following Wilde scholars: Davis Coakley, Joy Melville, David Rose, Professor John Stokes and Mark Samuels Lasner. I owe particular thanks to Donald Mead, Chairman of the Oscar Wilde Society, and to Neil McKenna, who liberally shared their extensive knowledge of Wilde with me, and also offered excellent practical advice regarding my research. In addition, I am indebted to two extremely gifted young scholars, Iain Ross and Paul Kinsella, who sent me copies of their unpublished Ph.D. theses, and answered my numerous questions on their respective fields of Wildean expertise.

I would like to express my appreciation for those who commented on early drafts. Penelope Hoare, my editor at Chatto, offered invaluable comments and suggestions. David Smith expertly edited the unwieldy first draft of *Oscar's Books*, and provided me with many extremely helpful criticisms and several fascinating snippets of research information.

My agent, Camilla Hornby, volunteered many useful comments on an earlier version of this book; she also made significant improvements to my proposal. I am greatly indebted to her, too, for the general advice and support she has given me over the last three years. I would like to take this opportunity to thank my former agent, the late Giles Gordon, a true Wildean, who offered enthusiastic and stimulating comments on the original outline.

I must register a more private debt to the friends with whom I have discussed Wilde, and many of the ideas that appear in this work, over the past twenty years: C. Robert Holloway, Gino Scatasta, Alan Barnard, Anthony Smith, A.C. Wilson, Simon Scardifield, Jamie Glazebrook and Costa Peristianis. My discussions with Dr Caroline Barnes and Andrew Fanning have been especially inspiring.

The greatest accolade must go to Mauro Nicolini and Anna Wright, who offered advice, ideas, editorial suggestions and fellowship, every step of the way; without them, my journey might never have been completed. Thanks, too, to the rest of my family and friends, for their unstinting support.

I also acknowledge the help of the following people: Tessa Milne of Sotheby's, Anthony Stokes (warder of Reading prison), Laura Barber, Stewart McLaughlin (historian of Wandsworth prison), Brother John, Clare and Charlie, Tommaso Aspetta, Rick Gekoski of Gekoski Rare Books and Manuscripts, Mary Fanning, Beppe Narizzano, the librarian at St Thomas More School, Bedford (1989–1991), Martin Mavellen, Dr Ninian Hewitt, Francesco Clichy, Enrico Masnata, George Washington Brown, Ago Loriga, Elena Grondona, Eric Warnakey, Parisa Ebrahimi of Chatto and Windus, Katherine Spears of Bernard Quaritch Rare Books, Chris Proud, Helga Barnes, A. Biavasco and Chiara Nicolini.

I would like to offer my profound thanks to the Royal Society of Literature/Jerwood Foundation, which awarded me a £5,000 prize for the second-best non-fiction book proposal of 2006.

Finally, I extend my sincere gratitude to Oscar Wilde's grandson, Merlin Holland, for his assistance in tracking down, and supplying me with, the illustrations in this book, and for all the encouragement and priceless advice he gave me at every stage of this project. Mr Holland also kindly granted me permission to reproduce quotations from Wilde's unpublished letters, annotations in his books and other miscellaneous unpublished sources, as well as quotations from Lady Wilde's letters and from Vyvyan Holland's *Son of Oscar Wilde*.

Notes

INTRODUCTION

1. *Hampshire Telegraph and Sussex Chronicle*, 27 April 1895.

2. See A.N.L. Munby (ed.), Sale Catalogues of Libraries of Eminent Persons, Vol. I (London, 1971), p.372, and also Lily Wilde to More Adey, 8 May 1897 'A great <u>many</u> things were stolen in Tite Street', Bodleian, MS. Walpole d. 18. Munby reproduces a facsimile of the 'Tite Street Catalogue' which lists some of the books from Wilde's library.

3. Stuart Mason, *Bibliography of Oscar Wilde* (London, 1914), p. 8. See also *Freeman's Journal and Commercial Daily Advertiser* (Dublin) 25 April 1895.

4. *Hampshire Telegraph and Sussex Chronicle*, 27 April 1895.

5. Robert Ross, Introduction to *A Florentine Tragedy* (John W. Luce, Boston, 1906).

6. Vyvyan Holland, *Son of Oscar Wilde* (London, 1954), p. 62.

7. *De Profundis, Selected Letters of Oscar Wilde* (Oxford, 1979) p. 179. Wilde's prison letter, which was penned to his lover Alfred Douglas, is not called *De Profundis* in this, or in any other, collection of Wilde's letters. The letter was given the name when it was partially published in 1905, five years after Wilde's death. As it is the title by which the letter is most commonly known, I have used it throughout this book for the sake of convenience.

8. These figures have been arrived at by an examination of the annotated catalogue reproduced in Munby and the notes relating to the sale written by the book dealer H. Parsons. These form part of the Eccles Bequest, which is in the British Library. I am extremely grateful to Sally Brown, Laura Fielder and Dr Elizabeth James of the British Library for giving me access to the Eccles Bequest. For Wilde's weekly expenditure see *De Profundis, Selected Letters*, p. 157.

9. Catalogue of the collection of H. Montgomery Hyde (1948), item 383. Eccles Bequest, the British Library. 'Most of the people, excepting a knot of artists, were brokers.' *Lloyd's Weekly Newspaper*, 28 April 1895.

10. *De Profundis, Selected Letters*, p. 180.

11. E.H. Mikhail (ed.), *Oscar Wilde:*

Interviews and Recollections, Vol. II (London, 1979), p. 375.

12. M. Holland and R. Hart-Davis (eds.), *The Complete Letters of Oscar Wilde* (London, 2000), p. 647. This volume is hereafter referred to as *Complete Letters*.

13. *De Profundis, Selected Letters*, p. 180.

14. *Complete Letters*, p. 190, n. 1.

15. Ibid., p. 911.

16. *Lady Windermere's Fan* and *Dorian Gray, Collected Works of Oscar Wilde* (Ware, 1997), p. 504 and p. 29.

17. *Complete Letters*, p. 553.

18. George Fleming, *Mirage* (London, 1877), p. 135.

19. *Complete Letters*, p. 880.

PART I: BUILT OUT OF BOOKS

CHAPTER I

1. Lord Henry Wotton, *Dorian Gray, Collected Works*, p. 134.

2. E.H. Mikhail (ed.), *Oscar Wilde: Interviews and Recollections*, Vol. I (London, 1979), p. 224.

3. Macpherson claimed that his poetry was compiled from the writings of Ossian, the ancient Celtic bard. The first of his Ossianic books was *Fingal: An Ancient Epic Poem in Six Books; Together with Several other Poems by Ossian, Son of Fingal* (London, 1762).

4. This is how W.B. Yeats describes the scene in his *Fairy and Folk-tales of the Irish Peasantry* (London, 1889), a book Wilde reviewed. See *Reviews by Oscar Wilde* (London, 1908) p. 406. For Wilde's markedly different oral version of this tale see 'Le Pays de la Jeunesse', in Guillot de Saix, *Contes et propos d'Oscar Wilde*, Les Oeuvres Libres, Nouvelle Série, no. 40. pp. 7–9 (Paris, 15 September 1949).

5. Davis Coakley, *Oscar Wilde: The Importance of Being Irish* (Dublin, 1994) p. 26.

6. Lady Wilde, letter to John Hilson, 16 December 1869, University of Reading archives.

7. Ibid., November 1852.

8. Owen Dudley Edwards, 'Impressions of an Irish Sphinx', in *Wilde the Irishman*, ed. J. McCormack (New Haven and London, 1998), p. 50.

9. Speranza included a number of tales concerning Oscar, the 'Lion hearted' hero, in her collection of Irish peasant folk tales, *Ancient Legends, Mystic Charms, and Superstitions of Ireland* (London, 1888). She was particularly fond of a poetic retelling of Oscar's death entitled 'The Cromlech of Howth', written by her friend Samuel Ferguson. (See Coakley, p. 24.) The young Wilde may have been familiar with another retelling of Oscar's death from Charlotte Brooke's *Reliques of Irish Poetry* (1816), a copy of which was owned by Wilde's father, Sir William Wilde. See the *Catalogue of the Library of the Late Sir William Wilde* (Dublin, 1879). I am very grateful to Davis Coakley for sending me a copy of the catalogue.

10. R. Sherard, *The Real Oscar Wilde* (London, 1917?), p. 250.

11. Lady Wilde, letter to John Hilson,

Monday, 1850, University of
Reading archives.

12. Sherard, *Real*, p. 250.

13. R.D. Pepper (ed.), *Irish Poets and
Poetry of the Nineteenth Century* (San
Francisco, 1972), p. 29. Wilde gave
this lecture in San Francisco in 1882.

14. 'The Portrait of Mr W.H.'
(extended version), in R. Ellmann
(ed.), *The Artist as Critic* (Chicago,
1968), p. 152.

15. Barbara Belford, *Oscar Wilde. A
Certain Genius* (London, 2000), p. 3.

16. Coakley, p. 25.

CHAPTER 2

1. See Coakley, pp. 29–30.

2. Quoted in D. Upchurch, *Wilde's Use
of Celtic Elements in 'The Picture of
Dorian Gray'* (New York, 1992), p.
11.

3. They were published in the
anthologies *Ancient Legends* and
*Ancient Cures, Charms, and Usages of
Ireland* (London, 1890). Wilde often
revised his mother's prose and
probably helped her with the
preparation of some of his father's
posthumous publications. See the
letter from Robert Ross to Walter
Ledger, 11 December 1907. Bodleian,
Walpole, Ross Ms. 4 and *Complete
Letters*, p. 25.

4. Anon., 'A Batch of Books',
reproduced in *Notes and Queries*,
August 1983, pp. 314–5. See also
Reviews, pp. 406–11.

5. Wilde and his parents were
extremely superstitious. Merlin
Holland has suggested that in the

earliest surviving photograph of
Wilde (see plate 1), he is dressed as
a girl in order to ward off the
fairies. According to popular
superstition, fairies preferred
stealing beautiful boys to girls. See
Complete Letters, opposite p. 694.

6. Lady Wilde, *Ancient Legends*, pp.
256–8.

7. Joy Melville, *Mother of Oscar Wilde*
(London, 1994), p. 228.

8. 'The Critic as Artist, Part II',
Collected Works, p. 1008. These words
are uttered by Gilbert, Wilde's
spokesman in the dialogue.

9. Wilde used the word 'mythopoetic'
in his review of *Sketches and Studies in
Italy* by J.A. Symonds, in the
Athenaeum, 14 June 1879, p. 755. He
quotes Symonds's definition of it as
that 'apprehension of primeval
powers in man, growing into shape
and substance on the borderland
between the world and the keen
human sympathies it stirs within
us'.

10. *Reviews*, p. 187.

11. Upchurch, p. 12.

12. See *Complete Letters*, p. 85.

13. 'Oscar Wilde', *Biograph*, Vol. 4,
(London, 1880) p. 132.

14. It now forms part of the Eccles
Bequest, the British Library.

15. Vyvyan Holland, p. 54.

16. *Complete Letters*, p. 60.

17. Ibid., p. 31. I am indebted to
Richard Pine for this comparison of
the West of Ireland to Tír na nOg
and for identifying Wilde's pun. See
Richard Pine, *The Thief of Reason:*

Oscar Wilde & Modern Ireland (Dublin,
1995), p. 121.

18. Lady Wilde, *Ancient Legends*, pp. 7–8
and 143–5.

19. *Biograph*, pp. 130–5.

20. 'The Critic as Artist, Part II',
Collected Works, p. 1007.

21. *Complete Letters*, p. 316. Irish folk tales
are political in a more general sense,
representing, in Yeats's words, 'the
innermost heart of the Celt in
moments he has grown to love
through years of persecution,
cushioning himself about with
dreams'. Wilde quoted this phrase
in his review of Yeats's *Fairy and Folk
Tales of the Irish Peasantry*. *Reviews*, p.
407.

22. R. Ellmann, *Oscar Wilde* (London,
1987), p. 332. All footnote references
in notes to 'Ellmann' are to this
biography.

23. Pepper (ed.), p. 28.

24. Some of the Irish tales Wilde
narrated are reproduced in Guillot
de Saix, *Contes et propos d'Oscar Wilde*,
pp. 5–9.

25. 'The Star Child' is a traditional
changeling narrative and the
conclusion of 'The Fisherman and
his Soul' owes a considerable debt
to 'The Priest's Soul', a folk tale
Wilde particularly liked.

26. See Upchurch's discussion of the
Celtic elements in *Dorian Gray*.

27. William Wilde, *Irish Popular
Superstitions* (Dublin, 1852), p. 99.

28. Vyvyan Holland, p. 54.

CHAPTER 3

1. *Biograph*, pp. 130–5.

2. Lady Wilde, letter to John Hilson,
16 Dec. 1869, University of Reading
archives.

3. For a portrait of Wilde the
storyteller see T. Wright, (ed.),
Table Talk: Oscar Wilde (London,
2000), which anthologises many of
Wilde's spoken stories. See also
T. Wright, 'The Talker as Artist:
the Spoken Stories of Oscar Wilde',
in G. Franci (ed.), *L'importanza di
essere frainteso: omaggio a Oscar Wilde*
(Bologna, 2001). Paul Kinsella's
unpublished thesis 'We Must
Return to the Voice: Oral
Traditions and Values in the
Works of Oscar Wilde' (University
of British Columbia, 2003) offers a
fascinating discussion of this
unjustly neglected part of Wilde's
oeuvre, and a brilliant analysis of the
oral residue contained in some of
his written works. The seminal
work of criticism, in this context, is
D. Toomey's 'The Story-Teller at
Fault: Oscar Wilde and Irish
Orality', in J. McCormack (ed.).
Some of the arguments in this
chapter are derived from Kinsella
and Toomey.

4. *Poems by Speranza* (Dublin, 1907).

5. Coakley, p. 73.

6. Lady Wilde, letter to John Hilson,
1855, University of Reading
archives.

7. Mikhail (ed.), Vol. I, p. 47.

8. Ibid., p. 139.

9. Letter to John Hilson, June 1848, University of Reading archives. Apropos of Macaulay's 'Battle of Naseby', she writes 'I could chant it forever.' Speranza is probably referring to solitary reading here which suggests that, even in private, she habitually read verse aloud.

10. 'The Critic as Artist, Part I', *Collected Works*, p. 973.

11. *Dorian Gray, Collected Works*, p. 17.

12. 'The Portrait of Mr W.H.', Ellmann (ed.), p. 199.

13. Lady Wilde, *Ancient Legends*, p. 182.

14. Pepper (ed.), p. 28.

15. 'The Decay of Lying', *Collected Works*, p. 942.

16. V. O'Sullivan, *Aspects of Wilde* (London, 1936), p. 32.

CHAPTER 4

1. Ellmann, p. 5.

2. *Complete Letters*, p. 606.

3. Pepper (ed.), p. 27.

4. Ibid. Wilde was probably introduced to the works of the poets he mentions in his lecture through volumes in his parents' libraries. Their sizeable book collections also contained anthologies of older Irish verse such as Dermody's *Harp of Erin* (1807), Brooke's *Reliques of Irish Poetry* (1816) and Hayne's *Ballads of Ireland*. Speranza was reading the last of these in 1858 and may have entertained the four-year-old Oscar with recitations from it (letter to John Hilson, 18 May 1858,

University of Reading archives.) Dermody and Brooke are listed in the *Catalogue of the Library of the Late Sir William Wilde*.

5. 'Inisfail', a poetic chronicle of the whole of Irish history, contains Bardic songs, ballads, an ode on 'The Curse of Cromwell', and verses that relate folk legends. De Vere inscribed a copy of *Antar and Zara, An Eastern Romance, Inisfail, and Other Poems* (London, 1877) to 'Oscar Wilde from A de V. May 21, 1877'. See the cuttings from auctioneer's and book dealers' catalogues contained in the Eccles Bequest, the British Library. These cuttings appear to have been compiled by Christopher Millard, possibly with the help of Robert Ross. Wilde's De Vere volume is now at the Pierpont Morgan Library, New York.

6. *Complete Letters*, p. 26.

7. E. Barrett Browning, *Aurora Leigh*, 14th edn (London, 1876). It is now in the Eccles Bequest, the British Library.

8. Ibid., p. 15.

9. *Complete Letters*, p. 26. See also Wilde's enthusiastic comments on Barrett Browning in *Miscellanies by Oscar Wilde* (London, 1908), pp. 110–15.

10. These passages appear on pp. 392, 196 and 32 of *Aurora Leigh*.

11. Page 88 of Wilde's unpublished lecture on Thomas Chatterton (1886?), William Andrews Clark Memorial Library, W6721M3 E78.

12. Tite Street Catalogue (London, 1895) p. 5.

13. This may be the volume that Wilde later recalled in *De Profundis. Selected Letters*, p. 200.

14. *Reviews*, p. 519.

15. Mikhail (ed.), Vol. II, p. 379.

16. 'Draft Review of Rossetti's *Poems* (1881)', William Andrews Clark Memorial Library, W6721M3 D758 (early 1880s?).

17. Wilde singled them out for praise in his draft review of Rossetti's *Poems*. See also, *Miscellanies*, p. 253.

18. *Complete Letters*, p. 157.

19. Ibid.

20. Ibid., p. 1133.

21. Tite Street Catalogue, p. 6.

22. *Complete Letters*, p. 880.

23. Holbrook Jackson, *The Anatomy of Bibliomania* (New York, 1981), p. 204.

24. *Miscellanies*, p. 66.

25. Coakley, p. 40.

26. Letters from Lady Wilde to her son. Lot 186, Sotheby's catalogue, 13 December 1990.

27. Melville, p. 139.

CHAPTER 5

1. Coakley, p. 38.

2. *Biograph*, pp. 130–5.

3. *Catalogue of the Library of the Late Sir William Wilde*.

4. Melville, p. 183.

5. Ibid., p. 246.

6. J.S. Laurie, *The First Steps to Reading* (London, 1862), p. 2.

7. Wilde frequently misplaced apostrophes and added an extra 'r' to certain words. See the

introduction to J. Bristow (ed.), *The Picture of Dorian Gray*, (Oxford, 2000), p. lxiii.

8. Mikhail (ed.), Vol. II, p. 294.

9. Wilde, 'Chatterton lecture' (1886?), pp. 10 and 21.

10. *Complete Letters*, p. 556.

11. *Reviews*, p. 388.

12. Wilde purchased a copy of the book from the dealer David Nutt on 22 February 1895. See Wilde's Nutt invoice in the Public Records Office File: B9/428.

13. *Complete Letters*, p. 204.

14. *Sidonia* also influenced Wilde's fairy tales. See I. Murray's introduction to I. Murray (ed.), *The Complete Shorter Fiction of Oscar Wilde* (Oxford, 1979), p. 3.

15. *Complete Letters*, pp. 1169–70.

16. Mikhail (ed.), Vol. II, p. 373.

17. *Complete Letters*, p. 1106.

18. A. Curse, *The Victorians and their Books* (London, 1935), p. 70.

19. D. Pryde, *The Highways of Literature* (Edinburgh, 1882), pp. 41–3.

20. *Complete Letters*, p. 789.

CHAPTER 6

1. G.L. Craik, *A Compendious History of English Literature and of the English Language* (New York, 1869), p. 8. Wilde's copy is mentioned by O'Sullivan, p. 143.

2. Ellmann, p. 21. For Wilde's derogatory reference to the book see Appendix I, p. 317.

3. Clippings from auctioneers' and book dealers' catalogues, the Eccles Bequest, the British Library.

4. Heather White, *Forgotten Schooldays* (Gortnaree, 2002), p. 92.
5. R. Sherard, *The Life of Oscar Wilde* (New York, 1906), p. 31.
6. Ibid., p. 154.
7. 'The Critic as Artist, Part I', *Collected Works*, p. 973.
8. *De Profundis, Selected Letters*, p. 211.
9. F. Harris, *Oscar Wilde, His Life and Confessions* (New York, 1930), p. 19.
10. Review of J.P. Mahaffy's *Greek Life and Thought* (London, 1887) in *Reviews*, p. 211. I am indebted to Iain Ross for drawing my attention to this issue.
11. C. Stray, *The Classics Transformed*, (Oxford, 1998).
12. White, p. 72.
13. *Complete Letters*, p. 366.
14. Coakley, p. 133.
15. Harris, p. 17.
16. Ibid.
17. These editions, which belonged to series such as F.A. Paley's *Biblioteca Classica*, were specifically aimed at 'the lower-reaches of the public school market', Stray, p. 100.
18. White, p. 124.
19. Tite Street Catalogue, p. 9.
20. Harris, p. 19.
21. Coakley, pp. 82–3.
22. Harris, p. 20.
23. Melville, p. 109.
24. Mason, p. 295.
25. Harris, pp. 18–19.

CHAPTER 7

1. Harris, pp. 18–9.
2. Ibid., p. 17.

3. W.E. Henley, *Views and Reviews* (London, 1890), p. 20.
4. Coakley, p. 40.
5. Curse, p. 331.
6. Melville, p. 204.
7. *Complete Letters*, p. 139.
8. *Reviews*, p. 440.
9. Coakley, p. 73.
10. Mikhail (ed.), Vol. I, p. 230.
11. *Biograph*, p. 132.
12. Ibid. See also Ellmann, p. 26.
13. Sherard, *The Life*, p. 92.
14. O'Sullivan, p. 36.
15. 'The Decay of Lying', *Collected Works*, p. 934.
16. *Reviews*, p. 79.
17. Harris, p. 48, Mikhail (ed.), Vol. II, p. 420, 'The Decay of Lying', *Collected Works*, p. 927.

CHAPTER 8

1. This bore the inscription 'Portora Royal School – Carpenter Prize – awarded to Oscar Wilde'. Clippings from auctioneers' and book dealers' catalogues, the Eccles Bequest, the British Library.
2. *Dublin University Calendar*, 1873, p. 28.
3. *Dublin University Calendar*, 1872–74, and *Dublin Examination Papers*, 1873–75.
4. *Dublin University Calendar*, 1873, p. 46.
5. Clippings from auctioneers, and book dealers' catalogues, the Eccles Bequest, the British Library.
6. (Oxford, 1868). The Eccles Bequest, The British Library.
7. Sherard, *Real*, p. 126.
8. (London, 1871). The Eccles Bequest, the British Library.

9. Wilde's annotations also attest to some broader aesthetic interests. Next to Tyrrell's comment that it is 'remarkable that Pentheus goes to spy on the Bacchantes', Wilde queries 'the weak point of the play?'

10. The book was edited by F.A. Paley and published in London in 1871. It is now owned by Julia Rosenthal, who very kindly allowed me to examine it, along with all the other items in her Wildean collection.

11. I am indebted to Iain Ross for this information.

12. Wilde's notes on *The Fragments of the Greek Comic Poets* (edited by Meineke) are held in the Berg Library in New York. I am grateful to Iain Ross for allowing me to consult his transcription of the notes and for his expert elucidation of them.

13. Mikhail (ed.), Vol. I, p. 16.

CHAPTER 9

1. *Complete Letters*, p. 562.

2. Ellmann, p. 27.

3. J.P. Mahaffy, *Social Life in Greece* (London, 1874), pp. 1–2.

4. It is anachronistic to refer to love between men, both in Greek society and in the late Victorian period, as 'homosexual'. I have, however, used the term throughout this book for the sake of convenience.

5. Ibid., p. 305.

6. Ibid., pp. 305–12.

7. Harris, p. 23.

8. *Studies of the Greek Poets* was published in two volumes: First Series (London, 1873) and Second Series

(London, 1876). Wilde's copies of these books are now in the Pierpont Morgan Library, New York. PML 125894 and PML 125905.

9. *Complete Letters*, p. 20. This particular comparison is marked in Wilde's copy of *Studies* (Second Series, p. 210).

10. See, for example, Philip E. Smith III and Michael S. Helfand (eds.), *Oscar Wilde's Oxford Notebooks: A Portrait of Mind in the Making* (Oxford, 1989), pp. 138–9.

11. *Studies* (Second Series), p. 129.

12. 'If the hammer,' Wilde paraphrased Aristotle's *Politics* in one of his Oxford notebooks, 'and shuttle [could] move themselves, slavery would be unnecessary' (Smith II and Helfand [eds.], pp. 155 and 204). It is, however, extremely difficult to accurately gauge the influence of Symonds and Mahaffy on Wilde's vision of the past. He was also encouraged to bring ancient ideas to bear on modern issues, and to compare and contrast different historical periods, by the *Literae Humaniores* or 'Greats' course he studied at Oxford. See W. Shuter, 'Pater, Wilde, Douglas and the Impact of "Greats"', *English Literature in Transition*, 46:3 (2003).

13. Alexander Grant (ed.) *The Ethics of Aristotle*, 2 Vols (London, 1857), Vol. I, p. 210.

14. J.E.T. Rodgers (ed.), Aristotle, *Ethica Nicomachea*, ed. J.E.T Rodgers (London, 1865). The Eccles Bequest, the British Library.

15. Ibid., opposite p. 183 and opposite p. 152.
16. Ibid., on the initial blank pages of the book.
17. Ibid., opposite p. 122.
18. Notes on the *Ethics* of Aristotle, William Andrews Clark Library, W6721M3 N911.
19. Aristotle, *Ethica*, opposite p. 67.
20. See Appendix I of this book (p. 317).
21. Benjamin Jowett, the architect of the 'Greats' course at Oxford, despised classical archaeology. Even as late as 1890, Oxford University rejected a proposal to include the discipline as part of their famous course. Harris, p. 23.
22. *Rambles and Studies in Greece*, enlarged edn (London, 1878), p. 18.
23. 'Notes on Travel in Greece' (*c.* 1877), Coll. MSS Wilde, Berg Library, New York. I am indebted to Iain Ross for showing me his transcription of Wilde's fragmentary notes. See also *Complete Letters*, p. 52.
24. *Complete Letters*, p. 45.
25. I am indebted to Iain Ross for this interpretation of the punishment meted out to Wilde.
26 Ellmann, p. 75.
27. *Biograph*, p. 134.
28. See *Complete Letters*, p. 79. Wilde's complex and often ambivalent attitude to historicism and to the past is discussed in Iain Ross's unpublished D.Phil. thesis, 'The New Hellenism: Oscar Wilde and Ancient Greece', Magdalen College, University of Oxford (2007).

29. J.P. Mahaffy, *History of Greek Literature*, Vol. I (London, 1880), p. 264.
30. Melville, p. 121.
31. Harris, p. 17.

CHAPTER 10

1. Mikhail (ed.), Vol. I, p. 12.
2. Ibid., p. 13. See also Ellmann, p. 42.
3. Ellmann, p. 37.
4. Mikhail (ed.), Vol. I, p. 19.
5. The idea of the Celt as protean, imaginative, humorous, myriad-minded and intellectually agile was a commonplace of the period. It can be found in the anthologies of folklore produced by Wilde's parents, and also in scholarly works such as Ernest Renan's *The Poetry of the Celtic Races* (London, 1896) and Matthew Arnold's *On the Study of Celtic Literature* (London, 1867), both of which Wilde knew.
6. *Reviews*, p. 22.
7. Harris, pp. 26–7.
8. *Reviews*, p. 23.
9. Ibid., p. 538.
10. Mikhail (ed.), Vol. I, p. 4.
11. Ibid., p. 47.
12. *Complete Letters*, p. 20.
13. Ibid., p. 27.
14. Thomas à Kempis, *The Imitation of Christ* (London, 1875). Inscribed 'Oscar F.O'F. Wills Wilde, S.M. Magdalen College, Oxford July 6th 76'. The Eccles Bequest, the British Library.
15. Mikhail (ed.), Vol. I, p. 5.
16. *De Profundis, Selected Letters*, p. 199.
17. *Complete Letters*, p. 25.

18. Ibid., p. 452.
19. An Oxford contemporary quoted in Ellmann, p. 52.
20. *Complete Letters*, p. 39.
21. It is reproduced in Mason, p. 245.
22. *Complete Letters*, p. 41.
23. Phillip E. Smith II, 'Wilde in the Bodleian, 1878–1881', *English Literature in Transition (1880–1920)*, 46:3 (2003), pp. 279–95. I am indebted to Merlin Holland for alerting me to the article's existence.
24. Ibid., pp. 282–9.
25. Ibid., p. 286.
26. See J. Newman, *The Idea of a University* (London, 1873), p. 7. Wilde was certainly familiar with this book.
27. *Miscellanies*, p. 177.
28. 'The Critic as Artist, Part II', *Collected Works*, pp. 1012–3.
29. *De Profundis, Selected Letters*, p. 155.
30. See Shuter, pp. 250–4. See also Linda Dowling, *Hellenism and Homosexuality in Victorian Oxford* (Ithaca and London, 1994), p. 119.
31. *Complete Letters*, pp. 102–3.
32. Ibid., pp. 19–20.
33. Ibid., p. 430.
34. In his letters to fellow Oxonians Wilde often includes Greek and Latin quotations; he also peppered his conversation with them, to the annoyance of those who had not received a classical education.
35. Ellmann, p. 302.
36. R. Shewan (ed.), 'A Wife's Tragedy', *Theatre Research International*, 7:2 (1982), pp. 86–8.
37. Dowling, pp. 72–3.

CHAPTER 11

1. *Miscellanies*, p. 60, and Mikhail (ed.), Vol. I, p. 5.
2. Mikhail (ed.), Vol. I, p. 4.
3. *The Dialogues of Plato*, trans. B. Jowett, 5 vol (Oxford, 1875).
4. Sold as part of lot 47 at the Tite Street auction, the book passed through several hands before it entered the Eccles Collection, now in the British Library.
5. *Phaedrus*, *Gorgias* and *Protagoras*, the *Republic* and the *Laws* were on the Greats syllabus. *Statutes of Oxford University, 1878* (Oxford, 1878), p. 55.
6. The Platonic quotation regarding children's education in 'The Critic as Artist Part II', is, for example, taken, almost verbatim, from a passage in Jowett's translation of the 'Republic'. *Collected Works*, p. 1007. Wilde marked these lines in his copy of the *Dialogues*.
7. 'Ion', *Dialogues of Plato*, Vol. I, p. 248.
8. I am indebted to Paul Kinsella for drawing my attention to the similarities between the two dialogues. In the light of Kinsella's description of the two works as defences of oral literary values, it is interesting that Wilde marked the famous passage in 'Phaedrus' where Socrates argues that the written word is inferior to the spoken. See 'Phaedrus', *Dialogues of Plato*, vol. II, p. 154.
9. Letter from Frank Harris to Wilde, 1 September 1892, the Eccles Bequest, the British Library.

10. *Complete Letters*, p. 911.

11. Ibid., p. 40. I am indebted to Linda Dowling for pointing out the Socratic resonance of this phrase.

12. Ellmann, pp. 334–5.

13. Mikhail (ed.), Vol. II, pp. 291–3.

14. 'Symposium', *Dialogues of Plato*, Vol. II, p. 67.

15. 'Phaedrus', *Dialogues of Plato*, Vol. II, p. 154.

16. See Book VIII of the 'Republic', *Dialogues of Plato*, Vol. III, p. 451.

17. 'Lysis', *Dialogues of Plato*, Vol. I, p. 62.

18. One critic accused Symonds of encouraging 'the worst passions and most carnal inclinations of humanity', see Dowling, p. 116, and p. 91.

19. *Studies* (First Series), p. 8. Wilde has written the word 'good' next to another passage in which Symonds argues that Achilles and Patroklos' 'fraternity in arms' played for the Greek race 'the same part as the idealisation of women for the knighthood of feudal Europe'. *Studies* (Second Series), p. 60.

20. These arguments actually come from the mouth of the goddess Diotima, but Socrates reports her speech with palpable approval.

21. *The Memoirs of John Addington Symonds* (London, 1983), pp. 99–100.

22. Ibid., p. 99.

23. Ibid., p. 102.

24. 'Charmides', *Dialogues of Plato*, Vol. I, p. 10 and p. 12.

25. Harris, p. 273. Wilde also marked a reference to this episode in his copy

of Symonds's *Studies* (First Series), p. 406.

26. 'Protagoras', *Dialogues of Plato*, Vol. I, p. 121.

27. Smith II and Helfand (eds.), pp. 121 and 147. Wilde has used the Greek equivalents for the words that appear in italics.

28. 'Symposium', *Dialogues of Plato*, Vol. II, p. 20.

29. Stray, p. 82.

30. *Dorian Gray, Collected Works*, p. 84 .

31. 'The Portrait of Mr W.H.' in Ellmann (ed.), p. 184.

32. *De Profundis, Selected Letters*, p. 154.

33. *Selected Letters*, p. 169.

34. See Lord Alfred Douglas, *A Plea and a Reminiscence*, introduced by Caspar Wintermans (Woubrugge, 2002), p. 33.

35. Ellmann, p. 435.

36. Ibid., p. 57.

CHAPTER 12

1. Wilde mentions his mother's passion for Schopenhauer in *Complete Letters*, p. 25. In *Sidonia the Sorceress*, Wilde's favourite reading in boyhood, there are several footnotes which refer to German philosophy and, in particular, to Hegel.

2. *Reviews*, pp. 476–82.

3. Smith II and Helfand (eds.), p. 150.

4. Ibid., p. 128.

5. The markings in Wilde's copy of Symonds's *Studies* (Second Series) evince his fascination with Hegelian dialectic, which Symonds alludes to on several occasions. See, for

example, *Studies* (Second Series), p. 389), which Wilde marked.

6. Mason, p. 245.

7. *Dorian Gray, Collected Works*, p. 12.

8. Smith II and Helfand (eds.), p. 169.

9. *Dialogues of Plato*, Introduction to 'Parmenides', Vol. IV, p. 155.

CHAPTER 13

1. Waler Pater: *The Renaissance: Studies in Art and Poetry* (Glasgow, 1961); first published (London, 1873), pp. 122–3.

2. 'The Critic as Artist. Part I,' *Collected Works*, p. 984.

3. Pater, pp. 222–4.

4. Quoted in K. Beckson, *The Oscar Wilde Encyclopaedia* (New York, 1998), p. 2.

5. Algernon Swinburne, *Essays and Studies*, 2nd edn (London 1876), p. 380. Wilde copied out these phrases in an undergraduate notebook. See Smith II and Helfand (eds.), pp. 145, 196–7.

6. Harris, p. 24. *The Philosophy of Kant*, Mahaffy's introductory work on the German philosopher, was a set text on the Classics course Wilde took at Trinity.

7. *Studies* (First Series) exemplifies 'aesthetic criticism', offering impressionistic and emotionally charged evocations of works of art rather than detached scholarly analysis. It also uses the word 'aesthetic' on a number of occasions.

8. Ellmann, p. 43.

9. Mikhail (ed.), Vol. I, p. 249.

10. Pater, p. 189; see also Dowling, p. 108.

11. Pater, p. 220, n.

12. *De Profundis, Selected Letters*, p. 199.

13. *Reviews*, p. 539. See also Sherard, *The Life*, p. 81.

14. *De Profundis, Selected Letters*, p. 199.

15. *Dorian Gray, Collected Works*, pp. 88–9.

16. Ibid., p. 102.

17. Ibid., p. 89.

18. *Miscellanies*, p. 12.

19. *Complete Letters*, p. 59.

20. *Reviews*, p. 538.

21. See B. Inman, *Walter Pater's Reading* (New York, 1981), p. 405 and Ellmann, p. 353.

22. L. Evans (ed.), *The Letters of Walter Pater* (Oxford, 1970), p. 26.

23. Harris, p. 29.

24. [John Paul Raynaud] and Charles Ricketts, *Oscar Wilde: Recollections*, (London, 1932), p. 37.

25. *Complete Letters*, p. 349.

26. *Miscellanies*, pp. 31–2.

27. Ibid., p. 32. For an excellent discussion of Wilde's engagement with Pater and Ruskin, and their influence on him, see Ellmann, pp. 46–50.

PART II: THE LIBRARY

CHAPTER 14

1. Sherard, *Real*, p. 188.

2. *Complete Letters*, p. 224.

3. See the Victorian manual of how to design, and furnish, a library *The Private Library* (London, 1897) by Wilde's friend, Arthur L. Humphreys (London, 1897) p. 119.

4. See H. Montgomery Hyde, 'Oscar Wilde and his Architect', *Architectural Review* (March 1951), p. 175.

5. *Complete Letters*, p. 237.

6. Ricketts, p. 33.

7. *Hampshire Telegraph & Sussex Chronicle*, 27 April 1895.

8. 'The House Beautiful', published in K. O'Brien, *Oscar Wilde in Canada* (Toronto, 1982), p. 171.

9. The benefactor was Sir Peter Daubeny. I am indebted to Anthony Smith, the former President of Magdalen, for information regarding the fireplace, which is in Room 3 on the Kitchen Staircase.

10. Tite Street Catalogue, pp. 13–4.

11. Mikhail (ed.), Vol. I, p. 39.

12. Tite Street Catalogue, p. 14.

13. *Complete Letters*, p. 915.

14. R. Sherard, *Oscar Wilde: The History of an Unhappy Friendship* (London, 1902), pp. 28–9.

15. T. Wratislaw, *Oscar Wilde: A Memoir* (London, 1979), p. 17 describes Wilde as 'sitting at a table in his ground-floor workroom overlooking the street'.

16. Tite Street Catalogue, pp. 13–4. For a description of the desk see the *Glasgow Herald*, 25 April 1895.

17. See Wilde's bills for cigarettes from the tobacconist Robert Lewis & Co. among Wilde's bankruptcy papers, PRO B9/429.

18. Vyvyan Holland, p. 41.

19. *Miscellanies*, p. 154.

20. 'The House Beautiful', O'Brien, p. 177.

21. 'The Decay of Lying', *Collected Works*, p. 934.

22. Ricketts, p. 35 and see also his *Self-Portrait* (London, 1939), p. 245.

CHAPTER 15

1. List of alterations and additions drawn up by Wilde on 13 January 1885. The Eccles Bequest, the British Library.

2. H. Montgomery Hyde, *Oscar Wilde* (London, 1976), p. 121.

3. Tite Street Catalogue, p. 14.

4. Humphreys, p. 129.

5. 'The House Beautiful', O'Brien, p. 177.

6. See Andrew Lang, *The Library* (London, 1881), p. 68 and Humphreys, p. 62.

7. 'The House Beautiful', O'Brien, p. 177.

8. Newspaper clipping, (no date) the Eccles Bequest, the British Library.

9. London Post Office Directory 1895 (London, 1895).

10. Vyvyan Holland, p. 51.

11. Ibid.

12. *Dorian Gray, Collected Works*, p. 44.

13. *Complete Letters*, p. 443.

14. Vyvyan Holland, p. 51.

15. Ibid., p. 41.

16. Ibid.

17. Lang, p. 34.

18. *De Profundis, Selected Letters*, p. 155.

19. Lang, p. 34.

20. Holbrook Jackson, p. 449.

CHAPTER 16

1. *Complete Letters*, p. 352.

2. PRO File B9/428. I am indebted to

Merlin Holland's paper 'Oscar Wilde: Plagiarist or Pioneer?' for alerting me to its existence. Holland's paper was published in C.G. Sandulescu (ed.), *Rediscovering Oscar Wilde* (Gerrards Cross, 1994).

3. *Complete Letters*, p. 372 and H. Pearson, *The Life of Oscar Wilde*, revised edn (London, 1954), p. 101.

4. Mikhail (ed.), Vol. II, p. 356.

5. *Collected Letters*, p. 372 and p. 2, n.

6. Mikhail (ed.), Vol. I, p. 45.

7. *Reviews*, p. 157.

8. Wilde's book bill from Franz Thimm has survived, but it is written in a scarcely legible hand. Made out to Oscar Wilde Esq. of 9 Charles Street and dated 8 September (the year is probably 1884), it appears to include, along with *The Virgin Soil* (*Les Tierres vierges*, probably in Viardot's 1879 translation), Paul de Saint-Victor's work of dramatic criticism *Hommes et dieux* (Paris, 1882) and Alphonse de Lamartine's *Oeuvres* (Paris, 1884). It also contains a request for another Turgenev volume, *Scènes de la vie Russe*, which seems to have been unobtainable. William Andrews Clark Memorial Library, T443Z W6721. I am very grateful to Bruce Whiteman for sending me information regarding the bill, and to Merlin Holland and Donald Mead for their help in deciphering it.

9. *Reviews*, pp. 157–8.

10. Ibid., p. 368 and *Complete Letters*, p. 399.

11. Mikhail (ed.), Vol. I, p. 173. All of these titles are listed in the Tite Street Catalogue.

12. 'The Critic as Artist, Part II', *Collected Works*, p. 1015.

13. All of these titles are listed in the Tite Street Catalogue pp. 7–10.

14. 'The Critic as Artist, Part I', *Collected Works*, p. 973. See also Wilde's notes on the *Poetics* in the 'Exercise book used for Greek and Latin at Trinity College Dublin, 1873?' William Andrews Clark Library, W6721M3 E96.

15. Aristotle, *Aristotle's Theory of Poetry and Fine Art* (London, 1895), p. 207.

16. See *Complete Letters*, p. 554.

17. Ibid.

18. Ibid., pp. 563–4.

19. Beckson, *Encyclopaedia*, p. 338.

20. Tite Street Catalogue, p. 7.

21. Ibid., p. 5.

22. Ibid., p. 4.

23. *The 'Eighty Club'* (London, 1890). The book is now in the William Andrews Clark Memorial Library, PR5828. E34. I am greatly indebted to Bruce Whiteman, Head Librarian of the Clark, for alerting me to its existence.

24. Tite Street Catalogue, p. 9.

25. Sherard, *The Life*, p. 91.

26. Nutt invoice. 'The Vision of MacConglinne: A Middle Irish Wonder Tale', ed. and trans. K. Meyer (London, 1891). Wilde purchased it on 1 November 1891.

27. Ibid. It was published in London in 1888.

28. Nutt invoice. Wilde purchased it on 27 March 1889.
29. *Reviews*, p. 430.
30. Clippings from auctioneers' and book dealers' catalogues, the Eccles Collection, the British Library.
31. *Reviews*, pp. 420–4.
32. Ibid., p. 356.
33. Ibid., pp. 448–9.
34. Ibid., p. 452.
35. 'The Decay of Lying', *Collected Works*, p. 928.
36. K. Beckson (ed.), *Oscar Wilde: The Critical Heritage* (London, 1970), p. 83.
37. 'The Soul of Man', *Collected Works*, p. 1053.
38. *Complete Letters*, p. 1052.
39. *Miscellanies*, p. 258.
40. Ellmann, pp. 323–4.
41. 'The Decay of Lying', *Collected Works*, p. 931.

CHAPTER 17

1. E. Behuke, *Voice Exercises* and Walton's *Compleat Angler*, Tite Street Catalogue, p. 7 and p. 10.
2. Edward Heron-Allen sent Wilde his *Violin-making* (London, 1884): see *Complete Letters*, p. 245. The Eccles Bequest, the British Library contains a copy of Amy Fay's *Music-Study in Germany* (Chicago, 1882) inscribed to Wilde. The cuttings from the auctioneers' and book dealers' catalogues in the Eccles Bequest also mention an inscribed copy of Leo Engel's *American & Other Drinks* (New York, 1878).
3. *The Theory of Theatrical Dancing*

(London, 1888). Tite Street Catalogue, p. 10,
4. Benjamin Williams was the author. The book was published in London in 1877.
5. *Complete Letters*, p. 617.
6. I. Small, *Oscar Wilde Revalued* (Greensboro, 1993), p. 144.
7. The book was published in London in 1889. See Tite Street Catalogue, p. 4.
8. Franz Hartmann, *The Life of Paracelsus* (London, 1887), it is listed in the Tite Street Catalogue on p. 7.
9. Hartmann, pp. v–vii.
10. 'The Critic as Artist', Part II, *Collected Works*, p. 997.
11. Tite Street Catalogue, p. 9.
12. (London, 1893), Tite Street Catalogue, p. 5.
13. The book was published in London in 1888. Tite Street Catalogue, p. 5.
14. *The Five Talents of Woman*, p. 112.
15. *Reviews*, p. 75 and p. 42.
16. 'The Decay of Lying', *Collected Works*, p. 925.
17. 'The Importance of Being Earnest', *Collected Works*, p. 712 and p. 685.
18. Comyns Carr, *Margaret Maliphant* (London, 1889), W. M. Hardinge, *Eugenia, An Episode* (London, 1883), and Blanche Roosevelt, *Hazel Fane* (London, 1891), Tite Street Catalogue, pp. 6–8.
19. This was published in London in 1894. Tite Street Catalogue p. 7.
20. Ibid., p. 11.
21. *Alison [A Novel] By the author of 'Miss Molly'* (London, 1883).
22. *Complete Letters*, pp. 623–4.

23. Ibid., n. p. 3 and p. 230.
24. (London, 1891), the Eccles Bequest, the British Library.
25. *Complete Letters*, p. 249.
26. See Kerry Powell, 'Tom Dick and Dorian Gray: Magic-Picture Mania in Late Victorian Fiction', *Philological Quarterly*, 62:2 (1983) and also his 'The Mesmerizing of Dorian Gray', *Victorian Newsletter*, 65 (1984).
27. Margot Asquith, *More Memories* (London, 1933), p. 119.
28. Anthony Hope, *The Dolly Dialogues* (London, 1894), p. 4.
29. *Alison*, p. 564.
30. *Dorian Gray, Collected Works*, p. 113.
31. *Reviews*, pp. 472–3.

CHAPTER 18

1. J. Clegg (ed.), *The Directory of Second-Hand Booksellers and List of Public Libraries British & Foreign* (London, 1888).
2. *Complete Letters*, p. 80.
3. See Charles Hirsch, 'Hirsch's Memoirs of Oscar Wilde and Smithers', Appendix D. P. Mendes, *Clandestine Erotic Fiction in English 1800–1930* (Aldershot, 1993), pp. 447–9.
4. Hodgson & Co., catalogue, no. 19 (1919–20) and Ellmann, p. 401.
5. Nutt invoice and *Complete Letters*, p. 540.
6. Ibid., p. 611.
7. See Wilde's bankruptcy papers, PRO File B9/428. Unfortunately Hatchards did not draw up an itemised invoice of Wilde's purchases.
8. The Eccles Bequest, the British Library.
9. Charles Hirsch, in Mendes, pp. 447–9.
10. Sherard, *Real*, p. 189.
11. *Complete Letters*, p. 588.
12. Holbrook Jackson, pp. 600 and 621.
13. This was published in London in 1893.
14. White purchased Wilde's copy of Harry Quilter, *Sententiae Artis* (London, 1886) soon after the Tite Street sale in 1895, and adorned it with his bookplate.
15. See introduction to *The Library of Edmund Gosse* (London, 1924).
16. Sherard, *Real*, p. 188.
17. *Complete Letters*, p. 917.
18. Ibid., p. 356.
19. Ibid., p. 501.
20. Stephen Calloway, 'Oscar Wilde and the Dandyism of the Senses', in P. Raby (ed.), *The Cambridge Companion to Oscar Wilde* (Cambridge, 1997), p. 48.
21. These books were published in London in 1869 and 1874 respectively.
22. Holbrook Jackson, p. 424.

CHAPTER 19

1. 'The Truth of Masks', *Collected Works*, p. 1037.
2. *De Profundis, Selected Letters*, p. 179.
3. *Complete Letters*, p. 569.
4. Ibid., p. 616 and p. 2, n. This book was offered for sale by John Hart in his catalogue no. 75, (2007) *Books of the Nineties*.
5. Tennyson, *Poems* (1858) 'with

Carlyle's autograph'. *Horæ Hellincæ* 'with Daniel O'Connell's autograph'. Tite Street Catalogue, pp. 5–6. *Horæ Hellinciæ* probably refers to John Stuart Blackie's *Horae Hellenicae: Essays and Discussions on Important Points of Greek Philology and Antiquity* (London, 1874), although Daniel O'Connell, who died in 1847, could not, of course, have owned this volume. Once again, the confusion must be due to the inaccuracy of the Tite Street Catalogue.

6. *Endymion* (London, 1818), *Lamia* (London, 1820) Cuttings from auctioneers' and book dealers' catalogues, the Eccles Bequest, the British Library.

7. The Schwob volume, which was published in Paris in 1894, is in the Eccles Bequest, the British Library.

8. *Complete Letters*, p. 624.

9. Rossetti, *Poems* (London, 1881), Michael Field, *The Tragic Mary* (London, 1890).

10. Michael Field, *Works and Days* (London, 1933), p. 139.

11. Wilde's *Sidonia* is in the collection of Dartmouth College, New Hampshire. I am indebted to Mark Samuels Lasner for alerting me to its existence.

12. *Dorian Gray, Collected Works*, p. 19.

13. *Complete Letters*, p. 984.

14. Mikhail (ed.), Vol. II, p. 380.

15. *Reviews*, p. 392.

16. *Complete Letters*, p. 395.

17. Ibid., p. 1173.

18. Ibid., p. 969.

19. Unpublished and undated letter offered for sale in January 2007 on abebooks.co.uk by Michael Silverman.

20. *Complete Letters*, p. 502.

21. *A House of Pomegranates* (London, 1891), *The Sphinx* (London, 1894). For further discussion of Wilde's idea of 'the Book Beautiful' and of his first editions, see Nicholas Frankel's study *Oscar Wilde's Decorated Books* (Michigan, 2000).

22. C. Millard, 'Memoir of Wilde', in H. Montgomery Hyde, *Christopher Sclater Millard* (London, 1990) p. 130.

23. *Dorian Gray, Collected Works*, p. 89.

24. Ibid., p. 34.

25. 'Pen, Pencil and Poison', *Collected Works*, p. 950.

26. 'The Critic as Artist' Part II, *Collected Works*, p. 994.

27. O'Sullivan, p. 217.

CHAPTER 20

1. Mikhail (ed.), Vol. II, p. 429.

2. *Complete Letters*, p. 453.

3. He was referring to William Morris's translation of the *Odyssey*. *Reviews*, pp. 154–5.

4. Of William Morris's *The Roots of the Mountain*. *Complete Letters*, p. 476.

5. *Reviews*, p. 339.

6. *Complete Letters*, p. 666.

7. *Reviews*, pp. 11–2.

8. *Dorian Gray, Collected Works*, p. 88.

9. Ibid., p. 114.

10. *Complete Letters*, p. 1144.

11. *Reviews*, p. 247.

12. 'The Critic as Artist, Part I', *Collected Works*, p. 972.

13. *Reviews*, p. 79.

14. Ibid., p. 389.
15. Sherard, *Real*, p. 188.
16. Both books are in the Eccles Bequest, the British Library.
17. Wilde, O. Notes on the *Fragments of the Greek Poets*.
18. (New edition, 1877), The book is in the Old Library at Magdalen College, Oxford. I am grateful to Magdalen's librarian, Dr Christine Ferdinand for showing it to me.
19. Wilde's copy of Symonds's *Studies* (First Series), p. 12.
20. *Complete Letters*, p. 287.
21. *Reviews*, p. 1.
22. 'The Critic as Artist', Part II, *Collected Works*, p. 1006.
23. Ibid.
24. *Biograph*, p. 131.
25. From the diary of George Ives, quoted in John Stokes, *Myths, Miracles and Imitations* (Cambridge, 1996), p. 83.
26. *De Profundis, Selected Letters*, p. 237.
27. 'The Critic as Artist, Part II', *Collected Works*, p. 1009.
28. 'The Young King', ibid., p. 248.
29. Mason, p. 368.
30. Vyvyan Holland, p. 54.
31. Sherard, *Real*, p. 84.
32. O'Sullivan, p. 96. The book was by W.E. Henley.
33. *Dorian Gray, Collected Works*, p. 90.
34. 'The Critic as Artist, Part I', *Collected Works*, p. 974.
35. *Miscellanies*, p. 273.
36. 'The Critic as Artist, Part II', *Collected Works*, p. 1005.
37. Ibid., p. 1003.
38. Ibid., p. 999.
39. *Dorian Gray*, ibid., pp. 99–100.
40. *Reviews*, p. 540.
41. The Critic as Artist, Part II,' *Collected Works*, p. 998.
42. Quoted in Philipe Jullian, *Oscar Wilde* (London, 1969), p. 200.
43. 'The Spirit Lamp', *The London Mercury*, 25: 148, (February 1932), p. 387.
44. Sherard, *The Life*, p. 23.
45. 'The Critic as Artist, Part I', *Collected Works*, p. 978.
46. *Complete Letters*, p. 855.
47. Ellmann, p. 235.
48. *Reviews*, p. 509.
49. W.B. Maxwell, *Time Gathered* (London, 1937), p. 142.
50. Ellmann, p. 21.
51. Holbrook Jackson, p. 434.
52. Maxwell, p. 142.
53. Ellmann, p. 21.
54. Mikhail (ed.), Vol. I, p. 192.
55. Ibid., p. 198. Wilde's friend later discovered that the quotation actually appeared on page 8 of Pater's book. We can only hope she was not heartless enough to inform Wilde of his slight error.

CHAPTER 21

1. W.B. Yeats, *Autobiographies* (New York, 1965) p. 136.
2. Ibid.
3. Ibid., p. 136.
4. The friend was Robbie Ross. *De Profundis, Selected Letters*, p. 157.
5. *Complete Letters*, pp. 911 and 688.
6. See, for example, Laurence Housman's *Echo de Paris* (London, 1923).
7. Wratislaw, p. 17.

8. Mikhail (ed.), Vol. II, p. 391.
9. William Andrews Clark Library, W6721M3.
10. Humphreys, pp. 127–8.
11. Pryde, p. 10.
12. Holbrook Jackson, p. 346.
13. Ibid., p. 286.
14. 'The Decay of Lying', *Collected Works*, p. 921.

CHAPTER 22

1. This is now at the Harry Ransom Humanities Center in Texas, shelfmark PN2597. I am indebted to John B. Thomas III for sending me this information.
2. Wilde's copy of George Meredith's *One of Our Conquerors* (London, 1891) is part of the Eccles Bequest, the British Library.
3. *Reviews*, p. 389.
4. See, for example, *Complete Letters*, p. 1, n; see also p. 531.
5. Ibid., p. 3, n; see also p. 1026.
6. Ibid., p. 898.
7. Ibid., p. 83.
8. The book was published in London in 1878. Sotheby's catalogue, 29 October 2004 (London), p. 21.
9. Mikhail (ed.), Vol. I, p. 139.
10. I am indebted to the owner of the book, Nali Dinshaw, for this information, and to Tessa Milne of Sotheby's for putting me in contact with her.
11. She was unable to do so. Letter from Nellie Sickert to Oscar Wilde *c.* 1881, in the Eccles Bequest, the British Library.
12. *Complete Letters*, p. 360.

13. Neil McKenna, *The Secret Life of Oscar Wilde* (London, 2003).
14. *Complete Letters*, p. 542.
15. *De Profundis, Selected Letters*, p. 157.
16. *Complete Letters*, pp. 407–8.
17. Ibid., p. 1229.
18. Ibid., p. 956.
19. Ibid., pp. 789–90.
20. It is now at Princeton. I am indebted to Mark Samuels Lasner for this information.
21. Arnold's 'Tristram and Iseult' appeared in his volume *Empedocles on Etna and Other Poems* (London, 1852). Swinburne's *Tristram of Lyonesse* was issued in London in 1882. Wilde would have known both books. See *Complete Letters*, ft. 1. p. 784.
22. Ibid., p. 1041.
23. Ibid., n. p. 1; see also p. 1128.
24. See Dowling, p. 34, n; see also p. 143.
25. The Eccles Bequest, The British Library.
26. Vyvyan Holland, p. 45.
27. I am indebted to Mark Samuels Lasner for this information.
28. It is now in the Eccles Collection, the British Library.
29. Sherard, *The Life*, pp. 317–8.
30. *Complete Letters*, pp. 241–2.
31. *De Profundis, Selected Letters*, p. 176.
32. *Complete Letters*, p. 785.
33. Ellmann, p. 222.
34. Ibid., p. 121.
35. Algernon Swinburne, *Erechtheus: A Tragedy* (London, 1876). The book is now in the William Andrews Clark Library, PR5828.S9E6.

36. Both of these books are in the Harry Ransom Humanities Center, University of Texas at Austin. I am indebted to John B. Thomas III, for alerting me to their existence.
37. Melville, pp. 227–8.
38. See, for example, a copy of *The Ballad* he gave to 'Alfred' (certainly not Alfred Douglas) in the Eccles Bequest, the British Library.
39. This volume is now at the Harry Ransom Humanities Center in Texas.
40. Catalogue of Hôtel Drouot, 2 April 1990 (Paris).
41. Mason, p. 9.
42. B. Fong and K. Beckson (eds.), *Poems and Poems in Prose: The Complete Works of Oscar Wilde* (Oxford, 2000), p. 167 and pp. 300–1.
43. Henry Danielson, A Catalogue of Books, no. 12, 1921 (London).
44. *De Profundis, Selected Letters*, p. 179.
45. *In a Music Hall and Other Poems* by John Davidson (London, 1891) given to Wilde on 7 January 1892. Clippings from auctioneers' and book dealers' catalogues, the Eccles Collection, the British Library.
46. Marcel Schwob, *Le Roi au masque d'or* (Paris, 1893). This book is now in the collection of Merlin Holland, who kindly alerted me to its existence.
47. I am indebted to Ludovica Piombino, Gino Scatasta and Paolo Trucco of the University of San Rocchino for identifying the poem.
48. Ellmann, ft p. 125. The Eccles Bequest, the British Library.

CHAPTER 23

1. *Complete Letters*, pp. 289–90.
2. Ibid., pp. 284–290.
3. Mikhail (ed.), Vol. I, p. 230.
4. Wilde, 'Chatterton Lecture' (1886?), pp. 6 and 82–4.
5. R. Rodd, *Social and Diplomatic Memories* (London, 1922), p. 22.
6. *Complete Letters*, p. 874.
7. See 'The Critic as Artist, Part I', *Collected Works*, p. 976.
8. *Complete Letters*, p. 1080.
9. Wilde, notes on *Fragments of the Greek Poets* (1873).
10. *Reviews*, p. 259.
11. Ibid., p. 92.
12. Ricketts, *Recollections*, p. 13.
13. *Reviews*, p. 86.
14. *Complete Letters*, p. 480.
15. *Reviews*, p. 542.
16. The manuscript of 'The Women of Homer' is held at the Pierpont Morgan Library, New York, MA 3574; the William Andrews Clark Library has a typescript version prepared by Robert Ross, which he re-christened 'Greek Women'. It has recently been published for the first time as the Oscar Wilde Society Publication: T. Wright and D. Mead (eds.), *Oscar Wilde: The Women of Homer* (London, 2008).
17. T. Wright and D. Mead (eds.), p. 33, and *Studies* (First Series), p. 97. Wilde's undergraduate essay represents the final stage of a systematic attempt to absorb Symonds's style. The markings in Wilde's copy of *Studies* suggest that

one of his primary aims, in reading it, was to learn tricks and effects from its prose. Thus he glosses marvellous metaphors with comments such as 'very charming'. In his undergraduate notebooks, Wilde also paraphases Symonds, as though in an attempt to assimilate his style. See introduction to T. Wright and D. Mead (eds.).

18. R. Miracco (ed.), *Oscar Wilde. Verso il Sole* (Napoli, 1981). p. 31.

19. This description of Wilde in full flow comes from his actress friend Elizabeth Robins and is reproduced in Sandulescu (ed.), p. 317.

20. Ellmann, p. 140.

21. For a discussion of Wilde's plagiarism see J. Guy and I. Small, *Oscar Wilde's Profession* (Oxford, 2000) and also I. Small, *Conditions of Criticism* (Oxford, 1991), from which I have derived some of the ideas contained in this chapter.

22. See letter of W.E. Henley to Wilde, 25 November 1888, reproduced in I. Small, *Oscar Wilde Revalued*, p. 78. For Wilde's reply to Henley see *Complete Letters*, p. 372.

23. See T. d'arch Smith and H. Schroeder, 'Feasting with Panthers', *Notes & Queries*, NS 45 (1995), pp. 201–2.

24. For example, Wilde plundered E. Lefébure's *Embroidery and Lace* (London, 1888), a book he had enthusiastically reviewed. *Reviews*, pp. 327–341.

25. R. Hart-Davis (ed.), Max Beerbohm, *Letters to Reggie Turner* (London, 1964), p. 36.

26. Quoted in Robert Ross, 'A Note on *Salome*', *Salome* (London, 1909), pp. 20–1.

27. *Complete Letters*, p. 915.

28. I have stolen this idea from Merlin Holland's paper 'Oscar Wilde: Plagiarist or Pioneer?'

29. Mikhail (ed.), Vol. II, p. 308.

30. Wilde, 'Chatterton Lecture' (1886?), pp. 84–7.

31. *Complete Letters*, p. 856.

CHAPTER 24

1. *Complete Letters*, p. 4, n; also see p. 453.

2. Ibid., p. 454.

3. I am indebted to Mark Samuels Lasner for this information. For further details regarding Wilde's relationship with Fitch see McKenna, pp. 111–4.

4. 'The Critic as Artist, Part II', *Collected Works*, p. 1009.

5. McKenna, p. 111.

6. Wratislaw, p. 17. See above, p. 000.

7. The details of Wilde's book gifts to Shelley came to light during the Queensberry Trial, at which Wilde's literary presents to another young man called Alfonso Conway were also mentioned. Wilde gave Conway a copy of W. Clark Russell's *The Wreck of the Grosvenor* (London, 1891) and Robert Louis Stevenson's *Treasure Island* (London, 1883). See M. Holland (ed.), *Irish Peacock and Scarlet Marquis: The Real Trial of Oscar Wilde* (London, 2003), pp. 316–17.

8. This theory was suggested by Merlin Holland in *Scarlet Marquis*, p. 142 and p. 316.

9. *Complete Letters*, p. 961.
10. This translation of Lionel Johnson's 'In Honorem Dorian Creatorisque Eius' was made by Richard Ellmann on p. 306 of his biography.
11. McKenna, p. 149.
12. *Dorian Gray, Collected Works*, pp. 33–4.
13. Ibid., p. 80.
14. *Complete Letters*, p. 585.
15. William Freeman, *The Life of Lord Alfred Douglas* (London, 1948), p. 282.
16. 'The Portrait of Mr W.H.', in Ellmann (ed.), p. 187.

CHAPTER 25

1. *Complete Letters*, p. 461.
2. Alfred Douglas, 'Notes for Frank Harris', the Eccles Bequest, the British Library. Typically, Douglas gave several versions of this anecdote, later claiming to have read the novel fourteen times *before* he had met Wilde (see McKenna, p. 149).
3. Ibid.
4. *Dorian Gray, Collected Works*, pp. 88–9.
5. Douglas, 'Notes for Frank Harris'.
6. *The Oscar Wilde Collection of John B. Stetson* (New York, 1920), item 14.
7. Ibid., item 51.
8. Ibid., item 84.
9. *Catalogue of Rare Books offered for Sale from the Collection of Giles Gordon. Oscar Wilde, Aubrey Beardsley and the 1890s.* Gekoski Catalogue no. 18 (1994), item 183 (London).
10. I am indebted to Caspar Wintermans for alerting me to the existence of the Marvell, which is in the collection of the late Sheila

Colman. *The Faithful Shepherdess* (1897) is inscribed 'Bosie from Oscar Paris'; like Douglas's copy of Thomson's poems, it forms part of the Eccles Bequest, the British Library.
11. *Complete Letters*, pp. 620–1.
12. *Ghazels from the Divan of Hafiz* (London, 1893), trans. Justin Huntley McCarthy, p. 97 and p. 12.
13. *De Profundis, Selected Letters*, pp. 165–6.
14. See W.H. Auden's perceptive 1962 review of *The Letters of Oscar Wilde* which is reproduced in R. Ellmann (ed.), *Oscar Wilde: A Collection of Critical Essays* (Englewood Cliffs, NJ, 1969).
15. *Complete Letters*, p. 948.
16. R. Croft-Cooke, *Bosie* (London, 1963), p. 67.
17. McKenna, p. 215.
18. Bonhams Catalogue, 30 September, 1997 (London, 1997).

CHAPTER 26

1. The Tite Street Catalogue, p. 10. mentions three volumes of the magazine *The Spirit Lamp* which Wilde must have received from its editor. See also *Collected Letters*, pp. 545–6.
2. For Wilde on Raffalovich see *Reviews*, p. 12. Wilde's copy of *Erotidia* (London, 1889) was sold by Hodgson's auctioneers at the start of the twentieth century. Clippings from auctioneers' and book dealers' catalogues, the Eccles Bequest, the British Library. Wilde refers to *Bertha* (London, 1885), which was published anonymously, in a letter reproduced in *Complete Letters*, p. 268.
3. *Complete Letters*, p. 268.

4. The book was published in London in 1871. Wilde's copy, which he autographed 'Oscar F. Wilde Magdalen College' is part of the Eccles Bequest, the British Library. Wilde refers to the volume in *Miscellanies*, p. 22.

5. Simeon Solomon, *A Vision of Love Revealed in Sleep*, pp. 17–9.

6. Sayle, *Bertha*. Epigraph to the poem 'étude en réaliste in August (A un jeune homme)'.

7. Quoted in C. White (ed.), *Nineteenth Century Writings on Homosexuality: A Sourcebook* (London, 1999). I am indebted to David Smith for drawing my attention to Carpenter's comments on Whitman, and for supplying me with some of the information concerning late Victorian homosexuals contained in this chapter. I have also drawn on Neil McKenna's *Secret Life*.

8. Beckson, p. 407.

9. *Complete Letters*, p. 96, p. 4, n.

10. Ellmann, pp. 161–4.

11. All of these titles are mentioned in the extended version of 'The Portrait of Mr W.H.'

12. Ellmann, p. 31.

13. Mahaffy lists a number of classical authors who refer to homosexuality in a footnote in *Social Life in Greece*, the book Wilde helped to edit. Mahaffy, *Social Life*, ft p. 311.

14. Wilde, Notes on the *Fragments of the Greek Poets*. Wilde's translations do not denote a particular prurience on his part. They simply demonstrate that homoerotic literature was studied, as a matter of course, by the superior classicists at Trinity.

15. Wilde, 'Notes on Travel in Greece' (c.1877).

16. See *Complete Letters*, p. 1070.

17. McKenna, p. 165. Krafft-Ebing's ideas inform a petition for early release that Wilde wrote to the Home Secretary during his imprisonment. See *Complete Letters*, p. 656.

18. *Complete Letters*, p. 1107.

19. Dowling, pp. 79, 130–1.

20. Symonds, *Studies* (Second Series), p. 67.

21. McKenna, p. 202.

22. *Complete Letters*, p. 1197.

23. E. Carpenter, *Civilisation: its Cause and its Cure* (London, 1899), p. 105.

24. Ellmann, p. 364, n.

25. Ives's books are now in the Harry Ransom Humanities Center Texas. I am grateful to John B. Thomas III for sending me information regarding Ives's books and for generously sharing his thoughts on Ives and Wilde with me.

26. Ibid. and *Complete Letters*, p. 1197.

27. McKenna, p. 201. I am heavily indebted to McKenna's book for the information on Ives contained in this chapter.

28. *Miscellanies*, p. 176.

29. *Complete Letters*, p. 625 and *Earnest, Collected Works*, p. 678.

30. McKenna, p. 201 and *Complete Letters*, p. 1197.

31. Letter from Alfred Douglas to George Ives, 23 December 1894. The letter is now in the possession of

the American publisher David
Deiss, who kindly sent me a copy of
it.

32. Quoted in Beckson, pp. 167–8.
33. O'Sullivan, p. 78.
34. John Stokes, p. 85.
35. *Complete Letters*, p. 1173.

CHAPTER 27

1. Published in London in 1886, the
   book is now in the collection of
   Jeremy Mason, who very kindly
   allowed me to consult it along with
   the other items in his interesting
   archive of Wildeana.
2. *Reviews*, pp. 110–5.
3. S. Weintraub (ed.), *Bernard Shaw: The
   Diaries 1885–1897*, Vol. I, (ed.). S.
   Weintraub (London, 1986).
4. All of the quotations from Quilter
   that appear in this chapter come
   from Anne Anderson's article
   'Oscar's Enemy . . . and neighbour:
   'Arry Quilter and the "Gospel of
   Intensity".' *The Wildean*, 27 (2005).
5. *Complete Letters*, p. 399.
6. *Reviews*, pp. 110–5.
7. Wilde's copy of Harry Quilter's
   Sententiæ Artis, p. 67.
8. Ibid., pp. 57 and 288.
9. Ibid., p. 177.
10. Ellmann, p. 352.
11. Wilde's copy of Quilter's *Sententiæ
    Artis*, p. 86.
12. Ibid., pp. 376–7.
13. Ibid., p. 377.
14. Wilde's unpublished letter to Cook
    is in the Eccles Bequest, the British
    Library. For both Quilter's letter of
    complaint and the editor's defence

of his reviewer see the *Pall Mall
Gazette*, 23 November 1886, pp. 11–2.

15. Tite Street Catalogue mentions a
    number of books Wilde reviewed,
    such as John Veitch's *The Feeling for
    Nature in Scottish Poetry*, W.G. Wills's
    Melchior, Lord Henry Somerset's
    Songs of Adieu and William Morris's
    A Tale of the House of the Wolfings. See
    Tite Street Catalogue, pp. 5–7. A
    reference to *Sententiæ Artis* appears on
    page 4 of the catalogue.

CHAPTER 28

1. Translation of the introduction to
   the 1934 edition of *Teleny*, published
   under the title 'Hirsch's memoirs',
   Mendes, pp. 447–9.
2. Sherard, *Real*, pp. 262–3.
3. 'The Critic as Artist, Part II',
   Collected Works, p. 994.
4. Ellmann, p. 254.
5. *Complete Letters*, p. 175.
6. Ellmann, p. 237.
7. *Hampshire Telegraph & Sussex Chronicle*
   27 April, 1895.
8. See Alexander Michaelson (Marc-
   André Raffalovich), 'Oscar Wilde',
   Blackfriars, November 1927 and
   Merlin Holland (ed.), *Scarlet Marquis*,
   p. 313, n. 140.
9. Neil Bartlett, *Who Was that Man?*
   (London, 1988), pp. 105–6, from
   which I have derived this plot
   summary and the immortal
   quotation.
10. Arthur Symons 'The Decadent
    Movement in Art and Literature',
    quoted in Beckson, p. 64.
11. Ibid.

12. Ellmann, p. 332.
13. Mikhail (ed.), Vol. I, p. 199.
14. *Complete Letters*, n. p. 1, p. 435.
15. Beckson, p. 328.
16. Mikhail (ed.), Vol. I, p. 188.
17. Ellmann, p. 327.
18. *Complete Letters*, p. 625.
19. Merlin Holland (ed.), *Scarlet Marquis*, pp. 69–70.
20. In 1888 Smithers wrote to Wilde to praise his fairy tale 'The Happy Prince'. Wilde was gratified by the praise and gave the publisher the manuscript of the story, which he cordially inscribed 'To Leonard Smithers from his friend & a grateful friend, Oscar Wilde' (Catalogue of Valuable Books, Sotheby's, 1932). As Wilde's manuscripts were either dispersed or placed in safe-keeping after the sale of his goods in 1895, this must have been presented to Smithers before his trials. The pair had, in any case, so many mutual friends in the small world of artistic and literary London that it is almost inconceivable that their paths never crossed in the first half of the 1890s. Smithers was an habitué of the Café Royal and the Crown, a pub which Wilde frequented; he also attended some of the first nights of Wilde's plays.
21. *Complete Letters*, p. 924.
22. Ibid., p. 1063.
23. Ibid., p. 972 evidences Wilde's familiarity with Sir Richard Burton and Leonard Smithers's translations of Catullus, which the latter issued

in 1894 under the title *The Carmina of Caius Valerius Catullus* (London, 1894). See also O'Sullivan, pp. 113–4.

24. Anon., *White Stains* (London, 1898).
25. *Complete Letters*, p. 1093 and Mendes, pp. 308–9.
26. 'Hirsch's memoirs', Mendes, p. 447.
27. Quoted in H. Montgomery Hyde, *The Other Love* (London, 1970), p. 122.
28. 'Hirsch's Memoirs', Mendes, p. 252.

CHAPTER 29

1. This phrase is taken on loan from Richard Ellmann.
2. *Complete Letters*, p. 810.
3. *Reviews*, pp. 260–1.
4. Mikhail (ed.), Vol. I, p. 43 and p. 90.
5. Pearson, p.231.
6. *Complete Letters*, pp. 588–9.
7. Letter from Alfred Douglas to George Ives, 23 December 1894. In the possession of David Deiss, who kindly sent me a photocopy of it.
8. Ellmann, p. 377.
9. Ibid., p. 314.
10. *De Profundis, Selected Letters*, p. 155.
11. Ibid., p. 194.
12. H. Montgomery Hyde, *The Trials of Oscar Wilde* (Edinburgh, 1948), p. 177.
13. Ellmann, p. 371.
14. Ibid., pp. 419–20.
15. Ibid., p. 424.
16. Ibid., p. 394.
17. Ibid., pp. 420–1 and *De Profundis, Selected Letters*, p. 167.
18. *Complete Letters*, p. 634.

19. Ellmann, p. 360.
20. Mikhail (ed.), Vol. II, p. 296.
21. See the introduction to Merlin Holland (ed.), *Scarlet Marquis.*
22. Ellmann, p. 429.
23. Hyde, *Trials,* p. 154, n. 1.
24. Ellmann, p. 430.

PART III: A LIBRARY OF LAMENTATIONS

CHAPTER 30

1. R. Jackson (ed.), *The Importance of Being Earnest* (London, 1980), p. 110.
2. *Complete Letters,* pp. 650–1.
3. Harris, p. 155.
4. 'The Decay of Lying', *Collected Works,* p. 924.
5. *Complete Letters,* pp. 647–8.
6. Ibid., p. 647.
7. Robert Ross, Introduction to *A Florentine Tragedy.*
8. Ellmann, pp. 435–6.
9. Ibid., p. 439.
10. Ibid.
11. Mikhail (ed.), Vol. I, p. 135.
12. Sherard, *History,* p. 171.
13. Sherard, *The Life,* p. 366.
14. Ellmann, p. 439.
15. Ada Leverson, *Letters to the Sphinx* (London, 1930), p. 42.
16. Ellmann, p. 441.
17. Quilter quotations are taken from Anne Anderson's article 'Oscar's Enemy . . . and Neighbour'.

CHAPTER 31

1. P. Priestley, *Victorian Prison Lives,* (London and New York, 1985), p. 289.

2. Anon., *Pentonville from Within* (London, 1904), p. 31.
3. I have been unable to ascertain whether the cells at Pentonville had built-in lavatories. The so-called 'slopping out system' was certainly used at Reading Gaol, where Wilde served out the bulk of his sentence. Cellular sanitation was not reinstated at Reading until the 1980s.
4. R. Sherard, *Twenty Years in Paris* (London, 1905), p. 428.
5. Mikhail (ed.), Vol. II, p. 100.
6. Priestley, p. 36.
7. Ibid., p. 37 and M. Foucault, *Discipline and Punish* (London, 1977), p. 237.
8. Ellmann, p. 451.
9. Rules of Wandsworth prison *c.*1910, p. 351. I am greatly indebted to Stewart McLaughlin, historian of the prison, for sending me photocopies of the relevant pages from the prison rule-book.
10. H. Montgomery Hyde, *Oscar Wilde: The Aftermath* (London, 1963), p. 275.
11. Mikhail (ed.), Vol. II, pp. 323–4.
12. Haldane to the Governor of Pentonville prison 28 June 1895, Prison Commission file 8/432, PRO.
13. Letter from the Governor of Pentonville to the Prison Commission, 2 July 1895, ibid.
14. Priestley, p. 289.
15. Letter from Irishwoman to the Governor of Pentonville 8 June 1895, Prison Commission file 8/434.

CHAPTER 32

1. Governor of Wandsworth to the Prison Commission, 17 August 1895, Prison Commission file 8/432, PRO.
2. The library at Reading Gaol. Hyde, *Aftermath*, p. 87.
3. Rules of Wandsworth prison, p. 10 and Priestley, p. 111.
4. Priestley, p. 107.
5. Ibid., p. 112.
6. M. Ross (ed.), *Robert Ross, Friend of Friends* (London, 1952), p. 40.
7. O'Sullivan, p. 219. O'Sullivan attributes these words to Haldane but it is hard to imagine such an enlightened man uttering them. They are far more likely to have come from the lips of Pentonville's governor. Perhaps Haldane quoted them to Wilde.
8. Pentonville prison's library stocked a copy of the book in the 1890s. *Pentonville from Within*, p. 175.
9. Walter Besant, *The Ivory Gate*, Vol. III (London, 1892), p. 287 and p. 293.
10. *Complete Letters*, p. 1047.
11. *Pentonville from Within*, p. 41.
12. M. Ross (ed.), p. 40.
13. Sherard, *Real*, p. 258.
14. Haldane to Ruggles-Brise, Chairman of the Prison Commission, 24 August 1895, ibid.
15. It is in the Eccles Bequest, the British Library.
16. Gilbert, in 'The Critic as Artist, Part II', calls this the 'most suggestive' story in Pater's volume.

For Wilde's initial response to the book see *Reviews*, pp. 172–5.

17. Wilde's copy of *Imaginary Portraits* (London, 1887), is part of the Eccles Bequest, the British Library, see pp. 122–3 and 170.
18. *Complete Letters*, p. 1047.
19. Ellmann, p. 465.
20. *Complete Letters*, p. 665, p. 2, n.
21. Anthony Stokes, *Pit of Shame* (Winchester, 2007), p. 82.

CHAPTER 33

1. *De Profundis, Selected Letters*, p. 219.
2. Isaacson to the Home Office, 9 November 1895. Prison Commission file 8/433, PRO.
3. Ellmann, p. 468.
4. *De Profundis, Selected Letters*, p. 186 and p. 224.
5. O'Sullivan, p. 63.
6. T. Wright and D. Mead (eds.), p. 45. The episode is recounted in Homer's *Odyssey*, Book XI, lines 148–221.
7. *Complete Letters*, p. 858.
8. Ellmann, p. 467.
9. *Complete Letters*, p. 654.
10. See Wilde's copy of Walter Pater's *Imaginary Portraits*, the Eccles Bequest, the British Library.
11. Beckson, pp. 1–2.
12. *Complete Letters*, p. 653.
13. M. Ross (ed.), p. 40.
14. Harris, p. 193.
15. Stokes, p. 85.
16. M. Ross (ed.), p. 40. Italicised by Ross.
17. *Complete Letters*, p. 657.
18. Prison Commission to Major

Nelson, 27 July 1896, quoted in
Hyde, *Aftermath*, pp. 77–8.

19. Governor of Reading Gaol to the
Prison Commission, 29 July 1896,
Prison Commission file 8/433,
PRO.

20. George Ives, Diary entry, 1926,
Harry Ransom Humanities Center,
Texas. I am greatly indebted to
John B. Thomas III for transcribing
this entry for me.

21. Mikhail (ed.), Vol. II, p. 329.

22. Sherard, *Twenty Years*, p. 427.

23. *Complete Letters*, p. 667.

24. Governor of Reading Gaol to the
Prison Commission, 10 November
1896, Prison Commission file 8/433,
PRO.

25. Notes Adey made after that
meeting: MS Walpole, d.18,
Bodleian Library.

26. Nelson to Adey, 11 February 1897,
the Eccles Bequest, the British
Library.

27. Governor of Reading Gaol to the
Prison Commission, 12 March 1897,
Prison Commission file 8/434, PRO.

CHAPTER 34

1. *De Profundis, Selected Letters*, p. 164.

2. Mikhail (ed.), Vol. II, p. 330.

3. Sherard, *Twenty Years*, p. 427.

4. *De Profundis, Selected Letters*, pp. 200–1.

5. T. Wright and D. Mead (eds.),
p. 51.

6. *De Profundis, Selected Letters*, p. 160.

7. *Complete Letters*, p. 957.

8. Ibid., p. 1002.

9. André Gide, *Oscar Wilde* (London,
1906), pp. 59–60.

10. *Complete Letters*, p. 1129.

11. Ibid., p. 166.

12. Letter from More Adey to Adela
Schuster, 16 March 1897, William
Andrews Clark Library (A233L S395
1897 Mar 16).

13. *De Profundis, Selected Letters*, p. 199.

14. Harris, p. 194.

15. Mikhail (ed.), Vol. II, p. 384.

16. Ibid., p. 379.

CHAPTER 35

1. *Complete Letters*, p. 789.

2. Ibid., p. 409.

3. Ibid., p. 669.

4. Ibid., p. 967.

5. See below p. 000.

6. *Complete Letters*, p. 884.

7. Ibid., pp. 780–1.

8. Mikhail (ed.), Vol. II, p. 332.

9. *Complete Letters*, p. 667.

10. *De Profundis, Selected Letters*, p. 211.

11. Ibid., p. 195 and p. 209.

12. *The Ballad of Reading Gaol, Collected
Works*, p. 896.

13. *Complete Letters*, p. 669.

14. *De Profundis, Selected Letters*,
p. 239.

15. Wilde's copy of *Imaginary Portraits*,
the Eccles Bequest, the British
Library, p. 170.

16. *Complete Letters*, p. 880.

17. Ellmann, p. 486.

18. Sherard, *Twenty Years*, pp. 420–1.

19. *Complete Letters*, n. 1, p. 660.

20. Ibid., p. 802.

21. Ibid.

22. Ibid., p. 790.

23. Ibid., p. 887.

24. Ibid., p. 673.

25. Ibid., p. 668.
26. Ibid., p. 880.

CHAPTER 36

1. Ellmann, p. 492.
2. *De Profundis, Selected Letters*, p. 196.
3. *Complete Letters*, pp. 790–1. The parentheses in this quotation are mine, not Wilde's.
4. Ibid.
5. Beckson, p. 352 and M.A. Belloc, *The Merry Wives of Westminster*, (London, 1946), p. 46.
6. See above p. 000.
7. F.G. Bettany, *Stewart Headlam* (London, 1926), p. 132.
8. *Complete Letters*, p. 841.
9. Hyde, *Aftermath*, p. 143.
10. Max Beerbohm, *Letters to Reggie Turner*, p. 118, n.
11. A letter from Reginald Turner to C.S. Millard, 29 October 1910, the William Andrews Clark Library, T951LM645.
12. *Complete Letters*, p. 844.
13. Ibid., p. 846.
14. Both buildings were bombed during the Second World War. The site of the Chalet is now marked by a pathway named 'sentier Oscar Wilde'.
15. See, for example, Gide, *Oscar Wilde*, p. 49.
16. *Complete Letters*, p. 856.
17. Ibid., p. 855.
18. Letter of 18 May 1897, Stetson Collection Catalogue, item 379. The book was *The Poetical Works of Aubrey de Vere. Volume V* (London, 1897).
19. Harris, p. 333.

20. Published in Paris in 1897.
21. *Complete Letters*, p. 874. Wilde's italics.
22. Ellmann, p. 509.
23. *Complete Letters*, p. 946.
24. This unpublished letter, which probably dates from the latter half of June 1897, is written in French. In the letter Wilde does not identify the books he received. It is in the collection of Julia Rosenthal who very kindly allowed me to see it.
25. London, 1896.
26. *Complete Letters*, p. 901.
27. Ellmann, p. 507.
28. Paris, 1896.
29. It is now part of the Eccles Bequest, the British Library.
30. *Complete Letters*, pp. 873–4.
31. Ibid,. p. 898. This is a reference to the yellow covers that adorned works of modern French literature.
32. Gide, *Oscar Wilde*, p. 52.
33. *Complete Letters*, p. 922.
34. Ibid., p. 1101 and p. 924.
35. London, 1896 and London, 1897.

CHAPTER 37

1. O'Sullivan, p. 221.
2. Letter from More Adey to Adela Schuster, 16 March 1897, William Andrews Clark Library.
3. I am assuming that Wilde was sent most, if not all, of the books that he requested.
4. London, 1897.
5. *Complete Letters*, p. 753.
6. Ellmann, p. 508.
7. *Complete Letters*, p. 1041.

8. Ibid., p. 1056.
9. Ricketts, *Recollections*, p. 48.
10. Quoted in Pearson, *Oscar Wilde*, p. 332.
11. London, 1895.
12. Paris, 1890.
13. *De Profundis, Selected Letters*, p. 196.
14. *Complete Letters*, p. 912.
15. Mikhail (ed.), Vol. II, p. 335.
16. *Complete Letters*, p. 911.
17. Sherard, *Twenty Years*, p. 423.
18. *Complete Letters*, p. 934.
19. The bill for the shipment of Wilde's possessions – Lettre de voiture made out to Sebastian Melmoth, 22 October 1897 – is in the William Andrews Clark Library, T7725Z, W6721.

CHAPTER 38

1. *Complete Letters*, p. 948.
2. Ibid., p. 946.
3. Bernard Shapero, *Oscar Wilde: A Collection*, (London, 1989).
4. *Complete Letters*, p. 1095.
5. *Miscellanies*, p. xiii.
6. T. Wright, (ed.), pp. 160–1.
7. Housman, p. 34.
8. *Complete Letters*, p. 895.
9 Mikhail (ed.), Vol. II, p. 380.

CHAPTER 39

1. Sherard, *Twenty Years*, p. 456. For a reference to Wilde's wine-stained book see above (p. 155).
2. Harris, p. 288.
3. Mikhail (ed.), Vol. II, p. 385.
4. Housman, pp. 26–7. The book may have been Housman's *All-Fellows* (London, 1896). See *Complete Letters*, p. 923.

5. Laurence Housman, p. 27.
6. *Complete Letters*, p. 1162.
7. Brentano invoice to Wilde, 3 December 1900, William Andrews Clark Memorial Library, W6721 1900 Dec 3. The bill lists items that were unpaid on Wilde's death, so it probably details some of the last book purchases he ever made.
8. 'The Decay of Lying', *Collected Works*, p. 924.
9. *Complete Letters*, p. 1118.
10. O'Sullivan, p. 36.
11. Mikhail (ed.), Vol. II, p. 375.
12. Letter from W. Cheeson to Wright & Jones Booksellers, in the 'Collection of H. Montgomery Hyde', the Eccles Bequest, the British Library.
13. Mikhail (ed.), Vol. II, pp. 378–9.
14. O'Sullivan, p. 143.
15. *Complete Letters*, p. 1037.
16. See Ellmann, p. 531. The book is now in the Robert Ross Memorial Collection, The Bodleian Library.
17. Wilde also received a copy of Jean Moreás's *L'Histoire de Jean de Paris* (Paris, 1899) which is now in the Eccles Bequest, the British Library. In addition he was given Edouard Dujardin's *Antonia* (Paris, 1899) and Paul Toulet's *Le Bréviaire des courtisanes* (Paris, 1899); his copies are now in the library of the University of San Francisco.
18. Published in London in 1898.
19. Stetson Collection Catalogue, item 129.
20. *Complete Letters*, p. 1022.

21. Ibid., p. 1128.
22. Ibid., p. 1179.
23. Ibid., p. 1171.
24. Wilkinson to Wilde, 10 December 1898, the Eccles Bequest, the British Library.
25. Wilkinson to Wilde, 13 February 1899, William Andrews Clark Library, W6721LW686 1898–1914.

CHAPTER 40

1. Sherard, *Real*, p. 419 and his *Twenty Years*, pp. 456–8 See also Harris, p. 307.
2. Leverson, p. 46.
3. Sherard, *Real*, p. 419.

4. Ellmann, p. 548.
5. Ibid., pp. 545–6.
6. *Complete Letters*, p. 1216.
7. Ellmann, p. 548.
8. *Complete Letters*, p. 166.
9. Ibid., p. 1218.
10. Lady Wilde, *Ancient Legends*, p. 82.
11. Diary of George Ives, 18 February 1922 quoted in Stokes, p. 84.
12. Mikhail (ed.), Vol. I, p. 198.
13. Ellmann, p. 284.
14. *Complete Letters*, p. 446.
15. Ellmann, p. 188.
16. H. Travers Smith, *Psychical Messages from Oscar Wilde* (London, 1923), pp. 18 and 38–40.

General Index

Index of Authors